I'M FINE

. . . and Other Lies

I'M FINE

. . . and Other Lies

WHITNEY CUMMINGS

G. P. PUTNAM'S SONS
NEW YORK

G. P. PUTNAM'S SONS
Publishers Since 1838
An imprint of Penguin Random House LLC
375 Hudson Street
New York, New York 10014

Library of Congress Cataloging-in-Publication Data

Names: Cummings, Whitney, author.
Title: I'm fine . . . and other lies / Whitney Cummings.
Description: New York : G. P. Putnam's Sons, 2017.
Identifiers: LCCN 2017017627 | ISBN 9780735212602 (hardcover)
Subjects: LCSH: Cummings, Whitney. | Comedians—United
    States—Biography. | Actors—United States—Biography. | Television
    producers and directors—United States—Biography.
Classification: LCC PN2287.C6945 A3 2017 | DDC 792.7/6028092 [B]—dc23
LC record available at https://lccn.loc.gov/2017017627
p.   m.

Printed in the United States of America
10 9 8 7 6 5 4 3 2 1

Book design by Ashley Tucker

For all the voices in my head who told me
I could never write a book, this book is for you.

CONTENTS

I'M FINE

. . . and Other Lies

INTRODUCTION

When I was about twelve years old, one of my favorite things to do, besides making desperate audition tapes for MTV's *The Real World*, was going to yard sales and perusing strangers' junk. I (of course) mean peruse the stuff they were selling, although I'm sure I also checked out a couple of dudes' actual junk on more than one occasion given I was a very curious child and this was before porn was free.

I loved looking at the tables of old trinkets and fabricating a narrative of what the sellers' lives were like. Old skis, a chessboard, and dusty encyclopedias inspired me to fantasize about the sellers' mysterious lives; maybe they were detectives, spies, or on the run from the law for some glamorous crime they'd committed! In retrospect, I now realize they were probably just going through a divorce and needed to get rid of their exes' shit ASAP, but at the time this activity was a romantic escape from reality and perhaps the first evidence that I wanted to make up stories for a living. I was also a pathological liar until I was, like, fifteen but that's a way less sexy genesis of my occupation.

During one of these garbage-ogling sessions I came across a book called *Couplehood* by Paul Reiser. At the time I was too young to know who Paul Reiser was (and some of you might still be), but in this book he hilariously recounted the daily confusions and humiliations of being in a committed relationship. At that point in my life I had never been in a committed relationship with anything except anxiety and head lice, and I'm pretty sure my imaginary marriage to Luke Perry didn't count.

I somehow related to the book anyway. Reading about Reiser's foibles made me feel relieved and weirdly understood. Whether I could articulate it or not back then, I had some sort of epiphany that other people's misfortune made me feel way better about my own problems. I believe the official term for this phenomenon is *schadenfreude*. Count on the Germans to have a specific word for something so sadistic.

Couplehood made me feel less ashamed of the twisted, often inverted way that I saw the world. It also made me feel better about how obsessed I got over minutiae that most people didn't even seem to notice. Nobody else seemed to care about how weird it was that the salad bar at the Sizzler had chocolate pudding right next to the chickpeas, but this took up space in my brain for days as I tried to figure out what kind of psychopath did the arranging of the fixin's. Nobody seemed as stressed out as I was that Band-Aids always felt slightly racist for not having a selection of different shades of skin colors. I'm sure by now they have a kaleidoscope of shades available, but in the late eighties only waxy white people could protect their wounds without drawing too much attention to them.

Nobody wanted to listen to my rants about the injustice of racially insensitive Band-Aids, so I was inspired to write down my observations whenever I could. I found an old typewriter in my aunt's basement and hacked away at it every chance I got. Yes, there were computers back then, but computers saved documents, and I didn't want to risk anyone reading my insane diatribes. Plus, the typewriter made me feel smart and sophisticated. I mean, to feel sophisticated I probably could've just stopped curling my bangs, but at that point in my life common sense wasn't really on my radar.

I always dreamed that these masturbatory ramblings would one day be the seed of a book, but my self-esteem has always been too low to follow through. I always told myself I'd wait to write a book until I had accumulated enough entertaining mistakes to actually make the read worth your time. I realize it's a big deal that you're even holding this given how much is available for entertainment these days: YouTube videos of babies eating lemons, girls falling off stripper poles, and apps that remix your face with a dog's. Look, it took me forever to finish writing this book because of these exact distractions, but when I got focused enough to be able to finally get this stuff down, please know I set the bar high, constantly asking myself, "Can this compete with a video of a guy falling off a ladder on the Home Shopping Network?"

I was finally able to stave off my social media and online shopping addictions long enough to give you a whole book's worth of yummy, humiliating schadenfreude. For example, I've shaved an entire eyebrow off after eating too much edible weed, started balding from not eating enough fat, broke my shoulder trying to impress a guy, and came very close to spending my life in a Guatemalan prison. For years, I've kept these stories as bullet points in overpriced journals, figuring I would eventually find the courage to talk about them onstage, but they were just too embarrassing. That said, I actually think these stories are better illustrated in book form or on virtual eyeball drones or whatever people are reading with by the time this book comes out.

In addition to hoarding mortifying situations that'll make you feel way better about your own choices, I've also accumulated a compendium of knowledge that I believe can save you a lot of time. Look, you're busy. You have a family, maybe even a secret family. You have a life, maybe even a double life. You have a husband, a wife, a Facebook page. I don't have any of those things, so think of me as your personal assistant who went to a billion doctors and got you all the information you don't have time to get yourself and that Wikipedia will lie to you about. Think of this book as the Internet if it was honest and didn't hate women so much.

When I do stand-up, I need to make a joke about every twenty seconds. If I see someone in the audience cringing at what I'm saying or generally looking traumatized by the subject matter, I have to lighten the mood by changing the subject or deflecting with a joke. Writing a book gave me the freedom not to be funny every now and then so I could dig into some raw truths that I think can be healing for everyone. With a book, I can't read the room or see your reaction so I'm able to go off the grid without y'all shaming me into keeping the material safe or socially acceptable. I'm finally able to share my most embarrassing foibles, whether it was lying to therapists, driving myself to the ER when I was hemorrhaging blood from my head, or having explosive diarrhea in a literal jungle.

I've spent the last five years rewiring my brain, ending toxic relationships, combating insomnia, experimenting with antidepressants, struggling with love (or what I thought was love), talking to an imaginary child, and freezing my eggs.

As a result, most of the time I spend with my friends is consumed by them asking me how I worked my ass off to change my brain and worked my ass on to get the body I want. Friends and even strangers ask me how I got good skin, kicked my eating disorder, stopped dating narcissists, quit letting my ego run the show, and generally ceased being cray cray. It would make my life way easier to be able to just say "How about you just read this book?" so I don't have to spend every social event rambling on about neurology when I'd much rather be spending the evening flirting with a guy who is terrible for me.

I've spent tens of thousands of dollars accruing information from a smorgasbord of doctors, psychiatrists, healers, teachers, and peo-ple who jammed things up my butt while making unflinching eye contact with me. Look, if you get anything out of this read, it's that you do not *ever* need to put anything up your bottom hole unless you really want to. Even then, you certainly don't have to pay for it.

So if I may be so bold, I straight-up want this book to change your life. I personally was sick of being a mess and I'm also sick of your being a mess, so let's get our shit together. Together.

THE SELF-HELP CHAPTER

I have some good news for you. I love you. And because I love you, you're about to get like a hundred thousand dollars' worth of psychological therapy for the measly price of this book. I'm not proud of this, but I've spent an embarrassing amount of money I never really had in the first place on mental health professionals, some of which I should probably put in quotes. Mental health "professionals." Traipsing along this yellow brick road of healers, I didn't get to Oz, although I did see pink horses a couple times due to low blood sugar from stupid cleanses.

The Butthead

I went to a "nutritionist" once who I should have known was trouble because he went only by his first name. Let's call him Dr. Bob, even though the real name he went by is even more ridiculous and sounds like a corny DJ who plays cheesy music you would have heard at your uncle's third wedding in the early nineties. Let me be clear: A doctor going by *Dr.* followed by his first name is a red flag, unless it's Dr. Dre, in which case it's at least worth going to for the story. The fact that I paid money to go to a nutritionist who went by his first name meant the kind of doctor I actually needed to go to was a psychiatrist.

Dr. Bob was the skinniest person I had ever met, and that's saying a lot, given how much time I spend around Hollywood actresses. He bragged that he slept on a treadmill, which he kept at a high angle so blood would flow to his head. Honestly, since I hate running, this actually seems like the best use of a treadmill I can think of, but to sleep on it upside down puts the *bat* in *batshit crazy*. I realize now that when I heard this, I should have swiftly exited the building, but I'm a sucker for men who have prevaricated for so long that they've not only started to believe their lies but also have the audacity to charge people to listen to them.

Dr. Bob's philosophy was that you should eat only food indigenous to where your ancestors are from, and since I'm a Western European mutt, I couldn't eat bananas, coconuts, cantaloupe, or basically anything delicious. Being from Europe, my ancestors pretty much consumed only potatoes, alcohol, and their own teeth. I asked Dr. Bob what would happen if I was in an airport and desperate for something healthy and happened to sneak a banana. His face went paler than it already was. With not one molecule of irony in his tone, he said, "You might as well put a gun in your mouth."

Dr. Bob's main obsession was colonics. Giving them, getting them, showing you pictures of them, telling me about other celebrities who got them. If you don't know what a colonic is, I'll save you the Internet search, because frankly I'm worried some very disturbing images will come up that will give you eternal nightmares. This is as elegant a description as I can give of a colonic: Dr. Bob puts a tube up your tushy and releases some water to scare out all your hidden poopies.

Nothing can prepare you for the feeling of a skeletal man without a last name slipping a hose into your anus, whilst whispering "You're doing great." Lying there with a tube inside my butt with a man who slept on exercise equipment was so uncomfortable and invasive that after every session I was tempted to call the police. I eventually stopped going to Dr. Bob because I realized that literally all the money I spent on him was being flushed down the toilet.

When he wasn't penetrating my reluctant crevice with Tupperware tubes, he did give me some helpful advice: Don't cook your veggies to the point of depleting them of all their vitamins. Veggies should be crunchy, not flaccid suggestions of their former selves. Apparently, if you're not farting, you're not eating your veggies right. And yes, I realize that even though this advice is great for your body, it's terrible for your personal life.

Other honorable mentions include: chew your water, drink apple cider vinegar, and you should be bent over when you use the toilet because as it turns out, toilets were designed by misogynists who want everyone to get colon cancer, so we're all using the bathroom the wrong way. Apparently when we use the bathroom, we should be in the posture we'd be in if we were hiding from zombies in our basements: squatting but crouched over instead of straight up. Our bodies are designed to "release" at a certain angle, and traditional toilets are not conducive to that angle, which also explains why a lot of women constantly have to pee . . . because we're not emptying our bladders completely. Sometimes we pee because we need an excuse to get out of a boring conversation with a weirdo, but that's a whole other thing that's less about physiology and more about people being annoying.

There is actually a contraption you can and should buy that raises your feet up so you're in a squat. Look, I didn't say it was sexy, I said it was healthy. I've found having a stool around my toilet is incredibly awkward when I have company over, but it's a total game changer for my peeing habits. If you don't have a stool to put your feet up on, you can just bend over like you're giving birth in a ditch in the 1200s. You might not be able to text as much while you're on the can, but at least you'll have to spend less time on it.

Lady Finger

In order to become a functioning human, I had to learn how to cry. Historically, I've really only cried at unexpected times, such as when a cartoon dinosaur loses its mother or when I accidentally step on my real animal's paw. I'm also no stranger to shedding a tear or two when I hear "I'll Be Missing You" by Puff Daddy and Faith Evans. I think his name is Diddy now, but who knows what his name will be when this book is released, and I don't have time to keep up with his indecisive nomenclature. The point is, the song makes me emotional, so if it comes on in a public place, I literally have to excuse myself to have a wistful sob in a bathroom. Maybe because it makes me nostalgic for when I was a teenager, back when I wanted to escape reality and couldn't wait to finally be an adult. This was of course before I realized that most of adult life is spent on the phone with customer service, making up lies to get out of plans, and thinking every ingrown hair is an STD. Regardless, I had a sort of emotional dyslexia when it came to releasing sadness; often when I heard terrible news, I would laugh hysterically, and when a jovial pop song would come on at the gym, I'd erupt in sobs. Dude, something was up in terms of my relationship to expressing healthy emotion.

My friend told me about this thing where you go sit with a woman who makes you cry out all the old repressed grief you carry around with you. This practice is called the Grinberg Method, and when I looked it up on Wikipedia I found this definition: "Practicing the methodology is intended to teach people to gain control and stop trying to avoid the pain, to be fully attentive to their body and experience of it. When this occurs, energy is freed to deal with the pain and related sensations, giving the body an opportunity to mend and heal." The woman I was meeting was named Evelyn. I know, already intimidating. When I went to her office, it took me a little while to find the front door. I always wonder if healers and therapists get offices in hard-to-find places on purpose to make sure you're as stressed out as possible when you arrive, so by the end of the session, when you've finally calmed down, they can be like, "See? My therapy is working! You were so stressed out when you walked in!" when in reality the biggest problem in your life is finding parking at your therapist's office. Evelyn had an office with a keypad entry system, and I struggled with punching in the numbers because if I'm over a minute late to something, I panic and my frontal lobe shuts down. After I frantically hacked at the keypad as if a bomb would go off and destroy Earth if I didn't get the code right in time, Evelyn opened the door from the inside. Even though I had an appointment, guilt and shame washed over me because I felt I interrupted whatever she was doing.

Evelyn's vibe is arresting to say the least. She has an inexplicable energy that's calming but also creepy at first because she doesn't mirror or entertain the behavior around her. It's like she's got this invisible orb shield thing around her that deflects people's needy energy. No matter how much toxicity you throw at her, it just bounces off, then hits you in the face, sort of like when you spit gum out of a moving car and then it gets stuck in your hair. And no, she's not on muscle relaxants. I asked. She had laugh lines on her face, but almost no forehead lines, which told the story that she smiled a lot but didn't stress out. Or maybe she had Botox, but I don't think so.

Evelyn looked like she slept eight hours a night, and I'll pay for advice from anyone who has figured out how to do that. She didn't talk much, which is very triggering for insecure people like me. Silence makes me so uncomfortable that it usually causes me to launch into a vagina monologue of jokes, apologies, and excuses for my existence. Most of us, without realizing it, are in a constant state of apology. I once tried to go twenty-four hours without apologizing and I lasted thirty minutes, basically as long as it took to encounter another human. I said to a receptionist, "Sorry I'm early." *Early.*

Evelyn truly doesn't give a shit if people like her or not, which of course makes everyone like her. Evelyn speaks only when she needs to and doesn't fill silences with nervous, insecure drivel the way a lot of us do when we need the approval of others. Her self-assured silence of course made me think she was mad at me, which is ridiculous, since she didn't even know me. When someone isn't talking, my brain tends to fill in the blanks with how I feel about myself, so I made the assumption that she was disappointed in me and I did what I do best: apologized when I had done nothing wrong. When I apologized to Evelyn, she looked deeply confused. After hearing my hemorrhaging litany of apologies, she made eye contact with me and sincerely asked, "Why?"

I immediately burst into tears.

Then, like any child conditioned to "calm down" and "stop crying," I felt the muscles in my face automatically clench up to stop the tears from coming. She looked even more confused.

"Why are you stopping yourself from crying?" Evelyn asked very gently. This was not a rhetorical question. She seemed genuinely confounded. Then I was genuinely confounded. The whole thing felt like a trick. What did she mean? We all stop ourselves from crying. Crying is pathetic, lame. It's a sign of weakness. I mean, crying in your car in a parking lot at two A.M. while eating old Hershey's Kisses you found half unwrapped in your purse is one thing, but in public with another person? Unconscionable.

"Crying is a solution," she said. This statement blindsided me, because I had always thought crying was a sign of failure. In our culture we're made to feel ashamed of showing our feelings, of being vulnerable. If a woman cries, she's crazy, emotional, has PMS, or whatever the most current pejorative dismissive term is. As I write this, "psycho" is pretty popular, but it seems like "hot mess" is making quite a comeback.

We're brainwashed with garbage idioms like "Big girls don't cry." Guys who "cry like a girl" are told to "man up." Or "She's crying like a baby," as if only babies have a reason to cry, which makes no sense to me, given babies have the fewest problems out of all of us. They don't have mortgages or jury duty, and they get the fun end of the whole birthing situation. The mother is the one who is pushing and bleeding and tearing, and the baby basically just gets to jet down a water slide. I think the ole "crying like a baby" idiom should be reversed: What we should say about babies is "Jesus, that baby is crying like a grown-up!"

The sessions with Evelyn were very uncomfortable at first. She had me get naked save my (granny) panties. I immediately apologized for those. Then I apologized for apologizing for them. By then she just ignored my apologies and moved on to staring at my feet for a ridiculously long time, which made me squirm due to how ugly I think my feet are. I mean, Western European people evolved to run from bears and balance on glaciers, not to be foot models. Seriously, I don't know if it's my Viking DNA or my mom's GMO-laced breast milk, but my feet look like a basket of french fries. To make things worse, I had fallen in love with a pair of New Balance shoes with Velcro straps a couple weeks prior, but they had only a size 9.5, and I'm a size 10 when I'm not bloated. That didn't stop me from buying and wearing them so much that one of my toenails straight-up fell off one night when I was onstage. I painted over it with nail polish, thinking nobody would notice. Right as I was about to trick people into thinking I had ten toenails, I made the blunderous choice of red polish, making my toe look like a Craisin.

I lay down on a padded table and Evelyn proceeded to beat the living shit out of me *with one finger*. Usually if someone is using one finger on you, it feels awesome, but this was literally an intolerable amount of pain. Now I know what they mean by the adage "location, location, location."

Evelyn jammed her finger into the side of my hip, the back of my shoulder, and the area between my jaw and ear because she discovered that's where I hold my tension and repressed emotional pain. She explained that since our bodies react to stress faster than our brains can, our bodies will tense when a situation reminds it of a previous trauma, which signals the brain to release the stress chemicals adrenaline and cortisol, which is what makes us feel anxious. Her goal is to neutralize these areas so your body halts that reaction cycle and you stop turning every benign situation into a fight-or-flight scenario. For example, when you're at the grocery store and someone leaves her cart in the middle of the aisle, you don't feel the need to end their life because of that time you got left in the car too long as a kid. This practice can also help you stop making every guy you date your dad and every girl you date your mom, because unlike what the popularity of MILF porn may indicate, that's not a cute look on anyone.

Evelyn taught me that crying is a healthy release and should be a part of our daily lives since we have so much repressed pain stored up in our bodies from our past. As corny as it sounds, I took with me the expression "You gotta feel it to heal it." When we repress our feelings, they build up and will eventually explode in random situations or end up getting expressed in unhealthy ways, like addictive compulsions, self-sabotage, or general assholery. Another adage that's always stuck with me is "If it's hysterical, it's historical." So when I suppress my feelings today, I know that it's a negative contribution to my future because it's eventually going to cause an inappropriate reaction where the punishment does not fit the crime. If I don't cry when my body and brain want to cry, you better believe that in two years when a form at a doctor's office innocently asks for my relationship status, I'll internalize it as a personal attack and have a full-on tantrum.

Today, crying is a part of my routine to maintain emotional equilibrium. We all carry a lot of grief around, and there's so much sadness in the world that we empathically take on but don't have the time to release on a daily basis. I look at crying like cleaning the lint out of the dryer before using it again so it can function better. I try to make crying a routine maintenance thing like vacuuming, emptying the garbage, or masturbating. But maybe don't cry and masturbate at the same time, because if the CIA really is watching us though our computer cameras, that footage is seriously going to thwart your political ambitions.

Crystal Balls

Look, I don't *not* believe in psychics. My theory is that they aren't necessarily divinely clairvoyant, but that they're just some of the few people that actually listen when someone else talks. Suppose I say, "The thing about James is, well, I don't know, he's just like . . . I don't know. *You know?*" Any truly awake person listening to me can tell that James and I are not going to live happily ever after, given how ambivalent I am when I talk about him. Whenever girls talk about guys with an expression like they just smelled a dead body, it's pretty clear that they aren't that into him or there's some red flag they're in denial about. So unless your friend has had a shocking amount of work done, it doesn't take metaphysical witchcraft to figure out what's going on by her facial expressions. I feel like being psychic might just be the natural result of what happens when you actually just listen to someone without being a distracted spaz plotting your next Instagram post during a conversation.

I go to the same psychic once a year. Again, I'm not sure I believe in psychics, but I do believe in this particular one because much to my chagrin, she has never been wrong. I won't give you her real name because I'm worried everyone will start booking her and I won't be able to get an appointment. I didn't say any of these healers made me stop being selfish, folks. Let's call her Beatrice. Beatrice's waiting room is full of lamps that look like rocks and seemingly endless yoga magazines, my least favorite magazine to have to flip through. To me, the only thing more boring than stretching is reading about stretching.

Beatrice records all of our sessions with a tape recorder. You heard me. Whenever I get skeptical about her psychic powers and assume she must have just looked me up online to get such accurate information, I remember that she still uses a tape recorder. The Luddite who still uses that obsolete a machine probably doesn't have too strong of a Google Alert game.

Here's how the session goes down. First, you have to give her a piece of your jewelry, which she cups in her hands during the session the way Gollum held the gold band in *The Lord of the Rings*. Then you tell her what you want to know about—that is to say, a guy, a job, a guy you wish had a job, whatever. She then closes her eyes and begins talking to your "spirit guides." From what I gather, these are spirits who guide and protect people, sort of like guardian angels or invisible bouncers. I wasn't a huge fan of my spirit guides at this point in my life because I felt very lost and like I had no guidance, invisible or otherwise, but Beatrice spoke to them regularly. She'd close her eyes, rock back and forth, then start reacting as if five people were sitting in chairs around her. As they speak to her, she quickly scribbles down notes as she nods and talks to the air. My guides seem to be a real gaggle of weirdos because sometimes she ends up arguing with them; other times it seems like she's flirting with them. The only thing more insane than someone flirting with ghosts? The fact that I've actually gotten jealous.

One time after chatting with the invisible people, Beatrice told me about my "past life regression," which is basically the idea of why you are the way you are based on who you were in past incarnations. Up to this point in my life, this was the craziest thing I had heard aside from recently learning that we have tons of bugs living in our eyelashes and that Jason Schwartzman is related to Nicolas Cage.

Beatrice told me that in a past life I had fought in the French Revolution and stood up for the proletariat who were starving to death while that selfish biatch Marie Antoinette pounded her pound cake. Apparently back in the day I was a voice for the voiceless, which I still do in other ways now through my stand-up and work with rescue animals. The whole ordeal mostly just made me feel old, but it did make a little more sense that I had dated two broke French guys.

One of the times I went to Beatrice, I was in a particularly sticky situation. I was in a very happy relationship and was blindsided by falling in lust with someone else. It was that instant electric, cellular connection that makes us throw around misleading words like *soul mate* and *love*, when it's probably just a confabulation of a bunch of adrenaline, fear, childhood conditioning, and your lizard brain thinking the person is your father. Beatrice told me the reason we were so magnetically attracted to each other was because we had died together in a volcanic eruption at Pompeii back in the day. As you can probably imagine, when I told my boyfriend I had fallen for someone else, the whole "but we died together in a past life" thing didn't go over particularly well, but I'm sure it helped him get over me way faster.

Beatrice also told me some pragmatic things, like that I had anemia and candida. I mean, psychic or not, anyone who saw me back then without makeup on could fairly easily ascertain that I was anemic, and I'm pretty sure we all have candida. She also told me I needed new brake pads, which was true, but you didn't have to be psychic to figure out that one. I was twenty-seven and it was obvious I couldn't swing the thousand bucks for new brakes, considering the last three checks I had written to her bounced. Back then, I justified not paying her by rationalizing that if she was really psychic, she should have known that I couldn't afford her services, and if she didn't know because she wasn't truly psychic, well, I deserve a refund.

Head Games

In my twenties, I was promiscuous with therapists the way most twenty-somethings are promiscuous with sexual partners. Quite frankly, I was a therapy slut. I tore through therapists with no strings attached, a different one-hour stand a couple days a week. Ultimately, the reason I couldn't land on one is because I realized I was so triggered by people, especially authority figures, that it was hard for me to be vulnerable with them. I'd go into a therapist's office and try to charm him or her, and make the therapist think that I didn't need to be there. I treated meeting new therapists more like a job interview than a time to reveal my struggles. Weirder, if a therapist didn't see through my performance of pretending to be normal, I'd lose respect for them and never go back.

I know. The whole thing is very dark. But in those days, I truly wasn't ready to admit I had flaws, much less fix them. I was way too paralyzed by my own denial and survival mechanisms to even know what the truth was, but what I *did* know was that I was sick of being crazy because, frankly, being crazy isn't cute once you turn thirty. Tweet it, blog it, retweet it, re-blog it, make it your screensaver, then take a photo of said screensaver and text it to all your friends. I mean, being crazy isn't particularly attractive in your twenties either, but at least you have an excuse.

One therapist I went to for a while was particularly annoying because he never gave me an opinion or suggestion. This meant he either wasn't listening or thought I was too fragile to hear the truth. Based on what some ex-boyfriends have yelled at me in fights, it was probably a little of both.

In retrospect, he was probably just trying to keep me dependent on him, which is especially cruel given one of the main reasons I was going to therapy was to stop being dependent on manipulative men. I could tell he'd try to be neutral, telling me what he thought

I wanted to hear, which essentially enabled my self-destructive behavior. I was in a very unhealthy relationship and he absolutely should have told me to get out of it ASAP, but every time I would ask for advice, he'd say, "What do you think?" This sort of talk therapy may work for some folks or may have been proven to be effective by very smart people, but it triples my crazy. I hate when psychiatrists ask me what I think I should do, because usually what I think I should do is wildly inappropriate and sometimes illegal. I just wanted someone to tell me what to do, because left to my own devices I was either acting like a sociopath or dating one.

After many Dr. Wrongs, I finally came across a Dr. Right. Someone that I respected enough to go back to a second time. The first sign that we were meant to be was that I could make appointments with her via text. If I have to call and leave a message, then wait for you to call me back, I'm already experiencing the very anxiety a therapist is supposed to be mitigating. I feel a therapist's job is to make a person feel safe enough to be able to come to terms with their wounds, so if I have to pick up the phone and call you, you're just creating more emotional wounds we're gonna need to heal.

When I first met Vera at her office, she was wearing a T-shirt with a wolf airbrushed on it. So. This probably goes without saying, but that's really all I needed in order to hire her on the spot.

Vera was the first therapist I had ever met who taught me about neurochemicals and helped me understand my brain on a biological level. She's very solution-oriented, whereas the therapists before her all seemed just fine talking about the problem ad nauseam. Instead of listening to me blather on about my delusions and further embed my negative thinking, Vera put me to work by starting EMDR (eye movement desensitization reprocessing), hypnosis, and giving me books to read about addiction and neurology. She was the first person who seemed to really want me to get better. I became the second.

I obviously had a lot of neural rewiring to do, which would take some time, but right off the bat she noticed that my picker was very off when it came to men. According to Harville Hendrix, we tend to be attracted to people with the negative qualities of our primary caretakers, and I was no exception. Although changing who you're attracted to takes a while, in the meantime Vera at least helped me stop the bleeding. She started by trying to keep me out of another draining relationship by giving me a psychology test created by Carl Jung. It's very simple, yet mysteriously profound. It's a couple of questions that can give insight into someone's psyche and values without having to ask them directly. Unfortunately, it's not socially acceptable to ask someone on the first date, "So are you a sex addict? It would be great if you could just let me know now before my brain starts producing oxytocin, which will make me all chemically attached to you, thanks!" Vera told me I'm required to perform these tests on the first and second dates with guys to find out who someone really is before I'm in too deep and putting some guy's name on my car insurance even though he has two DUIs.

On a date, ask the server for a piece of paper and a pen. If you don't have a server because you're at home watching Netflix for the first date, immediately leave the house and go to a public place because that is way too casual for a first date, ya nut. Also, do not bring your own piece of paper because that will make you look very crazy for being so prepared. You should play this game only if you're feeling safe and have clean motives; it should be spontaneous and fun. Your date should not feel like he or she is being interrogated by Tommy Lee Jones in a movie from the nineties, and you should not look like you're an insurance adjuster with a clipboard in your hand, investigating mold.

Once you find something to write on, give it to your date and have them write down their answers, which you should *not* see. Since this game illuminates a lot about the subconscious, how about you play the game first? Yeah, now. It's never too early to find out who you are so you can either fix it, celebrate it, or get a head start on being in denial about it.

Here goes: Write down your favorite animal. Don't just pick an animal you think is cute or funny. Really think about it. Pick an animal you admire. Also, it can't be an animal you know, such as your cat or the lizard from your childhood who was dead for a week before you noticed. When I first played this game, I chose a dog, but when I stopped texting and really focused on the question with my full attention, I ended up choosing a honey badger. This is one instance where I'm going to tell you not to trust your gut. Instead, overthink it a little. Once you choose your animal, write three reasons that you chose it in adjective form. This was what my quiz looked like:

FAVORITE ANIMAL: HONEY BADGER

    –SCRAPPY

    –FEARLESS

    –DON'T GIVE A SHIT

Next choose your favorite article of clothing. It can be anything from a hoodie to a ball gown to a Windbreaker. Or it can be a leotard or your favorite tube top if you get down like that. Then write three adjectives to describe that article of clothing. Mine was:

ARTICLE OF CLOTHING: HOODIE

    –VERSATILE

    –COMFORTABLE

    –WARM

Next up, choose your favorite body of water. It could be a river, an ocean, a glass of water, any iteration of H_2O. I once went white-water rafting on the New River in Virginia. It was a terrible experience and I am very confused about why people go white-water rafting when Mother Nature has proven over and over again that she gives zero craps if we live or die, but I do remember being in awe of the river. There was just something so amazing to me about its being so beautiful, but also able to kill you at any moment, a concept very sexy to me during the time in my life where I instantly became smitten with anything that was both attractive and treated me terribly.

BODY OF WATER: THE NEW RIVER
   –SOMETIMES ROUGH, SOMETIMES CALM
   –FUN
   –UNPREDICTABLE

The last element isn't listing a favorite thing, it's more about your instinctive reaction to an imaginary situation. So imagine you're in a white room with no windows or doors. List three emotions that you'd feel. Mine were:

WHITE ROOM
   –SURRENDER
   –CALM
   –RELIEF

Now comes the fun part! Now that you've written down all your answers, you can get to finding out who you really are, not who you pretend to be! If you're doing the quiz with others, ask them for their answers first before telling them what the answers mean for maximum insight and LOLs. Here goes. Your favorite animal apparently represents how you see yourself. So according to my quiz I see myself as a honey badger: fearless, scrappy, not giving a shit. This metaphor really held up when I also discovered that honey badgers are eager to pick fights even when they aren't hungry, their teeth can break the shell of a tortoise, and they'll eat literally *anything*. I mean, that's kind of me in a nutshell, which I would of course also eat. That said, if your date puts down honey badger as his or her favorite animal, I strongly suggest you leave immediately and fake your death. Animals that reflect well on a person: elephant, whale, lion, monkey. Animals that could be red flags: shark, snake, crocodile, recluse spider—okay, you get it.

I have a friend who did this quiz with a girl he was dating and the animal she chose was a leech. He assumed she was joking and laughed it off, but months later he found out she was gold-digging numerous guys at once. I highly recommend that when people tell you who they are, do yourself a favor and go ahead and believe them.

Now for the article of clothing. Your favorite article of clothing represents how you're perceived by others. I love this one because it's usually antithetical to the essence of the animal we pick—that is to say, how we perceive ourselves. So I think I'm a honey badger and other people think I'm a hoodie. There is quite an incongruity between who *I* think I am and who *others* think I am, which either means I have a self-perception issue or that I wear a mask around people and have an authenticity issue. Spoiler alert: I have both.

This juxtaposition usually shows that we're attached to an old story of who we are and/or the role we played as a child. I realized that if I could just figure out a way to see myself the way other people see me, that my life would get a lot easier, and my self-esteem could start hovering over zero.

Now to your favorite body of water. This one symbolizes how you view . . . drumroll, please . . . sex. Embarrassing as it was, mine was right on the money. I like it "sometimes rough, sometimes calm." Well, stranger, now you know pretty much everything about me. I've had a guy on a first date tell me his favorite body of water was a pond because it's "still and peaceful." We did not end up having a second date. It was pretty safe to assume he's a bottom, and that would never work out because, well, I have bad knees.

The white room metaphor gives insight into how we view death. This one is just sort of fun because I personally don't think you should judge people too harshly on how they view death, unless their response is "I like to create white rooms for other people to be in forever," because then they may be a good old-fashioned murderer. I've had some friends write "annoyed." It cracks me up to think about someone who's annoyed they're going to die, "Goddamn it! My flight was late, traffic is crazy, and I freaking have to go *die* at some point. Who has time for this shit?"

If you administer this quiz with your date and he or she passes without revealing any obvious psychotic tendencies, the second game to play to find out if there are red flags lurking beneath a charming, beguiling facade is word association. Again, Mr. Jung was big into this one. That dude knew how to party. You know the deal, you say a word and they have to say the first thing that comes to mind, which can reveal some random but often also horrifying peeks into someone's subconscious. One time I was doing word association on a second date with a guy, and we went back and forth on a bunch of words. We were cracking up laughing because his responses were so innocent and funny. When I got to the word "marriage," he went dark and he blurted out, "Cunt!"

Uh-oh.

A man using that word is grounds for leaving the table immediately, which of course meant I dated him for another four months.

Jung has specific words he uses which I'll include for you cuties, but I like to make up my own list based on what I need and specifically want to know about a person. You're probably not going to get something as clear as you saying "cheat" and your date responding "I will totally do that!" but a vague response may lead to a deeper conversation you wouldn't necessarily have had otherwise. Again, the goal with this is to learn as much about a person as early as possible so we aren't finding cocaine in our boyfriends' wallets at the Cancún airport. Don't worry, that story is coming up.

Here are the words I like to use when I play this game on dates.

Skin	Future	Write
Wife	Dad	Me
Animal	Play	Pain
Wet	Baby	Blood
Man	Fear	Want
Mother	Red	Test
Fresh	Mind	Religion
Sex	Brain	Rich
You	Girlfriend	Dead
Life	Fight	Fantasy
Give	Bitch	Work
Money	Family	Friend
Deep	Cheat	Sick
Taste	Song	Freedom

To make you feel less ashamed about your weird answers, here are mine in case you want to feel less crazy or judge me.

Skin SWEAT	Future JETSONS	Write JOB
Wife LADY	Dad LOVE	Me SAFE
Animal HUNGRY	Play HARD	Pain HEAD
Wet PANTS	Baby POWDER	Blood GUN
Man DAD	Fear ANNOYING	Want BAD
Mother EASTER (?)	Red CHINA	Test PREGNANCY
Fresh CANDLE	Mind WIRES	Religion MONEY
Sex NAKED	Brain DELICATE	Rich GOUT
You HI	Girlfriend TIRED	Dead END
Life GAME	Fight WIN	Fantasy PRETTY
Give HAND	Bitch FIGHT	Work TWERK
Money FREEDOM	Family ORIGIN	Friend FAMILY
Deep THROAT (!)	Cheat LOST	Sick HELP
Taste TEST	Song BIRD	Freedom SKY

And here are the words Jung used in the actual test in case you want to trust a trained professional instead of a comedian.

1.	head	19.	pride	37.	salt
2.	green	20.	to cook	38.	new
3.	water	21.	ink	39.	custom
4.	to sing	22.	angry	40.	to pray
5.	dead	23.	needle	41.	money
6.	long	24.	to swim	42.	foolish
7.	ship	25.	voyage	43.	pamphlet
8.	to pay	26.	blue	44.	despise
9.	window	27.	lamp	45.	finger
10.	friendly	28.	to sin	46.	expensive
11.	to cook	29.	bread	47.	bird
12.	to ask	30.	rich	48.	to fall
13.	cold	31.	tree	49.	book
14.	stem	32.	to prick	50.	unjust
15.	to dance	33.	pity	51.	frog
16.	village	34.	yellow	52.	to part
17.	lake	35.	mountain	53.	hunger
18.	sick	36.	to die	54.	white

I realize that my responses aren't funny, and I'm very insecure about that, but the idea isn't to be entertaining, it's to be as honest as possible with the first thing that comes to your head. The idea isn't to be a laugh riot, although that's always a bonus, but the point is to look for any major red flags—for example, you say "man" and she says "castrate," or you say "girl" and he says "poison." And I don't mean the band. That said, if he randomly yells out "Poison the band!" my advice is to marry him on the spot.

Now here's the hard part of all this: Once you do spot a red flag, your job is to actually read the writing on the wall. You don't get to pick up a pen and rewrite the writing on the wall. For most of my twenties I rewrote the writing on the wall, and frankly it's a miracle that as a result I'm not in court trying to get custody of my seven kids from numerous very handsome malignant narcissists.

Hopefully these tests save you some time and help you weed out some weirdos. Ultimately, even if the games don't yield poignant or revealing answers, I feel that if your date is down with being open and vulnerable enough to play the game, I already like them. Godspeed. And I better get an invite to the wedding.

But even if you don't invite me, I'll be fine.

THE CODEPENDENCE CHAPTER

A lot of people ask me why it took "so long" to write a book. I pretend it was because I didn't have time or didn't think I had enough to write about, but the truth is, I was scared. I was scared it wouldn't be good, that people wouldn't like it, that I'd be rejected or that you'd think I was a narcissist for writing a book about myself. I've felt this same paralyzing fear with every show, every joke, every performance. Even with my sexual performances. What I'm trying to avoid saying here is that I have a condition called codependence, which essentially means that for a long time I couldn't tolerate not being liked. Down, boys! I can't marry all of you!

I don't trust you to look up the condition online yourself, because if you're anything like me, you'll end up in a wormhole Googling your ex-boyfriend's new girlfriend. So, let me save you some time; here's a definition of codependence I remixed from a compendium of sources:

Codependents have low self-esteem and would rather focus on the needs of others than on their own. They find it hard to be themselves because they're more concerned with appeasing others and avoiding rejection than with doing what they want to do.

Codependents are people pleasers who have an extreme need for approval, feel a sense of guilt when standing up for themselves, and can't tolerate the discomfort of others. Guys, if that doesn't get you to swipe right on my Tinder bio, I don't know what will.

People throw the term *codependence* around pretty casually these days, like "Me and my boyfriend are sooo codependent!," basically implying that they spend a lot of time together. Spending time together can be part of it, but it's not necessarily about proximity. You can be in a long-distance codependent relationship where you don't see the person very often, yet still obsess over their needs and behavior, or you can even be in one with a person you've actually never met but that you think you're dating in your crazy haunted house of a head.

The type of codependence wired into my brain is pretty intense and can actually be quite dangerous. For some people, codependence can show itself in ways as extreme as buying drugs for a drug addict because you think you're "helping," having sex without a condom due to fear of conflict or abandonment, or getting into debt because you don't want to admit to others you can't afford certain things. However, codependence can rear its ugly head in seemingly more benign ways as well. Some of the less extreme ways my codependence complicates my life are being late due to an unrealistic number of commitments because I have a hard time saying no, losing sleep worrying about things I can't control, deriving my self-esteem from my productivity and achievements, and looking like a crackhead Muppet from cutting my own bangs because I don't make time for myself given how much I overbook my schedule.

My codependent brain has gotten me into endless quagmires, from trying to get an Australian stripper a job and a visa (the only reason I didn't is because she never e-mailed me back) to training strangers' dangerously aggressive dogs to staying in relationships years too long because I didn't want to hurt the other person's feelings.

Fine, I'll tell you the stripper story. One night my friend Zoe and I had a very random instinct to go to a strip club. It was actually technically a "bikini bar," but I had been before and remembered that they played late-nineties hip-hop, which always makes me feel deeply understood. It's also the only music I know how to dance to.

I'm not going to lie, I always get along very well with strippers. Maybe I was a stripper in a past life or maybe I'm going to be one in the future, I don't know. I have what I can only describe as fantastic chemistry with strippers, maybe because we likely have very similar childhoods and assumptions about what we have to offer the world.

Zoe and I were having a blast. We watched flexible girl after flexible girl dance her ass and tassels off. My codependence first kicked in when one of the girls was flying hands-free around a pole, using only her legs to propel her in circles. It was like watching an ice skater, which for me is very stressful because I spend most of the time wincing, anxious that she might fall and shatter her dreams of winning a gold medal and being on a cereal box or whatever ice skaters do after they retire at twenty-five. I found myself wincing watching the strippers as well—praying none of them went flying off the pole and into some perverted man's lap, or worse, my lap given I was very into wearing studded belts back then.

After a couple of girls did their thing with their things, an incredibly tan and dare I say emotionally buoyant girl stormed onto the stage to "Lady Marmalade," the version by Mýa, Lil' Kim, Christina Aguilera, and Pink. Maybe it was my deep appreciation for the song, or maybe it was the mostly ice cosmopolitan I was drinking out of a plastic cup, but this gal really lit up the room. She was a star, I tell you. She had a gorgeous body, but she had hardly any breasts, which made me root for her, given that most of the girls there were as buxom in the chest as they were lost in life. As Zoe and I watched this girl dance her heart out, I could tell that she was a little less lost in life and didn't really belong in this giant box of tears. I could see this girl had potential—to do what, I didn't know, but I had a strong magnetic pull to be the person to save her from her plight and get her on track to get her anthropology degree, which in my head was her obvious destiny.

After being hypnotized and quite frankly humbled by her dance, Zoe and I called her over to talk. She told us she was a dance teacher and had an abusive boyfriend from whom she was trying to escape. She was just making some extra money until she could get back on her feet. My codependent brain sprang into action. And she's a victim!? This was like my dream come true: someone needy and helpless who also liked possibly feminist but maybe also sexist music from the early aughts? Add to cart.

I told the stripper I'd help her out in any way I could. I'd get her a job as a production assistant on a TV show, pay her to help me around the house, whatever I could make up to get her a job. Turned out she also needed citizenship, so I promised her I could help her with whatever she needed to ensure she could stay in the country and live her best life, because my codependence told me that this was for some reason my responsibility, even though the only things that could actually help her would be years of psychoanalysis and a time machine.

I gave her my personal e-mail and prepared everyone I worked with the next day that we'd all be having a new employee on board. The only hang-up to my rescue operation was that the stripper never e-mailed me. I can't even believe I'm typing this sentence, but I was rejected by a stripper. There I was, prepared to marry her so she could get citizenship, and she never even reached out to receive my help. But that statement epitomizes what's so frustrating about codependence: We think we're helping, but the truth is most people don't need, don't want, or feel patronized by our "help."

My codependence caused me to do all sorts of things I thought were thoughtful and kind, yet I was blindsided by the lack of gratitude. I used to stay with guys years after I broke up with them in my head, worried I would hurt their feelings. I now understand that it's insane and selfish to think that staying with someone for an extra year is helping him, given you're basically stealing a year of his life. Codependence isn't about actual altruism, it's about being lost in the fallacy that you need to protect everyone from reality and uncomfortable feelings.

Codependence is a particularly insidious condition because it masquerades as being "super nice." It's a disease that tricks you into thinking that caretaking and people pleasing is kind, when it's actually condescending toward the other person and ends up making you resentful of the people you're "helping." Real quick, I know the word *disease* may sound harsh and icky, but I'm comfortable with calling it a disease because it's progressive and habitual and there's no panacea for it. From what I can gather about codependence, it's not something you can cure per se, but if you build up your self-awareness and self-esteem, it is something you can curb and manage. Calling it a disease also helps me to take it more seriously, since before my therapy for codependence I tended to see my behavior as "being a good person" or "doing the right thing" instead of how I routinely neglected myself while focusing on others, hurt myself with my expectations of reciprocal treatment, and auditioned for people's approval. That said, I now know that none of this information should be on my online dating profile.

Codependence can be tricky to diagnose because it's so socially acceptable and even rewarded in our culture. Buying gifts, lending someone money, driving a friend to the airport—these are all filed under being selfless or having good manners. But as a very wise friend of mine once said, "People pleasing is a form of assholery" because our seemingly benevolent behaviors often have sticky motives. These could include needing someone to like us, fear of abandonment, setting ourselves up for disappointment, victimizing ourselves, and trying to maintain a perfect reputation to give us an identity, since we tend not to have one without feedback or validation from others.

The motives part was very confusing to me at first because I had a hard time delineating what was and wasn't a clean motive. My brain commingled so many dynamics from my childhood that I truly always thought I was doing the right thing, but a lot of my behavior benefited nobody. For example, I now know that it's "nice" for me to drive you to the airport, but not so much if a week later I text you, and when I don't hear back in an hour, I think, "How dare she! After I *drove her to the airport on a weekday*!" followed by stewing in my self-righteousness and resentment, making myself the victim. See how this "nice" gesture is not at all nice given that there are strings attached in the form of impossible expectations? Doing kind things for people and then being angry when they don't reciprocate by behaving the way we need them to in our heads is how we re-create feelings of being a victim, which is a very easy comfort zone to get cozy in. This batshittery is often described as "taking poison and expecting the other person to die." Before I started working on overcoming my codependence, I used to pound that metaphorical poison with a metaphorical beer bong.

Before I rewired my brain on the codependence front, I was always micromanaging someone else's experience: I was always making sure everyone was eating, the right music was playing, the AC was at the right temperature. I would tiptoe around everyone else's needs (real or imaginary) and limitations, yet martyr myself by tolerating an endless amount of discomfort and stress. For example, I lived with giant cockroaches in my apartment for years because I didn't have the courage to stand up to my landlord. I ate food I was allergic to because I was afraid of offending a dinner-party host. In college, I answered to the name Wendy for years because I was too afraid to correct someone in my building who had misheard my name when we first met.

Now, for those of you who relate, welcome! Let's become besties and make a big mess! And for those of you who are baffled about why I'd engage in this kind of emotional cutting, the long and short of it is that being disappointed by people was my safe place, so when people *didn't* disappoint me, instead of enduring the anxiety of waiting for it, I'd jerry-rig the situation so that it would happen right away on my terms. From what I gather from the gaggle of experts I've overpaid to explain these emotional gymnastics to me, as adults we tend to re-create whatever happened to us as kids so our minds can maintain the chemical equilibrium that we've acclimated to. Being disappointed was my comfort zone so my brain would choose familiar insanity over unfamiliar sanity every time.

Okay, so you're getting the gist of what codependence is, but you're probably wondering how one becomes codependent in the first place. I'll tell you, because if you consult WebMD you'll just end up deducing that you have leprosy, so allow me to save you a bit of panic. There are a myriad of ways someone can end up being codependent, but in my case it was a couple of specific things. First, I believe some of my family members may have been codependent, which they got from their parents, who got it from their parents and into the matrix we go. I'm sure the generations before us had good intentions and did the best they could—in fact, most of them were probably straight-up heroes—but our grandparents and their grandparents were alive at a time when therapy and self-awareness weren't really a thing. There wasn't much time back then for self-help, given they had to spend most of their time dodging scurvy and cannonballs.

Codependence thrives in alcoholic households. And let me just throw out that when I say *alcoholic*, I understand that word as describing a dynamic of continually doing something despite negative consequences. I'm not an addiction specialist, but smart ones have told me that alcoholism doesn't just apply to cartoon bums pounding bourbon from brown paper bags, it can be used to describe overusing anything to anesthetize discomfort: eating, drinking, fighting, cheating, gambling, worrying, shopping, or in my case, controlling. And by controlling, I mean micromanaging circumstances so everyone is comfortable so there's no conflict. Why? So I can feel safe, ya silly goose. This behavior kept me safe as a child, but made me annoying as an adult.

Our parents and grandparents came by their alcoholic behavior honestly. Up until the early 1900s, even water contained alcohol in it as an antiseptic. If you didn't put alcohol in your water, you were at risk for dysentery, so everyone was pretty much shit-faced, which actually explains a lot about why men were so comfortable wearing white curly wigs. Until pretty recently, people were either wasted or taking care of someone who was, breeding a generation of caretakers who created a blueprint for future generations to emulate and, voilà, the insidious vortex that is present-day codependence.

I'd be remiss to ignore how codependence also could have some roots in our various religions, many of which transmit the message "Take care of people at all costs and put yourself last." I can't argue with "Do unto others as you would have them do unto you," assuming you aren't one of those people who likes to pierce his face and hang himself from hooks. In that case, maybe leave others out of it.

I went to some religious schools as a kid and I felt shame and guilt if I took care of myself because selflessness and sacrifice were so glorified there. In church I learned that if I care for others at all costs, I not only get to go to heaven but also got to eat yummy low-cal wafers. It always bummed me out that I had to imagine my tasty snacks as being the body of Christ, but once I was able to block out the image of eating the skin of a dying man from two thousand years ago, those wafers were the highlight of my day and made the emotional martyrdom very worth it.

I was working on the theory that capitalism and the "American way" was inculcated into our brains to do whatever was necessary to impress and get the approval of others, to live the American dream, but when I went to Asia, I felt the vibe over there was deeply codependent as well, so maybe this is more of a global or simply deeply tribal phenomenon. The truth is, it's deeply co-dependent of me to feel I need to impress you with how strong a handle I have on the origins of codependence, but I'm hoping you're gleaning a bit about how deeply the dynamic of people pleasing is rooted in our collective human history. I'm throwing out some educated-ish guesses, but codependence seems to be a dizzying mix of human nature, cultural conditioning, and people posting photos of themselves on social media looking way happier than they actually are.

I think it's pretty obvious that I'm not a psychiatrist. I'm essentially a professional party clown who tries to make drunk people laugh at night, but having grown up around codependence and suffering from it my entire life, I do feel I can say with authority that always needing to be perfect, polite, and generous breeds a toxic culture of shame, guilt, competition, and inauthenticity. I grew up in a fragile ecosystem in which the appearance of being happy eclipsed actually being happy. I learned that to be happy yourself, you must make others happy by dazzling them with hu-mor, compliments, gifts—basically anything material and ephem-eral. During Christmas at relatives' houses, no matter how much I could feel we all resented one another, there was always a giant mountain of gifts under the tree. It was always so confusing to me that people would spend the day arguing and then follow that by exchanging gifts. I learned that presents were a way to pretend everything was fine when it clearly wasn't, even though many of the presents were obvious regifts. My brain learned at an early age: As long as everything *looks* fine, everything *is* fine. Hence me in my twenties spending more money on bronzer and wrinkle cream than on food.

Another element of my codependence is doing things out of a feeling of obligation instead of out of the actual desire to do them. Growing up, I learned that wanting to do something had nothing to do with whether or not you actually did it. The messages I heard were "we *have* to swing by that holiday party" or "you *gotta* send that thank-you card." A lot of what we did felt rooted in obligation, which of course comes from a deep fear of disappointing other people and the desire to make sure everyone thought and spoke highly of us. This of course never worked, because every time I was dragged to an event out of obligation, I ruined our reputation by sulking in the corner and wearing way-too-tight clothes from the dELiA's catalogue. And if you don't know what dELiA's is, first of all, congratulations on being so young, and second, dELiA's was a catalogue in the nineties where emo girls got their cheap, overpriced tank tops.

We've probably all had the experience as kids of having a phone jammed in our faces and being told to "say hi to your aunt Glenda!" even though you've never liked, or worse, never even met Aunt Glenda. I don't have an aunt named Glenda, but the point is that I was often forced to be nice to people and had to learn very early on how to fake enthusiasm. I was never able to develop an organic desire to connect with my metaphorical aunt Glenda. I'm sure she would be lovely if she existed, but how could we ever have a healthy, mutually enjoyable relationship if I wasn't able to talk to her by choice instead of as a chore? I learned that if someone wants something from you, you don't get to say no; you have to be inauthentic and force a connection with people instead of letting it develop naturally. I understand our society labels a chat with Fake Aunt Glenda as "polite," but as a child I found this very confusing. It taught me to put other people's needs before my own, and when

I was an adult, it taught me to fake everything from happiness to interest to orgasms.

Birth order is another ingredient that factored into the development of my codependence. Being the youngest in the family doesn't guarantee that you'll be a codependent, but for me, being the last kid out of the tunnel meant I had to squeeze into an already established system, which meant morphing into whatever shape would get me some attention. I tried every antic I could think of: being funny, dramatic, overachieving, or sick. Naturally, as an adult I continued to do these things out of habit. Given we're basically fancy monkeys, we keep doing what worked as kids. When I was twenty-seven, I realized that I literally yelled during one-on-one conversations with people. As a kid I always had to talk so loudly to be heard that when I grew up, I didn't even know the appropriate decibel level to hit in a civilized conversation. Back then, every time I spoke it sounded like I was getting murdered.

As a kid I developed many a survival skill that came in handy when things were stressful: being quiet during family conflict as to not make things worse, making jokes when things were tense, or just being a general chameleon in all situations. Complaining or needing things just seemed to exacerbate the stress and push people into making me feel guilty, so I began stuffing down my feelings and resorting to very sexy behavior like passive aggression and dissociation into fantasy worlds to escape. I used to pretend I was Kelly Bundy from *Married . . . with Children*, which eventually went from fantasy to reality, leading to some unfortunate wardrobe choices, burnt eyeballs from dousing myself with Aqua Net, and at least one rolled ankle.

In my nascent years I learned all sorts of maladaptive skills, one of which was how to anticipate someone else's needs. I became an expert at walking on literal and figurative eggshells because I also found out that cooking for people made them like you, so I started doing that at an early age. This may sound sad, but if I may find a silver lining, being able to say you can poach an egg really rounds out the ole Match.com profile.

This all coalesced into my becoming an adult (I use that term loosely) who spent a tremendous amount of time taking care of other people and trying to be helpful, then resenting the people I helped. My vocabulary was littered with "I gotta" and "I have to." Again, I'm sure it seems like the honorable or polite thing to do, to attend someone's birthday or baby shower or whatever, but the underlying vibe was that of obligation, and often it felt like a chore. I literally looked at most social invitations the same way I looked at a jury duty summons.

As a codependent, I mastered the art of giving my energy away. Before I got a handle on this nasty beast, I was always exhausted. My days were booked solid with work and social obligations, chores, errands, things I thought I "had" to do. Even social events were depleting because I'd go out of obligation and I'd spend most of my time figuring out how to be useful. I was always the chump who would spend the whole party listening to someone else's problems for two hours while everyone else was doing shots. Mind you, these were problems that no one actually wanted to solve; they just wanted to blather on about them ad nauseam. I call such people "time vampires" because they suck you into their problems and don't actually want a solution to said problems. Oh, and the "problems" usually involve "drama" with guys named Tad or Jake.

And if I wasn't in the corner of a party trying to help people figure out if they should get a divorce or giving them phone numbers to doctors, I didn't really know what to do with myself, so I'd be in the kitchen cleaning up. I truly thought I was being nice, but chances are I came off as annoying and micromanagey. If I've learned anything, it's that the only thing worse than asking a woman her age in front of a group of people is going into her kitchen without her very explicitly asking you to do so. If you storm into another woman's kitchen without her consent, you might as well just have sex with her husband while you're at it; then after you're done, ask her how old she is in front of him. Then tweet it.

Aside from all the aforementioned lunacy, my codependence also made me kind of grating. I was the person who was so socially anxious that I'd be hovering over you at a party, offering you water or a drink as if you were terminally ill. I was the one giving you an extravagant gift that frankly you didn't deserve, which ended up making you feel awkward and guilty for not getting me one. Some of my codependent pals call this being "pathologically thoughtful." We care about people to the point of smothering them and making them uncomfortable. I was like a crackhead, fiending for connection and purpose so that I could feel useful, helpful, pretty, alive . . . anything but self-aware. I was an addict and being needed was my drug.

My point is that a "fun night out" always ended with me being some stranger's therapist, doctor, mother, godmother, dermatologist, or janitor. I could never leave a party without three phone numbers of time vampires so we could be "besties." I'm not a statistician, but I'm almost positive I've gotten more phone numbers of kooky girls than Stephen Dorff got at Playboy Mansion parties in the nineties. The problem is that I was literally hoarding friends. Even though I had an abundance of amazing friends that I already didn't have time for, I still continued to add to my contact list anyway, creating an unsustainable number of friendships I could never possibly nurture in a healthy way. Since I've been in codependence therapy, it's clear that today I'm at capacity and have no business taking on new friends. No vacancy, no new friend applications for now. Sorry to disappoint you, but to take on a new pal, I need someone in my circle to either go on a six-month silent retreat, move to a city without Internet, or vape when we're in public together, which would mean immediate excommunication from said circle.

My codependence drove me to be kind of a compulsive friend-aholic. My codependence told me that I had to be friends with everyone. I needed everyone to be obsessed with me. And if some-one didn't want to be friends with me? Oh, girl, I'm comin' for ya. You shall be mine. If you didn't fall in love with me immediately, that just meant I would work even harder for your approval. I'd shape-shift into what you needed me to be: funnier, quieter, shorter. You read that right. I have worn flats around people shorter than me so they didn't have to feel insecure about their height.

Once I became friends with someone, it wasn't really about girl talk or having fun, it was about entrenching. We couldn't just be pals, we had to be intertwined like all the classic duos: Thelma and Louise, Sid and Nancy, Cocaine and Rehab. I realize this may sound very predatory, but when you're codependent, attaching to needy people comes very naturally because that's how you derive your self-worth and meaning. I didn't really know who I was un-less I was rescuing someone or helping people with their problems, both real and imagined.

I think my addiction to energy suckers must also have been a way of dissociating so I didn't have to look inward at myself and my own shortcomings. Focusing on other people's problems meant I didn't have to look at myself in the mirror. When you're so con-sumed with other people's issues, you don't have time to look at your own. I mean, Googling myself is one thing, but looking at my flaws? Pass.

A major element of my codependence is that it's incredibly hard to say no to things or cancel if I find myself overcommitted. As soon as I made a plan, I'd immediately be overcome with dread and regret and spend most of the time between making it and the event itself trying to figure out a way to get out of it, sometimes praying I'd get injured or have a baby so I'd have an excuse. At the time I didn't realize how arrogant it is to fear saying no to an invite. This is something that cracks me up about my codependence—that I'm very insecure, yet still think if I say no to an invite, the person inviting me is going to have an emotional meltdown if I don't attend. When we fear canceling plans, essentially the thought process is "If I don't say yes, this person will implode with sadness and have no reason to live!" I didn't understand that no one's life is shattered because I declined an invitation. As Vera once said, "Codependents obsess over what other people think about us until we realize they're not." Trust me, at parties nobody is in a fetal position, sobbing over the fact that I didn't make it; they're preoccupied with taking selfies and picking a flattering filter for their aforementioned selfies.

Maybe this isn't always true. Let's say someone does freak out when you honor yourself and say no because you're too tired, or simply don't want to do whatever thing they ask. If that's the case, there's something going on with that person that's way bigger than you (self-absorption, immaturity, narcissism, borderline personality disorder, addiction, or just general punk-ass-ness), or they may be possessed by their own codependent demons, like I was, leading them to believe that friendships are about attendance sheets. If this type of person is in your life making you feel guilty for taking care of yourself, try *control alt delete*—that is, take control, make an alt choice, and delete their contact in your phone.

It took me a long time to understand that friendships shouldn't feel like work, and the ones that do eventually corrode because you grow resentful of them. But sometimes when relationships feel draining, it's because we're not being direct and honest about what we need; then when we don't get it, we're annoyed. I used to

exhibit what's called "magical thinking," in which I expected people to just know what I wanted, since I was too afraid to tell them
outright. I expected them to know that when I said "Sure, I'll go,"
what I really meant was "I would rather have hot-sauce-covered
sea urchins on my eyeball than do that." I was angry at people for
not knowing mysterious things about me, like that I didn't *really*
want to go to an art walk or whatever probably very fun thing
people do these days that gives me crippling anxiety.

Once I got a handle on my codependence, I faced my fear of saying no and canceling on people. It never occurred to me that I was
allowed to say, "Thanks for asking, but I'm gonna pass." I realized
that it's okay to not want to do things. For example, I really don't
vibe on karaoke. It's just not my thing. I know I come off as the
type of person who would love to get up there and belt out bad
ironic nineties songs, maybe even the actual nineties song "Ironic,"
since Alanis Morissette and I seem to have a shockingly similar
approach to relationships. But no, the truth is I do not like karaoke. There, I said it. I hate karaoke! Goddamn, that feels good to
say. I hate karaoke! Okay, I'm done. I can see why it's fun for people, but for me, bad singing is something I enjoy doing in the privacy of my own home, not for strangers and Snapchat. I yell into a
microphone and embarrass myself for a living, so I don't feel I need
to do it in my free time as well. Also, my singing is shockingly bad.
I promise I'm not being self-deprecating here. My singing voice is
truly horrendous, and not even, like, funny horrendous. It, like,
makes people sad. I can't tell you how many times I've forced myself to do karaoke with people. I'm terrible at singing and the
thought of being bad at something in front of a crowd is probably
my least favorite of every worst-case scenario, so I'd pretend to
have fun when the truth was I was consumed by anxiety as I
forced laughs and woo-hoos. After the third or fourth night of
waiting for three hours just to get up and yell "Wild Thing" with
three drunk girls I barely know, I finally hit rock bottom. I had to

find the courage to start saying no to things I didn't want to do because once you turn thirty, pretending starts taking a toll on your immune system. I had to learn how to say no to others and yes to myself, and today I no longer feel ashamed for not being "fun" and being down for every draining activity I'm asked to do. I'm no longer terrified I'll be judged, abandoned, rejected, or left out. And if I am, good. Turns out it's kind of my dream to be left out of doing things I don't want to do. What this means is that unless your invite involves cheese, Netflix, Mexican wrestling, Moscow mules, or actual mules, chances are, in the words of Randy Jackson, "That's gonna be a no for me, dog."

I've also learned that I am allowed to change my mind after I have already made a plan to do something. This was previously anathema to my codependent brain, because when I was a kid, I learned to always give in to guilt, no matter how uncomfortable the situation made me. I now know that I'm allowed to RSVP yes to a seventies theme party, but then the next day, once I realize I have to go to a vintage clothing store and wear musty-ass high-waisted bell-bottoms that give me a camel toe, I can rethink the plan and politely bow out. Instead, I can do what I really want to do, which is stay home and stare at photos of my dogs even though they're sitting right next to me.

Now I find it amusing to think how scared I used to be to cancel on people. When people cancel on me, I'm never upset. In fact, I'm usually downright thrilled. When someone texts, "Not feeling great tonight, rain check?" I almost pull a muscle doing a victory dance. I love my friends, I love spending time with them, but when one of them flakes on dinner plans, I feel even more love for them. If you truly want to be nice to someone, cancel if that's what you really want. Showing up to a plan feeling tired, sick, resentful, or rushed isn't nice or fair to you or the person you have the plan with. I realize now that when I cancel, I'm probably giving someone the greatest gift of all: the opportunity to stay home, throw on some Crest Whitestrips, and not have to hold in their farts for a night.

Before I rewired my brain, even my house reflected my codependent belief system. I had a closet in my office reserved for gifts I collected throughout the years. Whenever I saw something online or in a store that I thought a person I know might like, I'd get it and throw it in the ole Make People Like Me Gift Closet. Or if someone gave me a gift, I'd put it in the closet to give to someone else down the line. I know that may seem pragmatic or just downright frugal, but I even did this with gifts I actually wanted to keep for myself. I just felt compelled to give everything away—from my energy to my time and even to my gifts. This was also a closet I needed, a closet I could have used for much more useful things like to store bully sticks, since I very recently discovered that they're dried cow dicks that smell like dried dicks covered in dried balls and should be buried deep in faraway closets. I could have used the unnecessary gift closet for all the miscellaneous crap in my garage that I bump my car on every time I pull in. My point is, if you got a gift from me in my twenties, I want you to know that I did not buy it for you, you don't deserve it, and please give it back.

I even decorated my home with the comfort of my guests in mind instead of my own. I had chairs that only guests could sit on, while I sat on a wobbly, too-tall barstool at my kitchen counter, which caused me to sit like I was either throwing pottery or puking outside a nightclub. It never occurred to me that *I* could enjoy sitting on the cozy couch or leaning on the fancy pillows—*my* cozy couch and *my* fancy pillows that *I* had bought on sale at Anthropologie. Nope, those were reserved for guests. I also never used my own dinnerware. I had nice glasses that I never used because I didn't want to soil them in case someone came by who needed to be dazzled with faux Moroccan tumblers from Pier 1. Meanwhile, for four years I ate off plastic plates and drank out of the same weird Comedy Central mug that I stole from some guy.

My fridge and cabinets were stocked with food, but just not food for me. I had all sorts of fancy Himalayan pink salt, mānuka honey, olive spread with different-colored olives in it, dark chocolate covered in goji berries (or whatever the berry of the moment was). All unopened, all waiting for the day that someone whose approval I needed came over so I could impress them with my cornucopia of overpriced garnish that made me worthy of eternal love.

Perhaps the most obvious area in my life that codependence has kicked my ass is with romantic relationships. Until very recently, I thought that dating someone meant abandoning your own life and disappearing into the wormhole that is the studio apartment your boyfriend shares with his three roommates. When I started dating someone, I would literally go missing. I'm actually kind of offended that none of my friends put me on a milk carton or at least called the police, because when I was in a relationship I was gone, girl.

At a young age I learned to make a man my first priority. Revolving one's life around a man is the perfect medicine for someone with low self-esteem. "This guy wants to hang out with me, I can't be *that* terrible." I outsourced my self-worth: If someone else "loved" me, I didn't have to love myself. My philosophy was, if a man asked you to jump, you asked, "Off which cliff?" And I'd take a cab to the cliff so he could have my car after I die from the fall, since he probably didn't have his own car or had his license taken away for driving when drunk.

When I was growing up, all the behavior in my home was reactive to the men. We ate what the men wanted to eat. We had heat when the men paid the bills. When they didn't, we froze our tits off. When men wanted to cheat, the women chose to believe their lies, knowing full well that nobody got hung up at an office job overnight or were in "crazy traffic" at eleven P.M. To make this dynamic even more pernicious, I also had very entertaining men in my family; they primed me to think men were more fun to be around than women. My dad and uncles were hilarious and charismatic, always acting out scenes from the *Vacation* movies ("Big Ben! Parliament!") and skits from the old *Saturday Night Live* shows ("Land Shark!"), whereas the women in my family were tired and mercurial, complaining about how much work they had to do and always asking me to do boring chores. I learned pretty early on that "Guys are a blast! Women are a buzzkill!"

In retrospect, I now know the women in my life were like that because they were essentially the first generation with nine-to-five jobs who were also expected to be full-time homemakers. Of course they weren't laughing at Chevy Chase impressions—they were exhausted. They worked too hard and slept too little, while getting poisoned every morning by hair spray and being asphyxiated by those hateful control-top panty hose that get swampy and basically shut your intestines down.

When I was old enough to start dating, I applied my codependent chameleon ways to boys. I was so afraid of my real self being rejected that I would shape-shift into whatever I thought would make the relationship work. If we met and had nothing in common? No problem! I'll fix that by pretending we do! Camping? *Sure!* Never mind that I hate camping and am allergic to bees, not to mention I can hardly sleep in my own bed, much less in a tent on a fire ant hill. A bar crawl? *OMG, that sounds amazing.* Even though I don't like bars, beer gives me migraines, and I hate crawling. (Seriously, my parents said I started walking at like six months because crawling was so boring.) You're not funny? *No problem!* I'll laugh at your terrible jokes anyway! You're broke? *No worries,*

I'll max out my credit card so you can buy video games and protein powder! You're married? *Even better!* That means you're not afraid of commitment!

I could be any dude's soul mate. I had racks full of jerseys representing almost every football team: Jets, Seahawks, Dolphins. My closet looked like a Foot Locker. And not even a *Lady* Foot Locker. I would commit so hard to supporting a man's sports team that one time I went so far as to buy some Giants lingerie on Etsy with Giants helmets on the bra, which seriously almost amputated my nipples. Hot tip: If you're going to wear lingerie with your man's team on it, make sure the team didn't lose the day before, because that's all he'll be thinking about when you're having sex. Walking out in lingerie is a very vulnerable moment for a girl and nothing is worse than strutting out and seeing a guy's face fall from having to relive the previous night's disappointing performance on a football field by some player who doesn't even know he exists. Anyway, the point is that I'm from D.C. and I can finally admit that by blood I have no choice but to be a Redskins fan, or whatever the name of the D.C. team is when this book comes out.

I've been a very different person in every relationship I've had. Different style, look, everything. I went through more hair colors than a prostitute on the run: I had black, blond, and greenish hair from trying to do red hair by myself. When you're insecure and codependent, every day is Halloween. My style choices for guys included everything from English schoolgirl, western cowgirl, Goth apocalyptic princess who shopped in the children's section, and way-too-much-spandex girl. Basically the rule of thumb in getting dressed for a guy was if my body hated it, he loved it. After much soul searching, I found out that my authentic self is a jeans and T-shirt type gal and that's okay because I now know that if a guy isn't into that, he's either gay or very gay.

Looking back, I actually might have even switched ethnicities for a guy. I dated someone who had only dated South American girls, so naturally I doused myself in self-tanner. If you've seen me—even if only on the cover of this book—then you've realized that I'm basically an albino, so when I put on self-tanner, I end up looking tie-dyed and slightly ill. Because I also have no patience and won't sit still long enough to let the self-tanner dry, I end up having what look like brown skid marks all over my sheets. News flash: Brown stains in your bed are not an aphrodisiac. When I look back on how much I morphed my skin color, I'm shocked I wasn't arrested for a hate crime. Or at the very least, didn't get a Facebook message from Tan Mom.

Another reason to get a handle on codependence is that when your identity is contingent upon the person you're dating, you end up eating a lot of very weird shit. I put so many things in my mouth to avoid conflict in relationships and I'm not even talking about the thing you're thinking about. I ate pickled eggs. Once I ate prawns on a boat. *Prawns.* I don't really know what a prawn is, but I just Googled it and it seems to be a shrimp with a weave, so apparently I ate fishy hair.

I even put myself in physical danger because I couldn't say no or stand up for myself. I went scuba diving at night, which may sound really fun to some of you, but it's my living nightmare. You don't need to be Neil deGrasse Tyson to know that fish are designed to swim underwater while humans are clearly not. I felt like Clarice in *The Silence of the Lambs* when Buffalo Bill had his night-vision goggles on and could see her, but she couldn't see him. The only saving grace of night diving is you can piss yourself and nobody can tell.

I was so reckless in my codependent attraction to people that I should be rotting in a Guatemalan jail. It all started when I met a cute French guy on a flight. He slept most of the time, so I projected an awesome personality onto him. Once he woke up, he didn't live up to my fantasy, but he was interested in me, and that's usually all I needed to give a year of my life to someone. He spoke just enough English for us to communicate, but not enough for us to be able to argue too much. And due to the language barrier, whenever we did argue, we both thought we had won, when in fact we probably both lost.

I should've known it wasn't an excellent idea to travel with him after I came across a shoe box in his closet full of credit cards with his name spelled differently on each one. I also found another shoe box full of photos, one of a girl with whipped cream on her hoo-ha and boobs. This was pre-iCloud, when we had to *print* dirty photos. I found this stuff when he was at work, so I obviously couldn't confront him about it. I didn't know how to confront someone, I only knew how to quietly fester. I was eighteen—gimme a break. And to answer your question, no, he never tried to put whipped cream on my boobs, which really hurt my feelings. That being said, I'm thrilled that there aren't hard-copy photos of me with my tits looking like sad cupcakes available on eBay.

To make things weirder, he lived in Fort Lauderdale. I had been spending most weekends commuting there to see him, and one night out of nowhere he asked if I wanted fly to Mexico, then drive to Guatemala. At the time I thought it was romantic and spontaneous, although now I suspect he was probably avoiding some kind of legal issue. Since this was before I had any idea how to say no to things I didn't want to do and felt a lot of socially constructed pressure for us to be soul mates, I enthusiastically responded, "I've always wanted to go to Guatemala!" I mean, no offense to Guatemala, but I had *not* always wanted to go there. The country is gorgeous, but it's also corrupt and intimidating. The first thing I saw at the border were fourteen-year-olds with machine guns, so I felt a low-grade sense of anxiety the whole trip, as if at any moment we could be punished for being American. Luckily, my dude was French, and his accent made everyone want to rob us just a little less. He told me since I was American to just be quiet in public, which was very insulting and very hot.

I loved Guatemala, but I spent most of my time there trying to pretend that I didn't have headaches and explosive diarrhea. Again, as a codependent I can't admit that I have needs, ask for help, or allow anyone to know that I'm human. This was quite a challenge, since our hotel had one "toilet." You had to pull a rope to "flush" it, and it was about four inches away from the "bed." Clearly whoever built this hotel did not believe in love and was very interested in challenging others' belief in it. The good news is that the French guy had a habit of drinking a lot of tequila during the day, so when I knew I was going to have a gastrointestinal episode, I'd push even more tequila on him to ensure he was knocked out cold so I didn't wake him up with what felt like giving birth to triplets every night at two A.M.

Once he was asleep, I snuck as far away from our room as I could go without having to end up on Nancy Grace's show and would crap my head off in the Guatemalan jungle. The third day I got a system down of going into the jungle and releasing the horror show in my belly. One night, we came back to the room from eating yet another diarrhea-inducing dinner to find a giant bobcat asleep on our front steps. After much cajoling and praying in two different languages, we managed to scare it away, and I wondered if this was the night I'd have to forgo my secret jungle routine. But no, my fear of exposing myself as human to a guy I was dating was way stronger than my fear of being mauled by a bloody-toothed feral animal. So did I go out into the jungle that night knowing a wild bobcat was afoot? You bet I did. But the episodes were over much quicker because it turns out that worrying about a wild bobcat mauling you literally scares the crap out of you.

On our way back to Florida, we waited for our flight in the Cancún airport after driving back over the Guatemalan border. He had been acting paranoid and was sweating profusely, which is usually more my thing. Even for Guatemala in August, there was a comical amount of sweat on his forehead. Now, if any guys are reading this, first of all, God bless you, and second, I know how much you hate when we go through your stuff, but please know that we do it because our reptilian brains tell us it's a great way to keep us from getting hurt: Our amygdala (the fear center of our brain) tells our hippocampus (our memory center) that we're in danger, and when the hippocampus corroborates with our frontal lobe (our decision-maker), our frontal lobe is, like, "Hey girl, I sense some weird shit going on. He's shady as hell and the only logical solution I have right now is for you to go through his personal items so we can get more intel. Godspeed!"

French guy went to the bathroom and my primordial survival instincts took over. My hands went into his bag and opened his wallet before my conscious mind could even process what was happening. I don't even know why I chose his wallet to go through, given he was a bartender two nights a week and his credit cards were all fake; I'm not even sure why he needed a wallet in the first place. That said, my primordial brain was on to something, because inside the wallet I found three little Ziploc bags full of white powder.

Was I furious? Yes. Could I have been arrested at the Guatemalan border for possession of drugs and never have seen my Myspace top eight friends again? Yes. Could I have been killed by a teenage machete-happy Guatemalan who had an excellent excuse to kill me? You bet. Did I say anything to him about it? Of course not. I put the wallet back into his bag and pretended nothing happened, because, well, God forbid I do something that could lead to a breakup with a drug-addicted, sweaty bartender who I couldn't even have a lucid conversation with.

Annoyingly, I can't chalk this behavior up to being a stupid teenager because I was still martyring myself for dudes in my late twenties. I'm not proud of this, but I once pretended I knew how to snowboard for a guy. He was great at it and I wanted so badly to be the cool girl who knew how to snowboard, but you've seen my body—I'm a gangly mess of tendons and have no business being anywhere near ice. Or even marble floors for that matter.

The first week I was in Los Angeles, someone invited me to a party at Val Kilmer's house. I know, weird brag. Anyway, to get ready for my big Hollywood party debut, I went and bought myself a hot pair of pumps from Nine West. Unfortunately for me, Val Kilmer's floor at the time was made of some kind of impossibly shiny marble that could only have been made from porcelain doll eyes. In an attempt to make a sexy, dramatic entrance that was sure to catch the attention of a powerful Hollywood agent (back then I thought this was how Hollywood worked, not that I have any idea how it works now), I stormed into this party like an ostrich auditioning for *America's Next Top Model*. I'd say I made it about seven feet or so before I found myself on the floor, in a sideways Warrior 1 pose, trying to get up like a newborn deer on ice. I split my probably Wet Seal pants in half, revealing a red thong that made me look like I had a horrible accident in my nether regions. The point is, I can barely walk on fancy floors, much less do snow sports that require skill and balance.

I didn't grow up skiing or any of that, and when you don't have health insurance, going eighty miles per hour down wet ice while standing up certainly doesn't crack the top thousand on your to-do list. As kids, if we wanted to slide around on something slippery, we would put Palmolive dish soap on a laminated picnic tablecloth or my sister and I would roll ourselves up in a comforter and slide down a flight of stairs. That may sound insane, but I promise it's worth the rug burn and risk of death. Basically anything that was free and super dangerous is how we kept ourselves entertained. So, without snow sports, we still managed to have a total blast as kids, even though I occasionally ended up with splinters in my teeth.

Anyway, I may not know a lot about winter sports, but one thing I do know for sure is that you can't just pretend you know how to do them the way you can pretend you know what a movie's about based on the title. After telling my boyfriend I needed to "brush up" on my snowboarding skills with a refresh lesson (it was my first and only lesson ever), I begged the instructor to make me a pro in two hours. I remember him looking very panicked by my ambition and my complete denial of how learning a skill works. He just kept repeating the phrase "In snowboarding, you go where you look." I froze. Not just because I was genuinely freezing (I didn't have on enough warm clothes, having prioritized cuteness over warmth) but also because I felt it was the most profound advice I've gotten about life in general. *You go where you look.*

The at once wonderful and horrible thing about snowboarding is that you have to be completely in the moment or else you'll eat (hopefully white) snow. This made me particularly terrible at it, since I'm someone who multitasks and am usually torn between regretting what I did ten minutes ago and fearing what's gonna happen in ten years, so being in the moment is not my forte.

After practicing for about two hours, I lied to my boyfriend and told him I was ready to "board." The look on his face told me *board* is not a verb used by anyone who actually knows how to snowboard. He then responded with the news that we were going up to a black diamond, and unfortunately that had nothing to do with the ring Big got Carrie Bradshaw in *Sex and the City*. Because of my codependence, it didn't occur to me that I could protest or request a smaller, less murder-y hill. I had been so many things for so many guys, it didn't occur to me that "expert snowboarder" wasn't one of them. The idea of his thinking we weren't compatible was much scarier to me than cracking my face open on a giant mountain made of sociopathic stalagmites.

We finally got to the top of the black diamond, which they should just freaking call a blood diamond already. I had learned to snowboard, like, ten feet, so I figured I just had to do that ten-foot stretch about a thousand times and I could get down the mountain alive. Codependence has this magical ability to spin fear into confidence because the fear of seeming incapable eclipses your fear of hurting yourself, so off I went. My scam was actually working until I started doing so well that my inner voice crept in and said I wasn't doing well enough. I had mastered a toe turn, so my self-flagellating brain had the audacity to heckle me: "You can only do toe turns? You should be doing *heel* turns! You suck! No wonder your show got canceled!" Alas, *you go where you look.*

As I glided down the mountain, my boyfriend yelled something inaudible at me. Looking back, I'm sure it was something encouraging or supportive, but when I can't hear the words someone says to me, I make up what they've said based on what I think about myself. It becomes a real live fill-in-the-blank test where I insert something only a verbally abusive person would say. In my head, I heard him agree with my nasty inner monologue—"Do a heel turn!"—which I am now certain he would not have yelled. Unable to say no or acknowledge any human limits, I tried to do the move I had learned only a couple of hours ago, at a speed I had never gone before, on a mountain you can see from space. I looked down to see if I was doing it right. The thing is, *you go where you look.*

You know those giant body-shaped balloons in front of car dealerships that collapse, blow up, then violently collapse again? They fall sternum first and head last, which I guess for some reason is supposed to make you want to buy a new vehicle? Well, that's how I looked as I fell face-first into the snow, except the incline was so steep that just when I would have blown back up, I smashed into the icy ground. It happened too fast for me to fathom. All I could hear were snowboarders ripping past my head, filming one another with GoPros, since I guess there aren't already enough shitty snowboarding videos on YouTube with six views.

Perhaps it's the female predisposition of having a high tolerance for pain, perhaps it's not being coddled enough as a child, or perhaps it's the brain damage I got from years of gel manicures, but I promise you, I felt no physical pain after I fell. All I really felt was shame, so I tried to get up as quickly as possible in order to laugh it off and pretend I was fine. No dice. When I tried to lift my right arm, I simply couldn't. It wasn't painful; it was more like my arm wasn't responding, like it was "rebuffering stream." I pushed my ass up in the air, trying to roll onto my back with a very sad twerking motion.

When my guy finally got up to me, I had a smile on my frigid face and made a joke (probably a corny joke about cocaine/white powder in my nose if I were to guess). I promised I was fine and that I could snowboard down the hill myself, even though I not only still couldn't snowboard but was also seriously injured. But that wasn't going to stop me from being fine! I did snowboard the rest of the way down the hill, falling many times, this time mostly on my ass but catching myself with my arms. With each fall, my shoulder hurt more and more, but that pain paled in comparison to the thought of possibly being considered someone who needed help.

Back at the house, I started taking my gear off, only to realize I couldn't do anything with my right arm. Lift it, push with it, take a bra off with it, even gesticulate for comic effect—which my shoulder injury made me realize I do way too frequently. To distract everyone from how much trouble I was having putting clothes on or lifting things up, I did impressions of Kristen Wiig's tiny hands character on *SNL*, which I must admit, I am excellent at when my shoulder is intact.

Two days later, when I finally went home, I couldn't lift my right arm more than four inches or so and I couldn't put a bra on to save my life. I finally gave up and went to a doctor, who told me I had broken my humerus, which felt like a cruel prank the universe was playing on me, given all the ways I was trying to use humor to minimize the gravity of the situation. I had also bruised my rotator cuff, which as far as I knew, was a car part. Long story short, I needed three days a week of physical therapy for six months. He also told me my shoulder would "never be the same." The only thing more unsettling to me than a doctor saying something that dramatic and vague was that all of this could have been avoided had I just said no thanks to the snowboarding offer.

It just didn't occur to me that I could say no to men until very recently. I've gone on countless dates with guys I had no interest in because I felt guilty or didn't know how to turn them down without hurting their feelings. I've slept with guys I wasn't even attracted to because they "drove all this way" or "they split the bill at McCormick & Schmick's, and *I did* order the fancy salmon."

I regularly put my sexual health at risk because I was too insecure to say no or stand up for myself. I was so afraid of abandonment that I couldn't ask for simple things: "Hey, dude, how about we wash that before you put it inside my body?" or "Let's use the hole that's specifically engineered for intercourse instead!" and let me tell you, the sooner you can say these things, the sooner you'll stop getting UTIs.

It's healing for me to make light of it, but I also feel sad for the person I was back then, for that girl who had no boundaries and was terrified of being thought of as annoying or weak. The irony is as soon as I stopped pretending and performing for people, I started attracting way more amazing ones. When you're authentic, you attract people who want a self-actualized person, not some Mrs. Potato Head who is customized based on who she's with. I started meeting guys who were excited about the prospect of being with a girl who has her own identity instead of some blow-up doll who acquiesces to whatever they're into. To figure out who I was, I learned to look inward instead of outward. Folks, *you go where you look.*

So how did I stop focusing on what other people wanted and figure out what I wanted? I got to work with Vera. You already know she wears shirts with wolves on them, but her personality is just as awesome as her clothes. Vera is the epitome of self-actualized. She knows exactly who she is, a person who upholstered the chairs in her office with fabric that has tigers on it, which elevates her to luminary status. Since she does her own damn thing, I knew I could trust her with helping me figure out what my damn thing was. Vera realized I had never been specific about what I wanted in a partner, so she had me make three lists so I could get focused and stop letting codependence be my matchmaker. Read closely because you're about to make one, too, cutie.

She had me draw three columns and head them with MUSTS, WOULD BE COOL, and RED FLAGS. The musts are things you absolutely need from a mate—for example, wants kids, doesn't want kids, or has a credit score above 5. The traits that "would be cool" are nice but not essential—for example, plays tennis, is taller than you, hasn't been married, has a Pez dispenser collection, etc. And the last column contains the "deal breakers." I know for some of us red flags are actually an aphrodisiac, but that had to change for me so I didn't end up a bag of battered bones on the side of a mountain. Here are some examples of red flags in case you're as confused about them as I was: cups his screen with his hand when he texts, always has a just-cleared browser history, or has two cell phones. If you're a guy, some red flags for girls could include being engaged, sending private Snapchat photos, and being a fan of my stand-up.

I wanted to include my list so you could see how specific you should be when you make yours. And now that you have my list, I'm asking you to hold me accountable! If you ever see me with a guy who does crystal meth and hates dogs, I give you permission to throw trash at me in public. Unfollow me on Twitter, leave an old-lady emoticon as a comment under an Instagram selfie—whatever you think will hurt me the most.

MUSTS	WOULD BE NICE	RED FLAGS
Trustworthy	Cooks	Roomates
Reliable	Can fix shit	day drinking
Consistent	doesn't call exes	ego problem
Will sleep w/ Dog	"crazy"	Same day plans
Self aware	hasn't been married	gives me adrenaline
committed to growth	Knows computers	mean to wait staff
helps me grow	funny	Violent
no pressure to be funny	Okay with me talking	Social media addict.
affectionate	about him in stand up	entitled (DARK WEB
doesn't make me go to music festivals	aligned w/ me politically	tells me to
~~doesn't~~ alpha	~~In therapy.~~	"relax" or won't
not a comedian	cool family	engage in communicat.
self-aware	Knows dog training	travels for work/ lives in another city
not a narcissist	has a car	STDs, won't use a condom
passport	goes to sleep same time	anger issues
gives good advice	as m.	litters (litter Bug)
loyal	good relationship w/	Sociopathic
open to having kids	his family (women)	ostentatious car
financially responsible	reads books	negative thinking
has a job hes satisfied w/ the (happy, fulfilled outside home)	not closed minded	active alcoholic
Strong self care game	about the metaphysical	makes me feel insecure
hygienic	Understands addiction	actions and words
honestly likes me	Could contribute financially	are incongruous
don't take himself too serious	outdoorsy	in a band
Good taste in people/ clothes		liar, secretive
		dismissive

You can also make a list like this to manifest friends, jobs, or anything you want in your future. Many of us have been conditioned to chase unavailable people, settle for bad relationships, and stay in uncomfortable situations, so you should all use this as a guideline. You don't go to the grocery store without a list of what you want to get, so don't go out in the world without an idea of what you want from your life.

Today I still have codependent impulses and thoughts, but I rarely act on them. After doing a lot of work trying to rewire my brain and update the old software concerning what I thought was true, now when someone asks me what kind of takeout I want, I actually know the answer. If someone wants to set me up with a guy I'm not interested in, I don't go out of obligation. And when I do say no, I don't apologize ten times or make excuses because that's boring for everyone. If I change my mind later, I replay in my head one of my favorite sayings from Derek Sivers, entrepreneur and all around badass: "If it's not a hell yes, it's a no."

Since saying no can still be challenging for me, especially if I haven't eaten, I have some stock answers so I don't end up giving in, because when I do that, I usually end up at Build-A-Bear for a birthday party of some kid I hardly know. Some of my go-to's include "I need a couple of days to think about it" and "Can we circle back tomorrow?" If I know I can't do something, I'll say "I'm overcommitted at the moment and can't take on any more plans for a couple months. I'll reach out when my schedule clears up." Or if I downright don't want to do something, I say, "Thank you for thinking of me, but that's not really my speed. Let me know if you want to schedule something else, like an easy dinner." If you're codependent, it may sound like a nightmare to say this to people, but I promise that if you do, not one person will catch on fire. Almost everyone is grateful for honesty and directness, and the people who aren't? Well, that's why we have the option to "block this caller" on our phones.

I take a lot of pride in the fact that people can trust me now. They can trust that when I'm with them, I really want to be there, and that I don't do anything I don't want to do. I'm so grateful that because I give off an authentic vibe, I now attract people on a similar frequency who create that same safe space for me so I'm not consumed by self-doubt or insecurity about how they really feel about me. Today my relationships aren't laced with guilt or fear. These days I do only 50 percent in my relationships, whereas it used to be if someone gave me 20 percent, I'd overcompensate by giving back 80. If you feel yourself doing more than half your share in a relationship, maybe try pulling back and investing that time in more useful things, like stretching and creating dog memes.

I occasionally still feel my default wiring kicking in, telling me to mirror the people around me and give more energy than I have, but I can usually course-correct before I end up injured, engaged to a narcissist, or imprisoned in South America.

People tend to describe me as a "strong woman." I personally feel that phrase is redundant. All women are inherently strong. We regularly endure a screaming nine-pound mammal tearing through our bodies and live to post about it. I heard once that childbirth is apparently the pain equivalent of getting twenty bones fractured at once, so I think we can officially end the debate about whether women are strong or not.

Another reason I prefer to reject the term *strong* is because on some level it signifies enduring pain, whereas after a long reparenting process, I now view being strong as having enough self-respect and foresight to avoid pain. I now redefine *strong* as being brave and vulnerable enough to ask for help, whether it's from a doctor, a therapist, or from trusty Siri.

Today if someone calls me strong, it almost feels like an insult. It usually means I've fallen back into putting the needs of others before my own or am overworking myself. In my opinion, our society is plagued by an epidemic of self-sacrifice and self-deprivation.

We've become a culture of martyrs; we glorify busy and almost seem to celebrate exhaustion. In our workplaces, employees compete over who slept the least, who needs the most coffee, who worked the latest, who has the most packed schedule. There's obviously some other psychological phenomenon at play here because people who are truly that busy don't have time to blather on about how busy they are.

My point is, maybe I'm not strong. Maybe I'm fragile and vulnerable and terrible at snowboarding, and maybe that's just fine.

THE ROAST JOKE CHAPTER

People always ask me how I got funny. The short answer is: I had to figure out a way to be liked. The long answer is more complicated because humor also developed as a survival mechanism to protect myself and disarm or intimidate people when I didn't feel safe, to make fun of myself before other people could, to avoid having to feel sadness, or to mitigate the gravity of a situation because laughter was my anesthetic for pain. Also, my last name is Cummings, so as you can probably imagine, I had to learn to defend myself from insults pretty early on in life.

My parents were also very funny. My dad was a master of hyperbole and notorious for performing scenes from *¡Three Amigos!* in public, much to my chagrin as a kid with low self-esteem. When he would pick me up from school, he would hide behind a car, and caw like a nasal bird, yelling, "Look up here! Look up here!" à la Steve Martin in the scene where he's standing on the billboard. The later he picked me up, the louder his bird impressions were, always managing to make up for his lack of actual timing with impeccable comic timing.

My dad also had a very serious side, especially when it came to studying for tests. He'd drill me on spelling over and over, instilling a relentless work ethic and deep fear of failure in me. But every now and then, if I was nailing my vocabulary definitions or state capitals, he would look at the textbook I was memorizing from, bug his eyes out, and say, "You're right, but how do we know this book is right?!" He would momentarily look super panicked, which caused me to have a complete freak-out that the textbook was wrong. Once he got me, he would crack up laughing. Then I would crack up laughing. This could have been very damaging to my psyche and ability to trust men, but in our family, laughs were way more important than mental health.

My dad's all-time classic bit was at restaurants. After I had excused myself from the table to go to the restroom, he would dramatically shout "Hey!" Then when I'd turn back to the table, he'd wistfully announce, *"I'll wait here."* Again, this may not sound funny to you, but the fact that he did it so consistently and cracked himself up made it a timeless classic for us. My dad showed me that it's my responsibility to provide my own joy, and that every moment is a chance to find lightness.

My whole family had jokes like this, using humor to make us all think things were fine when they were far from it. Nebulous work situations, failed marriages, and financial uncertainty were constantly joked about. Some people take pills, some people drink, some people gamble—my family cracked jokes to make the pain go away. I'm sure some of them probably also took pills and drank, but that's another chapter I'll write after I've had a couple of pills and some drinks.

My mom's brand of humor was more of the *Ab Fab* slapstick genre. She's blond and beautiful, and always dressed very stylishly, so this wasn't a huge reach, given that she was always juggling way too many bags, balancing a coffee cup, and frantically looking for her glasses when there were two pairs on her head. I vividly remember as a kid getting stuck in a parking lot because my mom had lost the ticket. She bribed the parking attendant with whatever she could find in the car. *Vogue* magazine? A kid's thermos? Panicked and bombing, she snatched the bag of peanut butter crackers out of my hand and tried to make them appealing to the Hispanic parking attendant, who I can only guess was being given more ammunition to resent white people. It was humiliating at the time, but in retrospect, I can appreciate how hilarious it was that she was bartering with trash from her car in order to absolve us of a parking fee.

Everyone in my family loved to laugh. Looking back, I now realize they *needed* to laugh. Loud laughter was how we all said "We're fine!" even though in my gut, I didn't feel like anything was fine. Laughter's the universal sign for "Everything's cool! Let's keep it light!" The tenser things got, the more we laughed. My family also used passive-aggressive jokes to communicate what we couldn't say honestly. Conversations at our holiday gatherings were peppered with insults wrapped in jokes of the "I don't care that we had to sell the house to pay for Marcy's divorce! We hated that house anyway!" variety. These way-too-close-to-home backhanded "jokes" were always followed by uproarious laughter. It was around then that my brain's wiring was custom-designed; I learned never to tell anyone how you really feel and not to take people at face value. Kids, do not try this at home. Later in life this mentality morphs into a sort of emotional dyslexia. In my case, my brain always got things backward: When someone was nice to me, I'd get suspicious and wonder what their motives were, assuming they were trying either to manipulate me or to recruit me into a cult. And if people were mean to me, I'd immediately fall in love with them.

Since we communicated in loaded jabs, nobody was safe from a Cummings family roast. I remember being the target of ridicule at eight years old, around the time I became notorious for having a perpetual case of head lice. (What can I say? My scalp is delicious.) After I was sent home from school for the fifth time, my parents' only option was to cut my hair as short as possible so the lice were more easily exterminated by whatever Rite Aid poison was being marketed as lice shampoo. This resulted in a terrible bowl cut à la Jim Carrey's character in *Dumb and Dumber*. I was lambasted by my family for months for looking like Moe from the Three Stooges, a Shetland pony, and a wet poodle, in addition to some probably racist Polish jokes I was too young to understand.

I'm sure most kids would have been embarrassed or cried, which is of course the healthy reaction, but I learned pretty quickly that the best tactic was to just go numb and laugh along with them. That's the American way, right? Be strong, man up, pretend to not have feelings if you aren't lucky enough to be a psychopath. I developed the survival skill of giggling when I was uncomfortable. You should see me at the gyno; it's a goddamn laugh riot.

To avoid getting hurt or being vulnerable, my brain hatched the perfect plan: When people make fun of you, laugh. When people hurt you, laugh. When you feel unsafe, laugh. It tricks everyone into thinking you don't care, which is the best defense. One day when my family was ripping on my hair, I started making fun of it as well. I figured out that if you just make fun of yourself first, you can beat people to the punch. And if you can't beat them to the punch, just punch yourself. Anything for a laugh.

Of course we shouldn't take ourselves too seriously, but there's a difference between having a healthy perspective and emotional self-flagellation. For the first thirty years of my life, self-deprecation was my main approach, although I now feel that a little piece of you dies every time you put yourself down. Even as a joke. Seemingly meaningless quips like "God, I'm such an idiot" or "Of course I forgot my keys, I'm such a mess" are death by a thousand cuts to your soul. If anyone spoke to me the way I used to speak to myself, I would file a restraining order. Why am I so nice to complete strangers, who could be sociopathic murderers or felons, but when it comes to myself, someone I know is not a murderer or a felon, I'm Ike Turner. I'm sure there's a fresher domestic violence reference than Ike Turner, but I feel like he's oddly evergreen. His assholery really is timelessly classic. He's like the Audrey Hepburn of emotionally abusive dickheads.

Once I was in therapy with Vera, and per usual, I had done something self-defeating and inane as a result of my lack of self-awareness and self-respect. As I recounted the mistake, I kept saying, "I know, I'm a moron."

She got silent. Things got awkward and she genuinely asked, "Why would you say that about yourself?"

I thought hard about the question, wanting to come up with the perfect answer that would impress Vera and justify my habitual mindless behavior. Finally I came up with what I thought was an incredibly incisive and true answer: "I'm a comedian and being negative about myself is a comedian thing. Self-deprecating *is funny*." The only issue with my brilliant answer about how funny it was was that Vera was not laughing.

"It's actually not funny," she said.

The fact that Vera said this was literally shocking, which is in itself shocking, given whenever I've said "I'm an idiot," nobody has ever laughed. I should not have needed a professional to explain that an absence of laughter indicates when something's unfunny, but I guess my negative, fictitious inner monologue was too loud for me to even hear what was going on in real time. Now that I'm mentally awake, I can see that being negative about yourself actually makes people not only not laugh, but get uncomfortable. It really weirds out the vibe. When we're mean to ourselves, the people around us don't know whether they're supposed to agree, disagree, argue, or call a suicide hotline. Sarah Silverman has the most perfect response to people being self-deprecating. When someone says something like "I'm so dumb," she says, "Hey, don't talk about my friend like that."

Sometime in 2007, while self-deprecation wasn't working out particularly well for me, the ability to write hard-core roast jokes was. I was watching the Comedy Central roast of William Shatner, and after each setup, I was able to guess the punch lines, often predicting the exact ones that were said. I realized I had a somewhat unsettling knack for writing incredibly brutal jokes. I also realized my rent had been late for five years, so I asked my manager if I could apply to be a roast-joke writer for Comedy Central. He e-mailed me back saying the same five guys had written for the roasts since they started and that they generally don't take on new writers. So, no. Oddly motivated by the rejection, I decided I'd just have to prove myself. I refused to take no for an answer and I wrote eighteen pages of jokes for the impending roast, which was for the great who-knows-what-he-actually-does-for-a-living Flavor Flav. If you know anything about him, you know that coming up with premises for insulting him isn't rocket science, but I banged out as many as I could. I begged my manager to send them in.

From what I was told, the joke that got me the job was: "Flavor Flav, you look like what Magic Johnson should look like right now." So much for good karma.

Working for the roasts was my literal dream job. I loved being in the roast writers room, where sharp comedy writers sat around all day eatin' crap and talkin' shit. We threw around insults all day, pertaining to the talent on the show, but also to each other. Maybe I felt so at home because I was able to re-create my childhood circumstances of dodging emotional bullets and using caustic humor to avoid intimacy. It also distracted me from my inner monologue, which heckled me with even worse insults than we wrote for Flavor Flav.

Eventually I became one of the go-to people for roast jokes, which I now realize is something of a dubious honor. But Mommy had bills to pay, and it was better than getting paid forty bucks for doing focus group tests in which I would take pills that had not yet been approved by the FDA and probably never would be approved by the FDA. So when I got a call to write roast jokes for a variety show hosted by Carmen Electra, who wanted to perform self-deprecating stand-up, it was a no-brainer.

I spoke with Carmen on the phone, and she was as lovely as she is pretty. She seemed fearless to me at the time, because this is back when I thought fearlessness was a thing. She said that she really wanted to be edgy and that I should "go for it." This was music to my ears, given her colorful dating history. I Googled "Carmen Electra dating," and it not only gave me fodder for jokes, it instantly made me feel better about the pathological liar I was dating.

I wrote about fifteen pages of jokes about Carmen's personal life, professional life—you name it. In preparation for a meeting with her and the producers of the show, I printed ten copies at a local Kinko's. I got dressed in my comedy uniform of hoodie, vintage-looking New Balance sneakers, and wacky nail polish so there was no confusion in the meeting about who the comedian was in the room. Carmen showed up with what seemed to be a manager as well as a boyfriend who seemed to think he was her manager. I remember being perplexed by how pretty she was. I put a lot of energy into trying to figure out how she radiated a golden glow. It was either what they call star quality or the perfect self-tanner/body glitter–blending skills. Either way, it was titillating and slightly frustrating. I also noticed that she lined her lips slightly outside of her lip line. I immediately regretted not having written jokes about that and not having lined my lips that way all my life.

Once the small talk and nervous laughter subsided, I proudly handed out the packets of jokes. Everyone began to read over the first page of roast jokes about Carmen. On that page they found some of these zingy zings:

(CARMEN ELECTRA)

Things are going great for me. I had a really big audition yesterday. Don't worry, we used protection.

I'm in a great mood because I had sex this morning. But enough about my acting career.

I'm really glad they thought of me to host this show. It's kind of perfect, because right now I actually have some downtime between divorces.

Laughs. Whew. Carmen is loving it. We all flip the page.

People assume that all girls who are exotic dancers have daddy issues. I do not have issues with my dad. We have a great relationship: We talk a lot, I see him all the time, and the sex is great.

I was on Baywatch. *All the women on that show were hot. They say women's bodies are like a wonderland. Mine is more like a football field. Because I have a tight end and a lot of black dudes have been on it.*

Gasp. The room went quiet. Everyone looked to Carmen to see how they should react. She forced a smile like a pro, which I'm sure she had a lot of practice doing from having to tolerate Hugh Hefner for most of the nineties. I recognized her awkward smile because I myself have forced it many times, but with way less perfect teeth.

For example, I had forced this same smile when I got cheated on and found out the other woman was programmed in my boyfriend's phone as "Sandylicious." Realizing that this person was in pain and pretending she was fine, I thought to reach out my hand and take the stack of jokes from her. The only problem was that my body did not obey. I was too frozen in shock to do anything. Carmen held her head up high, took a deep breath, and turned the page. Fuck.

> It's sort of hard to date when guys can find naked photos of you all over the Internet. Seriously, if you Google me, your computer will get a virus.

Oof. Even as a desensitized comedian, I knew that one was rough. It managed to penetrate through whatever armor she had left and her eyes welled up, and the amount of eye makeup she had on indicated that she had not planned on crying that day.

This moment gave me compassion for guys when girls get mad at them and they're confused about why. I truly had no idea what I did wrong or how to fix it. I could also tell that, like all women when we cry, some of the tears were new, but some were very, very old. "They're just jokes," I kept saying as I tried to manage the warm pang in my chest that felt like my heart was defecating into my stomach.

This was the first time I realized that not everyone had the same acumen for self-annihilation I had. All my life I used myself as a punching bag. Didn't everyone? Wasn't everyone willing to put their self-esteem on the line for a laugh? Once I stepped outside the confines of my family system and the dingy hallways of comedy clubs, apparently the answer was no. Plot twist—turned out Carmen Electra had way more self-respect than I did.

This incident taught me that the coping skills I had learned in order to navigate my family didn't work in the outside world. I was wielding weapons I used to fight a battle that had been over for fifteen years. I was out of the boxing ring, sitting on the bench, but still had my boxing gloves on, jabbing at anyone who came near me like a half-blind kangaroo on Adderall.

Needless to say, Carmen quit the show. Before storming out, she barked rhetorical questions at me such as "Is this really what people think of me?" which led me to believe that she had some sort of awakening that day, too. Regardless, I'll always be grateful to her for making me realize that we can use jokes to get closer to people or to push them away. Turns out jokes are like knives. You can use them to cook a beautiful meal or to straight-up stab people. Life works in mysterious ways: Some people learn from Gandhi, some from Osho, others from the Dalai Lama. My spiritual teacher just happened to have been a Playboy Playmate who married Dennis Rodman. How, well, funny.

I hope that, like me, Carmen is doing just fine.

THE SEXISM CHAPTER

For the first couple of years that I was doing stand-up in L.A., I was doing shows wherever I could get up, hustling for spots via Myspace messages. Since I had no clout—or act, for that matter—the stages I graced ended up being bowling alleys, coffeehouses, dive bars, and youth hostels whose audiences, very appropriately, consisted of hostile youths. I even did a set in the parking lot of a fried chicken place, and if I must say so myself, I managed to get some laughs over the sounds of traffic and helicopters. I never knew, on any given night, what kind of audience I'd be up against, whether they'd respond to my jokes or even speak English for that matter.

Despite the wide array of venues I performed at, one constant up until a couple of years ago was that at every show there was always a guy or group of guys who were not thrilled with a female coming to the stage. As I grabbed the mic, I'd hear everything from a mutter of "Here we go" to a yell of "Take off your shirt!" to the sight of people checking their phones or straight up getting up and leaving. To be fair, I didn't have a great act back then, but they couldn't have known that yet.

Nevertheless, whenever people say, "Comedy is such a misogynistic field, right?" even I'm surprised that I'm not quite sure how to answer this question. Believe me, I've tried really hard to figure out a way to respond with a definite yes to this question, because clearly someone is saying yes to it and I wanna be liked by whoever that someone is. But no, I don't think the *field* is sexist. It feels ignorant to me to anthropomorphize a field, as if an abstract noun like archery has the capacity to be judgmental. I don't think fields are sexist, I think *people* are sexist, and in the comedy field it's just easier to see who they are because they're drunk and yelling at you. And I must say, that's actually something I appreciate about being a stand-up. I actually prefer in-your-face sexism to the more insidious institutionalized kind because dealing with the passive-aggressive, subtle sexism and gaslighting that women have to contend with in other professions sounds exhausting. There aren't that many jobs where you hear sexist insults in the workplace issued so bluntly. I'd much rather someone yell their insults to my face than have my boss DM me corny pickup lines or send dick pics on the sly after work.

From what I'm aware of, I don't think sexism has held me back in comedy per se. It may have fueled way more hateful comments on Reddit, but I have to own the fact that when I haven't been given an opportunity or job I wanted in comedy, it hasn't been because of sexism. The truth is, annoying as it is to say, I probably just didn't deserve it yet.

When I hear someone say, "Being a comedian must be so hard for women," I get annoyed because that's just going to discourage more girls from pursuing it, and could scare them out of living their dream. And trust me, the last thing we need is more people with the desire to be comedians doing other jobs. Us comedy folk need the outlet of stand-up or we get very grating. The people who should have been comics but didn't end up pursuing the craft have to hold all that energy in. These people end up becoming that dorky dentist who can't stop cracking inappropriate jokes or that sarcastic accountant who makes the weird vibe-killing speech at a wedding about how the groom used to bang "soooo many chicks" before he met the bride.

But look, the truth is, maybe I'm not even qualified to chime in on this topic because I'm still trying to figure out what sexism is exactly. These days it's too pernicious for me to even deconstruct and thanks to modern technology seems to constantly evolve into new incarnations I can hardly keep up with. We used to have more obvious sexism, such as being put on trial as witches and not having the right to vote, but now sexism is showing up in revenge porn, comments sections, and even offensive yet normalized names of shirts, i.e. "wife beaters." These days I'm even seeing sexism from women, so frankly I'm just trying to catch up with what exactly I need to be outraged about.

In a general sense, I feel like sexism can be broken down into a few different categories, which of course tend to be concentric. There's the classic blatant sexism, like slapping girls' asses, abusing women, and the sort of gross behavior that gets you fired or lands you in jail. There's also a more subtle strain of sexism, a general form of belittling that masquerades as helping. This, sadly, often lands you a girlfriend.

The problem with belittling is that it's often mislabeled as chivalry, which has a noble undertone. Chivalry is complicated because sometimes it makes me a hypocrite. If I'm dating a guy, chivalry is sexy, but if I'm not, it's insulting. Trust me, I'm very ashamed that I find it sexy when guys pay for dinner. Maybe it's my nasty lizard brain hardwiring that's always on the lookout for safety, the same primal monkey brain that makes me too insecure to date a guy who's shorter than me, that makes me think ice cream is delicious and kale disgusting, that makes me think nice and honest guys are "boring."

Chivalry is a tricky thing because as romantic as it may seem sometimes, it's actually obsolete. It originated in a time when city streets were covered in puddles of garbage and horse feces, back in the 1500s when a lady actually did need help from a man to do mundane tasks. She needed help getting out of a tiny carriage because she couldn't see over her giant hoopskirt. Stepping into sewage-y sludge could mean hepatitis, parasites, a septic infection, or a rat-bitten foot, which was probably already a club foot before the rat got to it. A man who didn't want his future wife to catch the bubonic plague had to hold the door for her because she literally couldn't do it herself. It took every ounce of her energy just to focus on breathing through a three-sizes-too-small corset made of knives. Holding the door was the least a guy could do to protect his lady from getting impaled by her outfit, even though death by undergarment might have been the least harrowing way to die back then.

It seems like it's only within the last thirty or so years that women's delicates evolved to be, well, delicate. The situation is finally at a place where we can hold our arms out or open a door without getting stabbed by some kind of rusty-ass wire that was designed to morph our body into the shape of a French braid. Women can move way more easily now that we have wireless bras and get to wear sneakers, so chivalry seems a little, well, unnecessary now that we can walk up a flight of stairs without the constant risk of toppling to our deaths.

The "chivalrous" act of paying for women's stuff wasn't much of a choice either until pretty recently. Before the 1950s, the majority of women couldn't pay for things themselves because it was rare that they could even get their own jobs. If women did have money, it was likely from working a dangerous factory job, so even if a gal could work, she probably had to use her money to treat the injuries she got from, well, working.

I'm still kept up at night thinking about a situation where a man thought he was being chivalrous but ended up deeply offending me. I was performing with a bunch of great comedians on a midnight show at a comedy festival in Chicago. Doing midnight shows is basically like offering to drive someone to the airport: it sounds like a good idea when you say yes, but then the day before you start dreading it and thinking of ways to get out of it. Also, the audience at a midnight show can be rough because anyone attending is either on drugs or should be on drugs.

A couple of other comics were ahead of me, so I didn't end up going on until about twelve-thirty. The crowd was rowdy, but that never scares me. Children who grew up in hectic homes often end up feeling comfortable in crisis as adults, so rowdy shows to me feel like a cocoon of safety. Conversely, a calm, serene vibe makes me anxious, because I get paranoid, always waiting for the other shoe to drop. Five hundred screaming drunk people yelling? Cozy as a bug in a rug. One-on-one eye contact over a daytime coffee date? Absolute panic that a metaphorical or literal shoe is going to fall on my head.

I got onstage and remember everything starting out well. I used to open with a joke where I would say, "My last name is Cummings, but don't worry, it's just a stage name. My real last name is Cumshot." Stupid as it seems now, I remember it getting a laugh, but after that, a group of guys in the crowd would not stop yelling "Cumshot!" at me.

It didn't bother me because when you grow up with this last name, there's literally nothing you haven't been taunted with. Cumface, Cummings-lingus, Cumwad. These are just a few of the litany of nicknames I had in high school. The yelling escalated to more vulgar stuff, but I truly don't mind hecklers. I worry saying this might encourage it, but interaction with the audience always keeps shows fresh; it keeps me awake and on my toes. I won't allow hecklers to ruin the show for those who have paid their hard-earned money for tickets, but I think a little back-and-forth here and there makes a stand-up show feel special. It gives the audience the opportunity to see a performance that nobody else has seen—a unique experience. So that's what I thought was happening.

I'm having a blast on stage, the hecklers and I actually have pretty good chemistry, which mostly means we agree on the insults they're yelling at me, and everyone seems to be enjoying themselves. Then out of nowhere, I started bombing. It got silent and awkward and I got very confused. Did I suddenly lose the crowd? Was my fly open? Did my tit fall out of my hoodie?

I saw in the front row that people were no longer looking at me; they were looking to my right. I instinctively snapped my head in that direction and saw that the host of the show, a male comic, was onstage next to me silently shushing the group that was heckling.

Now, we tend to break people down as fight, flight, or freeze. I promise you I'm usually fight. At the dog park, when dogs start fighting, I'm the first one in the melee while everyone else watches in shock. If a dog won't let go of another dog, I've even been known to stick my finger in their butthole because that's often the only way to get them to stop. I think that easily puts me in the fight category, even if it means "fighting a finger infection."

I'm not sure why I'm "fight," but I tend to snap into action before I even know what's happening. One time I saw a skinhead dangerously and seemingly drunkenly weaving through traffic and my brain kidnapped my body, and I ended up following him a mile. He crossed two lanes, pulled into a parking lot, parked his car in front of other people's cars, then got out and ran into a tobacco store. I pulled my car in and parked the front of mine against his bumper so he couldn't drive off. I calmly called the police. When he came out and noticed what was going on, he screamed in my face and threatened to kill me for a good seven minutes until the police arrived and arrested him for drunk driving. I don't fancy myself a hero or anything, but I just tend to err on the side of adrenaline rush. However, onstage when I realized this dude was standing next to me, taking it upon himself to scold the hecklers, *my* hecklers, I didn't default to my usual fight response.

I don't remember what I did or said, but knowing me, I defaulted to a codependent state of thanking someone for doing something totally dickish and making a joke, pretending like I was fine, even though I was fantasizing about all the ways I could end his life without going to jail.

As soon as I got offstage, I was filled with an inferno of rage. And not the Lewis Black kind of hilarious rage. It was a scary kind of rage that I thought my brain reserved for pedophiles and people who abuse animals. I looked around for the host, but another comedian immediately intercepted me, rushing me to the exit the way Kevin Costner enveloped Whitney Houston in *The Bodyguard*. He said that he saw in my face that I was about to do something crazy and that we should leave ASAP before I try to start a physical fight with a grown man.

Many of you may be thinking to yourselves: "That host sounds super nice! He was protecting you from those assholes! What a catch!" Honey, no.

Maybe in some jobs it's super cool if someone swoops in and helps you out; maybe they even alleviate your workload. But in stand-up, it's deeply insulting to have someone assume you need to be rescued from a situation you've been in a million times and then completely undermine you in front of your audience. And the dark part is he never would have done that if I were a guy. I pretended to be fine, but it was one of the most embarrassing moments of my life. If the audience was threatening my physical safety, maybe it would have made some sense, but under no circumstances is it ever cool to intervene during another comic's set.

The good news is, I realized in that moment that the fantasy of the knight in shining armor did as much harm to boys as it did to girls. It took me ages to reverse the damage of the stories that wired me to think I was so helpless that I needed a man on a horse to save me, but now I see that men have the pressure of being told they have to *be* that man on said horse. They've been taught to view women as damsels in distress who need rescuing. I was neither a damsel nor in distress, and this dude certainly was no knight in shining armor. He was a guy from New Jersey in a shitty blazer. In that moment, the whole fantasy crumbled. I didn't want a man to save me. Turns out, I wanted him to get the fuck out of my way.

I think something men and maybe women need to understand about women's being equal is that we should also be equal to suffer our own consequences and be exposed to pain. We don't need guys to protect us from circumstances and consequences that make us stronger. It means we have to fall down every now and then and get up on our own without anyone's help. Look, if I've learned anything, it's that it's okay to ask for help, but we shouldn't have help forced on us that we don't want or need. And sometimes even if we want help, we may not actually need it. Basically, there's nothing wrong with our asking for help and being helped, but wait for us to ask.

After I got back to the hotel, I started to think maybe I was crazy. Was I overreacting? Most guys I had dated up until that point told me that's what I did, so could that be what was going on? Was I "PMSing," like men always shamed me with whenever I had feelings? Did I need to "calm down," like my parents and every man after them always told me to do? Maybe I needed to "chill out" or "relax" or "stop being dramatic"?

I needed some perspective. I asked eight male comics what it would take for them to get onstage while another comic was performing. Seven said a version of "An audience member would have to be charging the stage or have already physically injured the comedian," and the eighth said, "I'd have to see someone with a gun." So it turns out I wasn't crazy. But that's the thing about crazy people; they make you feel like you're the crazy one.

The most interesting part of this story for me is that I didn't think the guys heckling obscenities at me were the ones that were out of line. Maybe I should have thought they were the sexist jerks, but I truly wasn't offended by them. Maybe I've gone completely numb to what's appropriate, but I feel like when guys heckle me, they're treating me as an equal. It's different than catcalling because I don't feel vulnerable or unsafe onstage; I have a microphone and security if something truly goes awry. When men heckle me, on some level I'm relieved, because I assume they'd do the same thing to men, and I appreciate that they're treating me just as shittily as they'd treat a male comic.

I entered into this field knowing that being yelled at and insulted by strangers was part of the deal, so I'm usually not blindsided or upset by it. Perhaps it's partly what attracted me to this job: the unpredictability and socially acceptable public sparring with strangers. I'm not saying it's healthy, but the heart wants what the heart wants.

What I didn't sign up for was the patronizing assumption that I couldn't handle myself. And let's say I couldn't handle myself and was in totally over my head that night; I should have been left to tread water and struggle so I could be given the dignity of having my own consequences. Protecting people from the aftermath of their choices isn't thoughtful or benevolent; it just takes away their ability to grow. The nicest thing that guy could have done was to let me suffer so I could become a stronger comic.

It's not just men who succumb to the old-fashioned, subtly sexist, outdated social constructs. I happen to think that our biology errs on the side of sexist dickhead, whether you have a dick or not. In fact, the kind of sexism that confuses me the most is the kind that comes from other women. It almost cuts deeper because I'm sure at some point they've been victims of it too, yet they aren't conscious that they're perpetuating it. Maybe some women have denial or have internalized it. Who knows, but my neck stiffens when a girl yells out to me: "Hey, hooker!" or "What's up, whore?"

I'm sorry?

If you're going to call me a name that relates to the prostitution industry, at least call me pimp. I mean, if you're going to call me a pejorative term for someone who sells sex for money, at least let me be the boss of the operation.

When I'm put in situations where sexism is directed at me, I'm ashamed to say a lot of the time I'm too stunned to react fast enough to do much about it, and because I'm codependent, often what comes out of my mouth when someone else does something wrong is "Sorry."

Once when I was ordering coffee at a café I never go to, I was taking a little extra time reading the menu. Trust me, I know there is nothing more annoying than someone *reading* a coffee menu at a coffee shop at eight in the morning and asking questions like "What's in the mocha, exactly? Is it like a powder?" but I was very confused by all the witty pun-themed drinks. If something is called a "thanks-a-latte," I'm going to have to ask what's in it because I have no idea what thanks tastes like.

As I was asking about the "capuccin-ho-ho-ho!" (it was Christmastime), two burly men behind me began to loudly order over me. They projected their voices over my head on a cloud of garlic-and-cigarette breath. While I was still talking.

While. I. Was. Still. Talking.

And look, I'm the first to admit that most of the time I talk way more than I need to and don't blame anyone who interrupts me when I'm getting redundant or boring. But this was not me bloviating in a conversation, this was me saying one pretty concise sentence to a stranger. They spoke right over me, as if I were the display case of scones between them and the barista. They took their money out, reached around me, and threw it on the counter before telling the barista to keep the change.

I was invisible.

You're probably assuming that I went apeshit on them, roasted them, did something fearless and insane. Nope. The second they started talking over me, I froze. The barista was so confused that he froze, too. As lame as it was, I'm kind of glad I didn't react because if I had, things would have gotten very Jerry Springer very quickly. Instead, I offered a permissive nod to the barista, giving him the go-ahead to serve them before me. He looked disappointed. At least twice a week I fantasize about handling that situation differently.

Like every woman I know, I've been made to feel uncomfortable and unsafe by aggressive men at one point or another, but this was the first time since my childhood that I felt literally unseen. These men didn't harass me, they just ignored me completely. I realized that day that it's very hard to defend yourself against someone who doesn't know you exist.

If you're asking yourself, "Jesus, how much attention does this bitch need?" let me reassure you, I just asked myself the same question. However, although this seems relatively benign compared to the sexism that makes news headlines, the reason I think this story is worth sharing is because the mentality of dismissing a woman's existence at a coffee shop could be the same mentality that in drunken moments could turn into a mentality that justifies worse behavior like violence. Not to bring a super fun winter activity into a conversation about sexual assault, but tolerating a small behavior can enable it to snowball into a bigger one.

So now that you know how much guilt I have complaining about this stuff, I feel like now I can dig into the even yuckier things that have happened to me.

Over the last five or so years as I've gained some much needed mental clarity, I've become able to wrap my head around a few specific cases of physical abuse and sexual harassment I've experienced. To me, sexual harassment is like what our moms used to say about gum: "It takes eight years to digest."

One experience was so bizarre that my reaction was to delete it from my memory for about seven years. When I was about twenty-three, I was jogging at night near my apartment in West Holly-wood. I had my headphones on, my Discman pumping my go-to jogging soundtrack *Now That's What I Call Music Vol. 43*. Despite my penchant for scary situations in my twenties, I tried to jog on safe, well-lit streets at night. In my neighborhood this meant running on a street called La Cienega, which is littered with trendy bars, clubs, and sushi places. I mean, what could possibly go wrong when there's edamame topped with sea salt in the vicinity?

There I was, jogging along, jamming to probably Usher, and out of nowhere a homeless man lunged at me and grabbed my vagina. Hard. This was of course before the concept of vagina grabbing was trendy; before Donald Trump put it in the zeitgeist. And since I used to run in loose Adidas shorts sans underwear, this was a legit vagina grab, not an over-two-layers-of-clothing type deal like we did in the back of Nissan Altimas in the nineties.

Thankfully I didn't get paralyzed by my freeze response the way I did in the coffee shop. I did the opposite. I just kept running—literally and figuratively. I don't know if anyone saw the incident or said anything, because my ability to see and hear went offline for about ten minutes. All I heard was a piercing white noise, like a faraway scream. Maybe it was me screaming, I don't know. A burst of adrenaline propelled me home like a spazzy Forrest Gump. I ran probably the fastest I'd ever run, yet my muscles weren't burning and my lungs weren't gasping for air. The irony was not lost on me that I raced past the infamous strip club the Seventh Veil, a grim purple building decorated with silhouettes of naked women. At least the women in there were getting paid for what I just suffered through for free.

Looking back, I realize the name of the strip club felt right on the nose, given I responded to the event with such a strong veil of denial. When I told the story to people the next day, I made jokes and laughed about it but nobody else thought it was funny. A couple of people even offered to take me to the doctor, which made me realize what happened wasn't as harmless as my psychological defenses were telling me it was.

That said, being violated by a complete stranger—as gross as it was—was a lot less traumatizing for me than being violated by someone I knew and trusted. When I was in college, I had a boyfriend force himself on me after we broke up. I know, LOL.

Back then I had no idea how to end a relationship, so I sort of just acted like an asshole until the guy I was dating eventually ended it himself. This was foolproof and foolish. After I spent weeks applying this method on one particularly stubborn boyfriend, he finally acquiesced after a three-hour melodramatic argument over my very obviously shady texting habits. He stormed out of the apartment, slamming the door. Success! I remember exhaling with relief that it was finally over, grateful that I was never going to see him again. Finally I could act like an asshole without someone constantly forcing me to lie about my behavior! (Just in case you're getting my mental health timeline confused, this was when I was twenty, way before I learned how to just tell people the truth.)

Within five minutes he stormed back into my apartment, coming at me with an erratic gait and a demonic fury in his eyes, like something had possessed him, or like he had just done an eight ball of cocaine. His energy was terrifying because it was at once aggressive and apologetic, like he knew he was about to do something terrible. I felt myself trying to scream, but my throat closed up. He forced me into the bedroom and onto the bed. I don't know if my thrashing was making him hit me by accident or if he was actually hitting me. Whatever it was, I was getting hit in the face a lot. It all got very blurry. He said a couple of things that I'm still too grossed-out to share, but I remember eventually surrendering, thinking it would be much easier to just make the situation consensual so I didn't have to live with being raped. He had been my boyfriend for a year, so what was the difference? I could just rationalize that it was breakup sex, makeup sex, whatever sex might justify something otherwise too terrible. I could feel my brain needing to spin the situation into something I would be able to live with.

Then some primal force inside me way more powerful than my conscious brain said, "Oh, fuck this shit." I don't know how, but out of nowhere I grabbed him by the face, and mind you I had very long acrylic nails at the time, and said quite calmly, "If you don't get off me I swear to God I will actually kill you." I specifically remember saying "actually." I must have been pretty convincing because he did back off enough for me to squirm out. I put a coat on and ran twelve blocks to a train station.

I took the train home to D.C. to my mom's apartment. I didn't tell her what happened because I didn't want to upset her. My codependence told me that it would be too stressful for her codependence.

Maybe the real point here is that as I write this, I'm starting to feel like an ungrateful brat, a spoiled asshole who doesn't even know what being victimized is or what real sexual assault feels like. I'm obsessing over you guys thinking, "This girl is white, she has an alarm system, that guy didn't kill her, she was able to escape . . . How dare this delusional snob complain about anything?" And perhaps that's where the crux of all this lies: That whenever I'm treated in a degrading way, all I can think is that other women have it so much worse than I do, so my experience doesn't matter. This is probably true by the way, but it's also a rationalization that just protects the people who acted in an inappropriate manner. What I'm thinking is: If we don't share our less severe experiences, we enable a mentality that could *snowball* into something that is way more severe.

For a long time I pretended that these experiences didn't

happen. But to discount them altogether would be implying that they don't matter or that other women's seemingly small wounds aren't worth attention either. Everyone's wounds count, no matter how seemingly infinitesimal. For me, these small offenses were like little cracks in a wall that bother you, but not enough to get the wall completely replastered. "Oh, they're barely visible," you think to yourself. But over time, little cracks become bigger cracks. Then all of a sudden the only thing that can make you feel better is, well, crack.

I feel lucky to have a job that allows me to talk about this kind of stuff publicly because after a show people feel safe to share their stories with me, which can be healing for both of us. I get to meet incredible, fascinating people all over the world. I also sometimes meet stupid morons. I would have to say the city with the highest concentration of stupid morons is probably Las Vegas. The reason I feel I can say this is that most of the people I meet in Vegas aren't from there and don't even live there. If you are a native, I've never met one of you, probably because you're too afraid to leave your home and run into one of the aforementioned stupid morons.

Vegas is simultaneously the best and worst place to perform stand-up. I mean, Belgium was pretty weird. When I performed in Antwerp, the whole crowd laughed in unison, which you'd think my anal-retentive perfectionist brain would love because of the predictable order, but it was actually super eerie given that us comedy folk are used to chaotic crowds and erratic laughter. Stand-up is like a mutual verbal assault: I yell at you guys, you yell back at me, but we love each other anyway.

Vegas can be a very useful place to perform because there is a big cross section of people in the audience, so if the material works, it probably works in like thirty states and a couple of random countries. Vegas also always makes me step up my game as a performer because I know good and well that I'm competing against beautiful naked women covered in glitter and feathers with zero cellulite right next door, dancing their tits off. I often can't even be bothered to wear a bra onstage, much less dance my tits off. So if people come see me in Vegas, I know I have to bring it, given the other yummy options available. Especially if you got confused and thought seeing "Cummings" on a marquee meant you were going to an erotic massage house, in which case my show will be very disappointing.

Vegas shows are always a blast save for the occasional audience members who puke on themselves. One time a woman in the second row was getting wasted and out of nowhere she puked in her hand, but that did not let this stop her from living her best life. Instead of leaving to clean herself off or avoid ridicule from strangers, she gently placed the puke on the floor next to her as delicately as you'd put your drink by your feet at a movie theater. She was hands down the coolest hot mess I've ever seen.

I'd say that at least every other show in Vegas there's a kid in the audience whose poker-addicted parent left for me to babysit. It usually takes me a couple of minutes to notice these kids, and I always manage to see them after I've talked graphically about anatomy they shouldn't learn about for at least ten more years. When I ask what they're doing there, they usually tell me their parents dropped them off because they had to "run an errand." Look, I don't know what it's like to be a parent or a gambling addict—well, not literal gambling; I'm more of an emotional gambling addict—but I can't begin to understand how hard it is to manage an obsession with craps while simultaneously trying to raise a kid, even though the first couple years of parenting is mostly dealing with literal craps.

I won't leave my dogs tied to a pole while I go into Starbucks, much less leave a child alone with a comedian for an hour. I'm just saying, if you're a poker-addicted parent, I'm not sure watching me talk about my humiliating sexual experiences is going to do less damage to a child than letting him watch you gamble away his college tuition.

I had one particularly rough night in Vegas. And let me preface this story with something about me: I don't do great with groups of big men. I love men dearly and have made many of them the center of my universe. That said, there's nothing scarier to me than a group of men who go to the gym a lot, wear tight shirts, and are out enjoying a "boy's night" fueled by vodka, Red Bull, and cologne from Walgreens.

One night after a show, I had carefully done my evening anti-insomnia ritual: stretched, meditated, put the yummy-smelling oil on my face that triggers my Pavlovian reaction to know it's time for bed. I creatively covered all the tiny blue and red lights on various electronics in the room because any suggestion of light keeps my brain awake. I didn't check my phone because going on Instagram before bed is like throwing a Molotov cocktail at my self-esteem, and I'll end up spending the whole night trying to figure out what parties I wasn't invited to. Finally at a point in my life where I was able to make sane choices before bed, I read some of a book and lay down. All signs pointed to a deep, juicy slumber and I was very much looking forward to not being a raging, exhausted bitch the next day. I closed my eyes, and after a couple breaths, felt a warm blooming in the pit of my stomach.

Our bodies have this amazing ability to react to something before we can even see or hear it. I'm sure this hypersensitivity served my ancestors very well when they were sleeping under rocks amongst lions and bears sans weapons, but there were no dangerous animals around my hotel room. What I was hearing wasn't the roar of a lion. It was the music of a Pitbull, and unfortunately it was Pitbull the human, not the dog.

FIREBALL! Do-do-do-dooo-doo-doop!

I peeked out my door to see what kind of hoedown I was up against and lo and behold, it was seven very muscly guys in those permanently ironed shirts, the ones that always look sort of wet for no reason. They paired their iridescent shirts with those jeans that have the stitching down the side as if to say, "I like to listen to house music, but I also want to look like a cross between a farmer and the guy from Creed." I don't know why they all decided to wear matching pants. Maybe there was a sale on them: "Buy six, get one free if you come with your CrossFit buddies?" Whatever was happening, it was a deeply tribal situation. When more than three people are in one place, wearing the same clothes, my reptilian brain deduces "It's *me against them*." And it was.

These monsters weren't even in their room. At one A.M. they were partying in the hallway with their door open, which I found shockingly rude, even for how low my bar is for people's manners in Las Vegas. They stood around a room-service table full of flavored vodkas, yelling and sort of punching each other between texting and taking pictures of themselves. As I walked toward them I saw that they all had that luminous helmet hair that can only be sculpted with the perfect mix of pomade, gel, and delusion.

Why not just turn the other way, Whitney? Why not just stay in your lane and let people have fun, you uptight meanie? Well, the only thing I want less than to confront seven agro psychos is to get no sleep, because then I become the agro psycho.

Since I spend so much time in hotels, I've mastered the art of telling people to shut up in a polite way that kind of makes shutting up their idea. For example: "Hey, just curious how long y'all are planning on being up?" subtly shames them into being quiet. When that doesn't go well, I ask something more vague and rhetorical like "Hey, guys, are you serious right now?" If you ask that question sincerely enough, it becomes a Rorschach test and people project their own anger and baggage about other stuff from their past. You become their disapproving high school coach, their drunk father, their ex-wife, whoever. And I don't care what or who you project onto me as long as it makes you stop blasting techno.

In this case I had a feeling that my sneaky reverse psychology mind games weren't going to work on this crew, but I walked up to them anyway, hoping to have a reasonable exchange. I promise you I had all the best intentions, but once I got within five feet of these dudes, they started to look me up and down in such a lecherous way that I couldn't possibly operate from a place of respect. The ogling probably just made me insecure and defensive, since I was in the least flattering pair of harem pajama pants I own, but instead of my usual gentle reverse psychology, I was slightly more direct.

"Hey, guys, it's one A.M. Do you mind taking the party into your room?"

"Why don't you mind your own fuckin' business?" the shortest one of the bunch quipped back.

I'm not going to lie; I did not react well to this. In fact, I straight-up snapped. My head lunged forward and I said some incarnation of "What do you know about business, given you're clearly unemployed?" The "oh shit!" reaction from the guys confirmed that I was somehow right that this guy didn't have a job, which didn't even make sense to me since he had a lot of money for steroids and lilac shirts. I'm pretty sure I said it because it was an old roast joke I had in my back pocket about The Situation from the Jersey Shore that was dying to finally get some airtime.

Now, look. Most of the time I'm pretty humble and willing to be wrong. This was not one of those times. I believe that when you get into an altercation with a stranger, you find out who you really are, because your brain has no point of reference about who this person is. It's like being face-to-face with a wild animal, which I have also had happen. One time I woke up and saw two coyotes in my yard. I know a *lot* about coyotes because they're rampant around L.A. and many of my friends have lost small dogs or their cats to them. Trust me, the first couple times I saw them, my instinct was to feed them, try and take them in, domesticate, and "rescue" them. But in fact it turns out they're sociopathic vampires masquerading as adorable dogs but who are nothing like dogs. They don't have empathy and they haven't evolved to read human faces the way dogs have. Learning to accept the limitations and motives of a coyote versus those of a dog helped a lot in learning to accept the same in the guys I dated. I often have to say to myself, "This guy is a just a coyote. He's always going to be a coyote. Stop expecting him to behave like a dog." And yes, most people call men *dogs* as a derogatory term. Not me. If I call someone a dog, it's the highest compliment I can give and basically means that person gets to live in my house forever and eat way more expensive food than I do as long as I can constantly take photos of you while you sleep.

So when I saw the coyotes, my civilized conscious mind took the day off and I had a total out-of-body experience. My dogs were in the house, so my momma bear pack-leader mentality eclipsed any sanity I had on deck. I snatched some deer antlers that my dogs play with off the floor, ran outside, and swung the antler around, flailing toward them. My phrase of choice to yell? "How *dare* you!" with a weird Katharine Hepburn type of accent.

"Howww dahhhh you?!" I kept yelling. The coyotes just stared at me, unfazed. They looked more embarrassed for me than anything. I was two feet away from them before they actually fled, and from the way they ran off, it seemed like they were doing it just to make me feel better. To this day I still hear the coyotes up in the hills howling, and I'll be damned if it doesn't sound exactly like mocking laughter.

So that's how I usually handle conflict with packs, but in the case of the Vegas tools, while my primal brain knew these heathens could kill me, my conscious brain figured they were so lathered up with self-tanner and cologne that their skin was very slippery, therefore I could probably slide away pretty easily if I had to. Amidst whatever yelling we were doing at each other, the guy with curly hair who worked very hard for his hair not to be curly said, "Why don't you shut the fuck up?" When I heard this, I did indeed shut the fuck up. It got very quiet in the hallway. *Fireball!* I walked up to him, as shut the fuck up as one can be, and got close enough to get a whiff of his Cool Water. I leaned in, almost close enough to get rug burn from his impossibly coarse stubble, and delivered a line that haunts me to this day.

"I would like to see you try."

Uh, what?

It got even quieter. The guys looked very confused. I also looked very confused, but I knew I had to be intimidating, so I raised my eyebrows, narrowed my eyes, and cracked a slight smile because that's what I've seen gangsters to do in movies.

One of the guys told me to shut up; then I told him to "try."

To what? To shut me up? Nobody knew what I meant, including me. Whenever I say something stupid, I have this Darwinian reaction to double down and believe in myself even more. Maybe it's a natural animal instinct to avoid showing any weakness, because in that moment I was very much losing the fight as well as embarrassing my entire gender.

I don't remember exactly what happened after that, but I did hear one of them yell the word *bitch* in my direction. Now, the word *bitch* actually doesn't bug me that much, mostly because of how unoriginal it is. It's borderline played out at this point. If you're still running around calling a woman a bitch, you might as well be on Friendster.

To be clear, I absolutely am a bitch, but these guys had no way of really knowing that yet. They could have maybe deduced that I was nervous, unhinged, reckless, and a sartorial train wreck, but I wasn't quite acting like a bitch yet. If you've known me a couple months, you can call me a bitch and chances are I'll agree with you, but if you don't even know me, I'd rather hear a fresh take. Like, if I were this guy, seeing a girl storm out of her room in pajamas and stomp toward five giant drunk men, yelling "I would like to see you try!" like a mobster from the forties, I wouldn't dismiss her as a bitch. I'd say something like "Ma'am, you seem mentally unstable. Can I help you find your medication?"

Since *bitch* has become the go-to insult for any female who expresses an emotion and since for the most part it signifies that the insulter has run out of jabs, the tension deflated and I was snapped out of my adrenaline response. Once such a boring insult was employed, my amygdala realized I no longer needed its services because for me *bitch* is like the chloroform of words.

Hearing *bitch* also calmed me down because whenever a guy calls me that in an argument, it's usually because he's losing or is all out of interesting angles. In a moment of clarity, I realized that I wasn't in a televised political debate. I didn't have to keep arguing with these animals. I could just calmly call security and have them removed. I always want to give people the courtesy of telling them I'm calling security so they can at least get their shit together and have a fair chance of leaving with some dignity. These guys probably had duffel bags full of Axe body spray and toupee glue to gather up, and I wouldn't want them to forget anything on their way back to (probably) Miami. I calmly said, "Anyway, guys, sorry about all this. I'm gonna go call security."

I had taken no more than two steps when I heard one of them yell, "You know what you need? Some dick!"

The guys exploded in laughter.

Now, this was a situation I had not yet had the privilege of being in. Did these people really think that a penis was going to solve this conflict? Frankly, the last thing I needed was an anonymous dick anywhere near me. Look, I'm a big fan of dicks, but I have yet to come across a problem a dick can actually solve besides wanting to become a mother. Even most men I know would agree that their own dick is the source of most of their problems, so adding a miscellaneous dick to the equation would just further complicate things.

Look, dicks are great. I think we can all agree on that. They're very awesome for, like, an hour at a time, but there are some drawbacks. Sometimes that awesome hour is accompanied by a bummer aftermath like a UTI or a visit to Planned Parenthood. Dicks also have the ability to give me a baby, which is the most stressful thing I can think of. But even without these side effects, dick was not going to get me out of this pickle.

I've never been trying to sleep with noisy people in the hallway and thought, "You know what this situation needs? A dick." I mean, maybe if I can use your dick as an earplug? If each of them put a dick in their mouths so they'd stop being able to yell? Or maybe they could put all their flaccid dicks under the door so I couldn't hear the racket from the hallway? Or if they used the most impressive dick of the bunch to cajole the women at the front desk to get me a later checkout so I can sleep in? Maybe if their dicks shot out sleeping pills so I could actually fall asleep? I'm genuinely trying to figure out why guys think dicks are these magical wands that contain the panacea for all stress. Unless they're covered in Xanax and Nutella, in the long run most dicks cause me way more anxiety than they alleviate.

This weird night in Vegas haunts me to this day. I'm always trying to own my part in situations because that's the only way for me to feel some power, especially in a case where I specifically feel powerless. Ultimately I think I could have handled this one with more grace and class, and likely should have just called security first, but my fear of "wasting time" usually prohibits me from asking someone to help me with something because I figure it'll just be faster if I do it myself, a belief that has yet to yield a single positive result.

Now I'm not trying to solve sexism with this chapter. I can't do that. I can hardly write about it as comprehensively as I would like to, much less solve it. Sometimes I can't even see or feel sexism, but I'm going to try and do my part in trying to deconstruct it. Maybe cultural conditioning is to blame, maybe primal neurology, mis-guided parenting, the media. Or maybe it's a tight knot of all of these things that needs to be delicately untied.

I lose a lot of sleep at night thinking about why some men need to be dismissive to women. When I look back at those guys in the Vegas hallway, I don't feel anger, just overwhelming sadness for them. After learning that anger is just pain all dressed up in a scary yet cheap Halloween costume, I feel we're somehow doing our men wrong. After all, "hurt people hurt people." Maybe our men aren't being seen or heard, or maybe they're not growing up with role models that treat women with respect so they have no blueprint. Maybe nobody's given them the tools to solve problem without their dicks. I'm not a sociologist, so I'll let someone else more qualified dig into all that pathos, but I want to do my part in illuminating my experience because hearing other people share theirs is what gave me the courage to come to terms with mine.

Anyway, I hope this chapter doesn't make you feel sorry for me or anything because I'm obviously fine.

THE EGG FREEZING CHAPTER

"Good for you!"

This is a phrase you really need to get used to hearing if you decide to freeze your eggs. But if you decide not to freeze your eggs, good for you!

My egg-freezing journey started a long time ago. Specifically, thirty-four years ago when I was endowed with two X chromosomes. My fate was sealed when I grew up listening to Dolly Parton sing about working "nine to five" and watching *Roseanne*, who imprinted on my brain when I was twelve that children are an irksome financial drain. *Roseanne* also crystallized my worst nightmare about having a family: the presence of a hideous brown plaid couch in your living room with a crocheted blanket on it that can't actually keep anyone warm.

My indifference toward motherhood was solidified by my extremely hardworking mother who had an all-consuming job. She worked in fashion, and it was very glamorous to me because when I was ten, going the mall was the epitome of glamour. The ladies spraying perfume testers! The generic, monotonous music blaring from Macy's! The toe ring kiosks!

I would go to my mom's office every day after school and wait for her to finish work. When I wasn't busy shoplifting, I'd sit at her desk and play with her colored paper clips and acrylic stapler, dreaming about the day when I'd have my own office supplies. This seems like a silly dream, but back then, office work was much more charming because people used cute pens, notepads, and colored paper clips. Flash-forward to my office life now, which mostly consists of forgetting my passwords and constantly reinstalling Adobe Acrobat Reader.

The point is, the women I was influenced by either didn't have kids, had kids and regretted it, or refused to be slowed down by the ones they (probably accidentally) had. I just wasn't exposed to a paradigm that glorified having children. That may not be totally true. I did religiously watch *Small Wonder*, but it didn't make me want kids, it made me want to be a robot, which I think I actually accomplished for a couple years in my twenties.

As a child I didn't play with baby dolls or even Barbies. For whatever reason, I had the maternal instincts of a fire hydrant, so I felt it was a cruel joke when at seventeen, I got pregnant.

I used to get benign cysts on my ovaries when I was a teenager due to a steady diet of caffeine and adrenaline. One day I was getting them checked with some sort of internal camera-type thing that goes up your most valuable crevice and the doctor said, "Well, we got rid of the cysts but not the pregnancy." He directed me downstairs to a doctor who would "terminate" said pregnancy. It was said with such nonchalance that it didn't even occur to me that it was a thing. It felt more like another chore: Do math homework, pick up Vidal Sassoon hot oil, get a mani, terminate pregnancy.

In this other doctor's office, who in retrospect I really hope was a gynecologist, I was given a clipboard with a comical number of papers on it to read and sign. One of them had a list of side effects of the vacuum aspiration procedure (of course I just had to Google that, since "vacuum thing" felt slightly insensitive and crass). One of the warnings was that the procedure could "possibly cause infertility." My heart puked. Even though I had absolutely no ostensible proof that motherhood was fun, I guess my primal instincts took over. I may not have dreamed of being a mom, but I wasn't ready to shut my uterus down before I knew who I was and what I wanted out of life. My imagination got the best of me, recoiling at how brutal a procedure must be to render a woman barren. I didn't have enough life experience yet to know that the chances of something going wrong were tiny and that the procedure's totally safe, but this was pre-WebMD, folks. I refused to sign it.

The doctor came in, and when he asked for my paperwork, I tried to speak, but ended up making erratic breathy grunts in an attempt to explain that I was too scared to do it. He seemed delighted to offer me an alternative solution. He told me he was working on an experimental procedure I should try: a cancer treatment in the form of a suppository that had a side effect of killing fetal cells. It had a 75 percent chance of working, and if I was scared of the invasive method, I should try this instead. I was too obtuse to understand what he was actually saying, but it seemed to make more sense at the time to my naive, completely uneducated brain. I uttered another primal noise that rhymed with "okay."

I went home, and once my mom was asleep I jammed the suppository thing into myself and hoped for the best. For the next five days I was tired and dizzy, which I remember feeling like I deserved. I wasn't particularly scared or crestfallen about the whole thing, maybe because I hadn't told anyone, which would have made it all real. A week later, I put on my best Urban Outfitters tank top and went back to the doctor. I remember this tank top well. It was purple with lace around the top and had a little rose bow on it. I used to think it was my "good top," but looking back, it's hardly appropriate to wear as an undershirt. After I sat in the waiting room for an hour, the doctor called me in, gave me a sonogram, and casually told me the medication didn't take.

The doc explained that I'd have to populate my undercarriage with the capsule yet again. He said something about the fetal cells growing. *Growing? Excuse me? Growing?* For whatever reason, that's the word that made me realize what was actually happening. "Growing" triggered an emotional avalanche of seemingly endless tears and snot.

The next time I used the medication, it "worked." I put that word in quotes because I don't consider sitting in a bathtub crying and bleeding to be a feasible solution to one of the most complicated emotional issues a teenager could ever face. It might be an ideal solution to waking up in Mexico and discovering you're missing a kidney, but not this.

I don't know if the FDA ever approved this medication, and if it didn't, I don't think I want to know why, although it might explain a couple weird rashes and random eye-twitching I've had over the years.

I find regret to be an immense waste of time and energy, but I did learn a lot from that fiasco. Notably, shame sucks. I was too ashamed to ask questions or ask for help from someone who had terminated a pregnancy, so I ended up putting my health and trust into the hands of a mercenary, callous doctor who made me a guinea pig for his new product. I decided that from now on I would take responsibility for my body. I mean, that wouldn't be the last weird, emotionally damaging thing that ended up inside me, but certainly it was the last unapproved medical suppository.

Fast-forward to me thirteen years later in yet another gynecologist's office, this time without a life-changing, emotionally overwhelming predicament on my hands. She was poking around and suggested I get my fertility checked. She was staring right down the barrel of my orifice, so I'm really hoping the sight of it wasn't what reminded her about my waning fertility. I like to tell myself she probably saw how gorgeous and unused it was, hence assumed I wasn't out there in them streets getting sprayed with a deluge of sperm every night, thus I clearly needed to put some huevos on ice for when I did decide to hand-pick from my throng of enamored suitors. Yeah, let's go with that.

It didn't seem right. Why do I have to freeze my eggs when guys can have kids well into their sixties? I was so outraged by the biological injustice that I refused to make the appointment for two years. I made childish proclamations to justify my stubbornness: "I can have a kid whenever I want. I mean, I eat kale!" and "I'll just adopt. So many kids need homes. At this point having your own kid is basically like buying a dog from a breeder."

To be fair, some of my excuses may actually be true, but my motives for making them were coming from a deep denial of reality. The truth is, biology simply has not evolved fast enough to catch up with feminism. It will take a long time for our bodies to evolve to accommodate this whole ladies-having-dreams thing, which makes me want to punch Darwin in the face.

Worse, admitting I had to freeze my eggs made me feel like a failure. I failed to manage my time properly, I failed at taking care of my health therefore my ovaries broke, I failed at figuring out how to want to marry someone, I failed at being a woman, I failed at being lovable. The only thing worse than feeling like I wasn't loved was that it ultimately just made me feel old. Old people freeze their eggs, I thought. That's what women do when they're desperate, lonely, wrinkly. In my head, freezing your eggs basically came with a walker and a free set of cats.

My brain made up all sorts of conspiracy theories to justify my stubbornness. It was a scam, a pyramid scheme, a misogynistic racket, just another bullshit lie to keep women scared. The fact that egg freezing isn't covered by insurance is outrageous, but in America neither is a lot of birth control, so I don't even know where to direct my fury at this point. The two things that would postpone women's having children aren't covered by insurance. So in America, it's literally cheaper to just have a kid before you're ready.

After a big breakup with a guy I thought I'd marry (don't ask), I finally lost enough hope for my future to be motivated enough to make an appointment with a fertility specialist. It was what I like to call a "fear-mality." A fear-mality is something I like to pretend is a casual formality, but the undercurrent is paralyzing fear. Also filed under fear-mality: laser hair removal, dating, stretching, voting.

I explicitly remember not knowing what to wear to my fertility check. My instinct was to overcompensate and look super fertile. Like, maybe wear pink or something, since that's always the color of ovaries in textbooks and educational posters. While searching for something perfectly pink, I realized I'd have to get naked for the exam, so I decided to just go with plaid pajama pants. And that decision basically sums up the theme of turning thirty: My laziness finally eclipsed my desperation.

I was shocked when I walked into the fertility clinic waiting room. I expected it to look like the set of *Designing Women*: overweight ladies who couldn't find a husband having a midlife crisis, sitting in wicker rocking chairs with giant palm trees on the cushions, leafing through self-help books. Imagine my surprise when I walked into a room that looked like a sexy spaceship decorated by Christian Grey's interior designer filled with gorgeous women on the latest iPhones. Modern walls, modern art, modern tables, modern women. It made me realize this problem is, well, modern. Women postponing motherhood is a new thing, so there's no blueprint on how to deal with it, which made me feel slightly better about my immature behavior and the passive-aggressive pajama pants I was wearing.

So, as you've already concluded, I had been a sexist punk. These were not lonely, pathetic, unlovable women. One of the women was on her knees behind the mid-century modern sofa looking for an outlet to plug her phone into, so she was already very loved by me. Her phone was out of juice at ten A.M. That's a busy-ass, in-demand bitch. My battery was at 90 percent, so I was clearly the loneliest, least e-mailed person there.

I was pleasantly surprised by the doctor I met with. Let's call him Dr. Dong because if I was reading a chapter about this depressing topic, I'd want some levity and the word *dong* to appear every couple sentences. Dr. Dong was lovely. I don't know why that surprised me so much. In my experience doctors can be patronizing and annoyed by vulnerability, but he seemed genuinely happy to meet me and patient with my being a female. Although when I explained my situation, he turned sympathetic, which pissed me off. I was thirty. I wasn't dying. "I would like to get my fertility checked and possibly freeze my eggs," I said. "Good for you," he responded, nodding his head slowly. I didn't realize then this would be the first of 327 times I would hear that phrase over the next five years.

I'm obviously being unfair. Anything short of him saying "You're way too young for egg freezing, ya knucklehead; get out of my office and go live your life, ya tiny fertile fetus!" would have annoyed me. It also didn't help that his office was decorated with endless photos of babies and on his desk he had an array of glass jars full of colorful Starburst. If you're in a room full of photos of children and tubs of candy, you're either in a pedophile den or at a fertility doctor.

Dr. Dong scooped out a handful of colored Starburst and spread them across the table with the smoothness of a card dealer that made it clear he did this countless times a day. He demonstrated with my least favorite candy how the quality of a lady's eggs declines with age. He used yellow to represent "good" eggs, which was offensive given yellow is the shittiest Starburst flavor. It's the buttered popcorn Jelly Belly of Starburst. I facetiously said, "Can you at least use the cherry ones to represent my good eggs?" He didn't laugh. However, he did offer me a Starburst seconds after he told me eating sugar isn't good for you during the egg-freezing process. This oddly made me like him more, but I sort of lost my appetite for candy after imagining it as my future zygote.

I wish I could describe to you how egg freezing works, but I didn't hear anything Dr. Dong said in his monologue. I have a mental wiring issue where I short-circuit and black out when someone smart starts explaining something complicated that I really need to know. As soon as they start saying important things, I totally power down. I've worked so hard to achieve mental serenity and bliss through meditation, therapy, marijuana—you name it—but I can only really transcend into complete Zen when people tell me incredibly important information. When I ask for driving directions, I instantly zone out and stare at the person's pores and fantasize about squeezing the gook out of each one of them.

After I pretended to listen for twenty minutes, Dr. Dong snapped me out of my haze by asking, "Have you ever terminated a pregnancy?"

"No," I said.

This would be the first of many lies I told Dr. Dong and myself during the egg-freezing process.

Dr. Dong could tell I wasn't sold on his whole operation, so he figured out how to appeal to my ornery nature. "Look, this may not be for your first or even second kid. It might be for your third kid after having two naturally. Or when you're forty-five, maybe you want a surrogate . . ." The word *surrogate* pulled me out of my entitled zombie state. You mean freezing my eggs could mean another woman could have my kid for me? Now we're getting somewhere.

I asked if I should come back in five years when I'd be closer to knowing if I had the patience for a kid or a possible baby daddy on the horizon. Dr. Dong explained that the technology is finally available to freeze and de-thaw (what?) eggs ten years later without defrosting, since the eggs are now freeze-dried (seriously, *what?*). I can't pretend to understand how it's done, but clearly the universe was urging me to increase my chances of creating another generation of neurotic children chock-full of my alcoholic, giant-feet-making DNA. To refuse modern technology felt oddly ungrateful and even—might I say—unpatriotic, given how much a future crazy Cummings child would stimulate the economy with her purchases of antidepressants, self-help books, and dog costumes.

After I grabbed a couple of cherry Starbursts for the road, I was led into another room down the hall and left to disrobe. This was the one moment I didn't regret wearing my pajamas. It did feel weird, though. Usually when you take your pants off during the day, your life is going either really well or really not well, and I couldn't tell which category I fell into.

A chipper nurse burst into the room and asked how my day was going, possibly trying to distract me from the fact that what was about to happen was gonna cost me twenty thousand dollars. While she fluttered about, she expertly put a condom on a sonogram wand with a smooth swooping movement that was downright humbling. Frankly, I was jealous. I don't want to brag, but I've put a couple condoms on in my day. However, after being sexually active for more than fifteen years, I still don't know which part of the condom is supposed to face up. I noticed the nurse was wearing a wedding ring, and all I could think about was if Chipper is ever single again, she'll have to pretend to fumble with condoms in front of men just so they don't think she's a prostitute. As if the condom swoop wasn't impressive enough, she then slipped the wand inside my female entry point without even looking, like a world-class fencing champion. I was taken aback by way of my front.

Suddenly my innards showed up on a TV screen. Let me be very clear with you about my next realization: My uterus is very ugly. Having inner beauty is pretty much my main goal in life, and I'll be the first to admit that I've failed miserably. Turns out my uterus looks like a moldy shipwreck crashed into GoPro footage of a haunted house on a snowy night.

Chipper swiveled the wand into the corners of my insides and pointed at a screen, saying, "Look, there's one follicle, two follicles . . ." I remember thinking, "Of course I have hairy ovaries." That's how little I knew about my own reproductive organs. She explained to me that follicles produce hormones and release eggs during ovulation. I figured this was probably covered in the Starburst lecture I tuned out earlier.

After examining the TV for a bit longer, Chipper unceremoniously removed the wand from my lower half and breezed out of the room rather quickly, which made me think she knew the glob of lube left inside me was now sliding down my leg with aplomb. And to answer your question, yes, I did throw my back out trying to wipe it off.

And that was that. I was on track to freeze my eggs. The first step was going off birth control and waiting for my period. For a myriad of reasons it took a while for my period to "start up again." After hearing all the phrases used to describe how my innards function, I now get why people use a female pronoun for cars.

Later I did end up learning all the important crap I was too dissociative in the consultation to absorb. I found out that us lassies lose a whopping 90 percent of our eggs by the time we're thirty years old. "Fertility peaks in your teens and twenties," I kept reading. Suffice to say I had a very hard time accepting that my fertility had its shining moment when I was slamming back Amaretto sours and dry-humping to 50 Cent.

I realize this is, like, Sex Ed 101 to most people, but I guess it just never crystallized in my brain that us gals hit our "fertile peak" between the ages of twenty-three and thirty-one. This fact sunk in when I was at the ironic age of thirty-two, the exact year I fell off the aforementioned peak. It just baffles me how badly evolution is bombing on the fertility front; it makes no sense that when I was the least equipped mentally and financially to have a kid, I was the most able to. I've said it once, and I'll say it again: Biology is a raging sexist psychopath.

Anyway, back to my uterus. Three weeks after the consultation, my period finally came. I texted Dr. Dong to give him the news. I was a little rusty at this, given that the last time I urgently texted a guy about my period, I was in high school and it was to my panicking boyfriend. Dr. Dong told me since I finally started ovulating, it was now time to start the fertility shots. Yay?

I feel like I worked so hard not to be the kind of person who desperately injects herself with an expensive substance every day, but here I was, doing exactly that. Only it wasn't something as glamorous or cinematic as heroin. It was a hormone called gonadotropins. Even though I spent a good hour with a nurse learning how to inject myself delicately, I kept puncturing my tummy with the kind of anger with which I'd stab at an Ann Coulter voodoo doll. Maybe I had spatial intelligence issues due to my body dysmorphia. Maybe it was yet another manifestation of my seemingly endless masochism. Or maybe it was to punish myself for not being younger.

After a couple days my stomach was covered in blue and green bruises. I injected myself twice daily until my torso eventually looked like a Monet. I found this both funny and a source of pride, both of which seem like the wrong reaction to have, and perhaps yet another indication that I was doing the right thing by postponing motherhood.

As if you weren't seething with jealousy enough, dear reader, it gets even sexier. In addition to shooting myself up with hormones every day, which caused brutal headaches and dizziness, I had to go into the office every other day to get penetrated by Chipper with the cold slimy phallus to reveal how, if, where, and at what size my eggs were growing. Every time I went to one of these appointments, not only did I lose three hours of my life driving there and back and thus a large chunk of my sanity, but I also had to drop about four hundred dollars per visit. I *know*. A heroin habit would actually have been way cheaper than egg freezing, and frankly, might actually have also increased my chances of getting pregnant before forty.

After a couple of weeks, my belly started swelling up. I had terrible cramps, felt like I constantly had to poop even though I didn't, and got migraines that felt like a tiny woodpecker was going to town on my right eyeball. I think this is what Shania Twain was talking about when she sang "Man! I Feel Like a Woman!" Finally, about three weeks and fifty sloppy bloody stabs later, it was time for me to have my eggs sucked out and put into the fridge.

The retrieval was shockingly fast and somewhat anticlimactic. I had to go to another place for this procedure, and this waiting room was full of bloated women furiously typing on their phones awaiting their retrievals. We were like a bunch of busy cows waiting to be milked.

I don't remember much about the egg retrieval because I was given the drug Michael Jackson died from overdosing on. I love Michael Jackson, and after having a dose of that drug, I can confidently say he died doing what he loved.

I woke up after the procedure to the doctor telling me to "take it easy." Now, I have a pretty type A personality, so for me "take it easy" means no paragliding or riding mechanical bulls. I had shows booked that weekend because I, like many women, have a job and I couldn't just clear my schedule for three months to do silly things like "heal." Plus, I needed to work in order to afford the insane cost of this process. Side note: If you attended any of my stand-up shows from May through July 2015, you basically paid for my frozen eggs, so thank you.

The day after the retrieval, I felt a sharp pain in my abdomen. I was able to ignore the pain because, well, ignoring pain is pretty much the skill I'm best at. And by design, women always seem to be in some kind of discomfort, so if I reacted every time my body hurt, I'd live in a cannabis dispensary.

That night I drove out to Irvine, California, to do two stand-up shows. Halfway through the second show, I suddenly felt an intense stabbing on either side of my lower stomach. There was a minute there where I was sure I was actually in labor and was perhaps having an "I didn't know I was pregnant" type situation on my hands. Adrenaline and audience laughter anesthetized me enough to get me through it, but once I got in the car, the only thing I could do was scream at the windshield and tell myself what my way-too-intense-for-nine-in-the-morning Spinning class instructor yells in my face a lot: "Pain is temporary!"

I texted a friend who had frozen her eggs before. I asked her if I was dying and she responded, "Did your doctor tell you to 'take it easy'?" I racked my brain. All I could remember anyone saying was "good for you." Turns out, her doctor told her to take it easy as well, and she's employed and has dreams too, so the same thing happened to her.

I had hyperstimulation, which is when the holes in your ovaries from the extractions fill up with water, then swell up. "You're supposed to be on *bed rest*," she said. I texted another girlfriend. Same thing. She told me to cancel all my plans for the next three days and to waste no time purchasing a laxative.

It was then I realized that the generation of women I'm proud to be a part of have no idea how to "take it easy." Women have had to "take it easy" for thousands of years. We've been on involuntary bed rest for most of the time and we're kind of over it. We're off the bench and ready to play. I realized the exact qualities that put me in the position of needing to freeze my eggs were the qualities that were making the procedure so harrowing. Even within my surrendering to my biology, I refused to surrender to my biology. I wanted to live life my way, have kids my way, freeze my eggs my way.

In a deep twist of irony, the only relief from the severe abdominal pain was lying in the fetal position. As I lay there, I moaned and whimpered and cursed Dr. Dong among pretty much anyone else I could think of: my parents for having me, my ex-boyfriends for not being father material, whatever incarnation of God I was believing in at the time, Dr. Dong for not coming over and giving me more of that Michael Jackson–y painkiller reality-eraser stuff.

I had to cancel the next night's show. It was heartbreaking. I know that canceling a show doesn't sound like a big deal and you probably think I'm being dramatic and victimy, but I take people's buying tickets to come see a show very seriously. As I've told you, I've encountered sexist treatment before, but this is the first time my own body was the one doing the sexist, discriminating behavior. I called my therapist, who as you know by now always cuts right through my ego and entitlement: "Get over it. You didn't settle for a bad marriage. You didn't have a kid before you were ready. You can afford to freeze your eggs. This is not a real problem." Well, there you have it. I had become so spoiled by the fruits of feminism and modern technology that having pain from a fertility-prolonging procedure had become something to complain about.

I learned from this that I needed to get some goddamn perspective about and gratitude for the time I was born into. Yes, it's very annoying to have a body that has an expiration date, but it's insane not to acknowledge the progress science has made. I also can't help but think that in fifty years women will be, like, "Thank God we weren't alive back in the Dark Ages when women had to pay for egg freezing! Remember when women were *having their own babies out of their bodies? Yuck!"*

I also had a rude awakening about how little people know about egg freezing, myself included. When I showed up to my rescheduled stand-up performance, the manager of the club ran up to me looking very concerned. He blurted, "Are you okay? I heard you had your ovaries removed!" It was then I decided I'd write about my experience and talk about it publicly to possibly help lessen the stigma and confusion about the procedure. I figure this is the only way we can start the process of making it accessible to more women, covered by insurance, and all that smooth jazz. Hopefully one day freezing your eggs will be as commonplace as getting a teeth cleaning or a bikini wax. Someone call *Shark Tank* because if there was a service that could wax me *while* I was under sedation getting my eggs extracted, I would have taken all this way more seriously. Whoever patents that business, you are welcome for the billion dollars you're about to make.

After the hyperstimulation madness passed and I was back to my old self, and by *old* I mean former, I truly felt an invisible weight lifted off my shoulders. I hear that cliché a lot but figured I would never have that feeling, given the gigantic size of the purses I carry and the fact that I've actually broken my right shoulder, so it always feels like it has weight on it.

Something about having my eggs on ice gave me an enormous sense of relief and filled my lungs with just a little more oxygen. I didn't feel an incessant hum of anxiety in my stomach. I stopped feeling guilty about taking on jobs that would mean working long hours or being out of town, which would prohibit me from being able to date or nurture a relationship. My inner monologue wasn't populated with misogynist hecklers yelling, "You'll never meet a man in time!" or "Motherhood just isn't in the cards for you, godless weirdo!"

This sense of relief manifested itself in ways I take a lot of pride in. Before I froze my eggs, I'd flirt with literally any guy who had real hair and a car. Post-freezing, I suddenly had these weird things called *standards*. Today if my gut tells me I'm not into a guy, I don't go out with him. I realize that concept may be very obvious to most people, but I used to talk myself into going on dates with guys I didn't like because I was so scared of running out of time or ending up alone. I mean, if I'm going to be very honest, I'm not scared of being alone; I love being alone. I was more scared of people *thinking* I was alone and that my life wasn't congruous with the socially acceptable timeline of when we're "supposed" to be paired up with someone. I rationalized dating guys I wasn't really into by defending their deficiencies and making excuses for them: "He cheated on his last girlfriend? Well, technically monogamy isn't natural . . . Monogamy was invented when our life expectancy was thirty! Maybe that just means he's a great multitasker." I adopted philosophies I didn't even believe to justify going out with mediocre guys. "He drinks eight glasses of wine a night? Well, science has found that wine has lots of antioxidants! I gotta meet this health nut!"

When I do go on dates, my biological clock is no longer my plus-one to the party. I can enjoy hanging out with a man without constantly trying to ascertain whether or not he's going to make a good father. I don't feel the need to ask manipulative questions or pretend I don't want a serious future with someone so they'll perceive me as carefree and cool. I can now just be carefree and cool.

Even though freezing my eggs gave me a new sense of levity, I also try to be realistic about how few problems it actually solves. Here's what egg freezing does *not* promise to do: make you happy, deliver your soul mate to your front door, ensure you're a good mother when you do use the eggs for a kid. It doesn't fix your shitty childhood, pay your bills, prevent cancer, or make you look younger. Guys, it doesn't even promise to give you a freaking baby. In fact, most of the time, the process doesn't even work. The statistics aren't even on our side on this one. There's apparently a 77 percent failure rate in IVF procedures with frozen eggs among women aged thirty and over and a 91 percent failure rate in women aged forty and over, which means most women have to do the procedure multiple times. I know, science can be a real asshole. Hopefully that statistic has improved by the time you read this, and continues to improve swiftly so we can all just start 3-D printing kids already.

Even if I did beat the odds and get a baby out of my chilly eggs, that isn't a promise for happiness either. My vagina could tear during childbirth, the kid I have could be weird, or when it gets older, it could become an addict or make me take it to water parks. The point is, I'm not saying egg freezing solves your problems, but what it *can* do is help us all step in the right direction toward extending our fertility. What I needed at that point in my life was to change my paradigm from feeling like a puppet of my biology to being somewhat in control of my future. Even if the chances are small, I needed some relief from the panic of the bleak fertility timeline. What we all need is for this procedure to be viable. The more we do this procedure and show interest in fertility extension, the harder scientists are going to work at perfecting it and getting the percentages to a promising place so we can all be wrinkled old ladies in nursing homes having babies well after menopause, changing diapers while we're wearing diapers.

It's our responsibility to invest in what we want and fight for our future selves and our (possibly IVF-conceived) kids' future selves. Whether it's quitting smoking, not texting our exes, or freezing our eggs. If I've learned anything in this life, it's that it's short and the line of people dedicated to making your dreams come true is even shorter. We have to champion ourselves, and sometimes that means saving lots of money to impale ourselves in the stomach with needles. Maybe it means cutting out lattes, maybe it means launching a kickstarter campaign, or campaigning for the procedure to be covered by insurance. Whatever it is, your time won't be wasted because girl, you're worth it.

I have a history of passively sitting on the bench when I want something, so when it didn't work out the way I hoped, I could find solace in telling myself that I didn't try that hard anyway. I used to avoid taking risks because I was so scared of rejection and failure. If I got anything out of the egg-freezing debacle, it's that I finally started accepting what *is* instead of what I think should be. Unfortunately, idealism and ambition don't change biology. I'm the first person to tell you to challenge the social norm, to defend yourself against a shitty boss or abusive boyfriend, but when it comes to our bodies, for the most part I think it may behoove us to be a doormat.

Women may have fewer and fewer social and professional limitations, but we still have very real biological ones. To pretend we don't isn't feminist, it's just misinformed, delusional, and unfair to your future self. I'm not saying I think it's fair, but I've had to accept a lot of biological annoyances: I have to floss, I can't eat more than three pieces of cheese without a gastrointestinal revolt, I can't change a guy's values over dinner, and I can't magically be attracted to a man who's a foot shorter than me.

Look, after this ordeal, I still may never even have kids. I may sell the eggs I froze on eBay. Or I may have kids from my eggs, then sell the kids on eBay. Who knows? The point is, I did something to increase my chances of having choices. If you can increase your chances of not getting leveled by your primal biology by even 20 percent, I believe you owe that to yourself. And if you're now thinking about freezing your eggs, good for you. Just take it easy. You'll be fine.

THE EATING DISORDER CHAPTER

I know, an actress with an eating disorder—how original.

To be fair, I did have an eating disorder long before I thought about acting in case that makes me seem any less derivative.

A myriad of things conspired to give me an eating disorder. I say *give* as if it was some kind of generous present from Santa or a surprise hit to my PayPal account, but I'm not sure how else to say it. I *developed* an eating disorder? I *caught* an eating disorder? I *downloaded* an eating disorder? I think for the most part my eating disorder was cued up the day I was born, so I think of it as being a latent beast inside me waiting patiently to take over and ruin my adolescence and bone density. So maybe I was *possessed* by an eating disorder is the more accurate way to go? Nope, that sounds weird too.

Weight was a concept in my purview way too early in life. My mom was very thin, but every time someone complimented her, she would always respond with "No, no, I need to lose five pounds." But she did not need to lose five pounds. She was tiny. That was confusing to my nascent, very literal brain. I mean, this was back when I thought McDonald's Chicken McNuggets were actually made of chicken.

I remember drinking a lot of diet soda as a kid. I don't blame my parents for this; it was the late eighties, way before we knew a lot of important information. We didn't know yet that artificial sweetener is bad for you, that Bill Cosby is a sociopath, and that denim shouldn't be bedazzled.

My stepmother was also very body conscious and had thighs that didn't touch each other, which I now know is not possible without excessive dieting or liposuction. I don't remember ever seeing her eat, but I do remember her smoking Virginia Slims. Even the cigarettes in my house were diet.

Despite all the diet food around, I was not a small child by any means. By the time I was ten, I was already five-nine thanks to still-cold-on-the-inside fish sticks and thinking Flintstones vitamins were food. I had developed a pretty intense obsession with candy and would go down to a local store called Sugars most days after school and buy some. And by *buy*, I mean put in my pocket and not pay for it. I was alone a lot as a kid and food became a dependable source of happiness. People can let you down, but food never will. Mike and Ike were the only two boys who I knew would never hurt me. They gave me a lot of cavities, but never a broken heart.

Around age twelve, I started playing sports and fell deeply in love with basketball. It was the only time I wasn't embarrassed about how tall and husky I was. What I was once bullied for, I was now praised for. But once I started practicing nonstop, I began losing weight and getting in shape. I also started getting the ultimate drug: attention. My family complimented me, coaches praised me, boys flirted with me. I imagine on a subconscious level my brain associated thinness with deserving love. I was hooked.

As a kid I felt like I had no control over anything—who my dad married, where my mom was and what she ate, who my friends were, whether D.J.'s date would go well on *Full House* . . . All I wanted was some predictable order, and my weight was literally the only thing I could control. This was of course incredibly unhealthy, but it soothed my brain to be in charge of something for the first time in my life. I learned from reading *The Female Brain* that organizing things reduces cortisol, our brain's stress chemical, so maybe that's why taking the marshmallows out of the Lucky Charms, sorting them by color, and eating them one by one felt so good.

From fourteen to eighteen, I ate mostly rice cakes, nonfat yogurt, and apples. I became irrationally terrified of fat. I of course now know that fat doesn't make you fat, but at the time I was impervious to things like science or facts. Eating disorders can be all-consuming brain take-overs that blind you to reality, so my brain became a labyrinth of self-deception. I knew it was bad when my hair started falling out, especially when it was wet. I remember going to my friend's house to swim in her pool. I was in a brown J.Crew bathing suit. That's how little I thought I deserved: Of the kaleidoscope of colors bathing suits came in, I chose poop brown. Anyway, I remember getting out of the water and seeing my silhouette in the form of a willowy stick figure. My shadow was a mere suggestion of a person. I was grossly proud of how small my body was; it was more my whisper of a ponytail I was concerned about. So much hair had fallen out it looked like a skinny rattail. Every time I brushed it, the brush would end up full of my hair, so much so that when I cleaned it off and threw the hair away, it looked like my trash can was full of Yorkies.

By the time I was fourteen, my eating disorder consumed my priorities, behavior, and thoughts. I didn't have real friendships because in order to be friends with someone, you have to eat with them at some point, and I wasn't willing to take that risk. Eating out means restaurants, and restaurants mean butter. In high school, every day for lunch, instead of going to the cafeteria with the other kids, I would go to my car and eat a bag of dried fruit alone. I didn't hang out after school either; I'd always leave immediately so I could get home and go for a five-mile run to burn off the afore-mentioned dried fruit.

Around fifteen, I started getting alarmingly thin. I had severe cheekbones, prominent shoulder blades, and ribs for days. I looked like the shadow of Jared Leto. The only people I allowed to get close to me were those who would joke about my weight instead of attempt a real intervention. I didn't mind being called Olive Oyl—in fact I took that as a compliment—but a real conversation about my weight was out of the question because it threatened my small, safe world of diet soda, dried fruit, and steamed vegetables.

The thinner I got, the thinner I thought I needed to get. I hadn't heard the term *body dysmorphia* back then, not that I would have thought I had it, but I now understand that's what I was experiencing. My perception of myself and my body was incredibly warped. It was as if I were looking in a funhouse mirror that makes your hips comically large. I literally could not see myself how others did. One time I was jogging up a busy street in D.C. called Wisconsin Avenue past a row of shops. A car driving by slowed down for a moment, and a man yelled out, "Eat something!" I remember stopping in my tracks. Today it breaks my heart to think that even strangers were motivated to try to help me, although, guys, I promise you that yelling from cars at women will never get you the result you want. This guy was not at all flirting with me, but if I'd had enough fat on my body to inspire him to, my suggestion would be to pull over and approach me. I might not respond how you want me to but at least you aren't perpetuating a boring stereotype. Post a missed connections ad on Craigslist, Catfish me—anything but yelling from a car.

I look back now and see the scenario as being particularly poignant given it happened in front of a store called Sullivan's Toy Store, my favorite place on Earth when I was a kid. The little girl who was once so obsessed with colored pencils and stuffed animals was now all grown up, with that passion for fun having been replaced with an obsession with calories, carbs, and food labels.

Although my mom dieted herself and was likely battling her own cunning demons, she started trying to help me. I can't even begin to fathom the pain it must cause a mother to see her child starve herself. I can hardly go into work if my dog looks the slightest bit sad.

I actually admire how my mom tricked me into going to an eating disorder specialist. She cleverly sold her to me as a nutritionist, so I thought she could help me figure out which foods had the fewest calories. However, as soon as I met the woman, I knew she was my enemy. Since my eating disorder behaved like an addiction, anyone who challenged my comfort zone was very threatening, and I instantly felt like a tiger in a cage. The beast in my head made me think in extremes—people were either with me or against me, food was either good or bad, you ate the whole box or none at all. In psych lingo, this is often referred to as black-and-white thinking, but this was way before I could see in color. As far as my addictive brain knew, this bitch was trying to kill me, which is ironic, since I was the one killing myself.

When I sat across from the specialist, she looked way too concerned about me for my liking. Her concern made me feel things, and feeling things was something I made a point to avoid. She started talking about how many calories we need in a day just for our organs to function. She talked about how protein keeps our hair follicles strong, and how fat keeps our skin bright and healthy. She was clearly trying to appeal to my vanity, but what she didn't yet know was that my disorder wasn't about trying to be pretty. It was about being in control and shrinking my body as much as I could to get the attention I couldn't seem to get when I looked too healthy.

She got up and pulled a giant sheet of paper from a huge roll hanging from the ceiling. She pushed aside a coffee table full of random objects and Rubik's cubes, which I always figured were a therapist's way of setting psychological traps for their patients, making judgments based on what you picked up. Distrustful, I never touched anything, which of course told her everything she needed to know. The specialist then had me lie down on a big piece of paper. She kneeled next to me, and with big black Sharpie, she outlined my body. When she was finished she told me to get up and look at the drawing.

"Did you know that that's the size of your body?"

As I looked at the outline of my frame, all I could think about were those chalk outlines of dead bodies at a crime scene. And Kate Moss. The two worst things you'd ever want an outline of your body to remind you of. But at that point, the sick perfectionism had taken my frontal lobe hostage, and instead of horror, I felt a sense of accomplishment. My isolating, lying, jogging, and starving had paid off. Anorexia is a disease of the mind that makes being thin your primary source of self-esteem and purpose, so the concern on this woman's face felt like even more of a win. When I was alarmingly thin, people cared, they fussed over me, they wanted to see me again.

In fact, she asked if I could come in the *next day*. See? Being thin worked! She was obsessed with me!

However, I didn't go back the next day because we couldn't afford it. If nothing else deters you from succumbing to an eating disorder, please listen to this: It costs a fortune. Between the low productivity due to the constant mental distractions, pricey fat-free foods, and the medical specialists, it drains your bank account as much as it drains your energy from low blood sugar. I'm not sure how my mom figured out how to afford it, but I agreed to see the doctor once a week solely because I could tell she was having a complete meltdown underneath the crystallized shell of denial about how thin I was.

Going to this "nutritionist," who I now realize was an eating disorder specialist, was a big obstacle in my ambitions for skeletal glory. She made me keep a food journal in which I had to write down everything I ate each day. This was perhaps my first piece of published fiction since everything I wrote down was a lie. At this point, I had lost sight of what normal people even ate, so I just wrote down whatever I saw on dinner tables in commercials.

When I went back to see the therapist, she read through my journal. She might as well have been reading *Harry Potter*. After she skimmed a couple of pages, it was clear that she saw right through my scam. She then asked me to stand on a scale to see if my eating had helped me put on weight, what with all the imaginary roast beef I had been consuming. The first time she weighed me, I remember trying to make myself heavier by bending my knees a bit and leaning back and forth. That's how cunning eating disorders can be; I actually thought that would work. I thought I could literally defy the laws of gravity. Whenever I get frustrated with the people in my life who struggle with addiction or dysmorphia, I remember how delusional I once was, thinking I could magically put on weight with mental force.

The next session, I was more prepared for the whole scale rigmarole. I had a whole system down: I'd arrive twenty minutes early with four fifty-ounce bottles of water, the ones you see someone carrying at the gym and you roll your eyes at. Like, dude, if you're *that* dehydrated, you should probably take the day off. Anyway, I would chug all of them before going into my appointment. As you can imagine, this was as uncomfortable as it was insane, but it actually worked. This time, when I stepped on the scale, I was four pounds heavier due to the water I was holding in my stomach and I guess the pee I was holding in my kidneys. She looked at me half confused, half impressed.

I really hope being pregnant doesn't hurt as much as drinking four giant bottles of water in a row because I was certain my ribs were going to shatter and that my body would tear open, causing the entire building to flood.

In my experience, eating disorders are all about control, so treating them is incredibly difficult because the more people try to help you, the further you recoil into your disease. Trying to help someone get better can actually make them worse. If you've ever had to deal with someone in active addiction or with a personality disorder, you know that it's very hard to make someone who is sick understand that they're sick given how many layers of denial shroud their perception. I was no different and since this woman was a little too aggressive with things like "logic" and "concern," I stopped going to her.

I pretended to go a couple of times, but of course the narc called my mom and told her I didn't show up. Since for me anorexia was a progressive disease, things kept getting more and more extreme. I became increasingly isolated and dysmorphic. I am not exaggerating when I tell you that I was terrified of some foods. Some people fear heights, others fear sharks; I feared olive oil. When an event was approaching, like a homecoming dance, prom, or a holiday gathering, for weeks prior I would have a knot in the pit of my stomach—not that I would ever eat a knot because it would have been way too many calories. I panicked thinking about what I was going to order at restaurants, how I could pretend to eat at dinner, or what I was going to say to get out of eating altogether. I've said every iteration of every prevarication to avoid eating in public: I'm vegan, I have acid reflux, I have celiac disease, wheat gives me migraines . . . The aforementioned is actually sort of true, but I didn't know that until pretty recently, so for all intents and purposes it was a lie at the time of the telling.

As I've mentioned, eating disorders aren't just about food obsession and restriction. In order to successfully starve yourself, you have to engage in a massive amount of lying to others and to yourself. My friends Jenny and Dori and I laugh about how much I used to lie to them in my early twenties. Now that I'm out of the woods, we make fun of how I used to order at restaurants to avoid eating calories: I would pretend to consider the most fattening meals on the menu, and then fake getting flustered at the buzzer and go for a salad with dressing on the side. When you have an eating disorder, your brain tricks you into thinking other people are absolute morons who are convinced by terrible acting. Knowing full well that I would have a panic attack if a carb came within a foot of my face, I would pretend to be indecisive even though I knew exactly what I was going to order: "So should I get the cheeseburger or the spaghetti with a milk shake? Hmm . . . ugh, I can't decide. I guess I'll just get the side salad and a Diet Coke."

I continued to be the puppet of my eating disorder through college. Being in college was kind of the glory days of my eating disorder because I was alone and could finally engage in all my weird food rituals without having to hide them from my mom. I didn't have to pray that she would buy the food I could eat, I could just go buy it myself. Once I lived on my own, what I ate started morphing from weird to just straight-up horrific. I know many people with eating disorders have "safe" foods, but mine were so few that I ended up eating only one or two foods for months at a time. That was the kind of rigid control my brain needed to feel calm. I went on a couple of very disturbing culinary tears that give me chills when I look back: I went about a month eating only dried mangoes, for example. I delved into the carcinogenic vortex as well, thoroughly enjoying the wave of new foods that were coming out before the FDA or the organic moms movement took super-toxic products off the shelves. Sugar-free Twizzlers, anything with aspartame, Olestra potato chips. If you don't remember these chips, they literally had a warning on them saying they deplete your body of vitamin D and give you "runny stools." But that was not a deterrent for me; I could not give less of a shit about having the shits. Today when people compliment me on having nice skin, I seriously think it may be because I embalmed myself with so many chemicals in my twenties.

Granted, this wasn't my first foray into artificial foods. I ate so much candy as a kid that the first time I actually ate a grape at around eight years old, I gagged. "There is something very wrong with this grape!" I said, spitting out what I thought was rotten fruit. It tasted nothing like the grape Bubblicious or the Runts I ate on a daily basis. I eventually learned that real grapes didn't taste anything like my beloved synthetic candy. Perhaps it wasn't a coincidence that my favorite philosopher is Jean Baudrillard, who wrote about the idea of simulacra, about how in modern civilization people tend to prefer the simulation of something to the original. After eating fruit-flavored candy for so long, actual fruit was a real letdown.

By the time I was twenty-two, my safe "food" choices were incredibly unhealthy, if not downright inedible. I got pretty obsessed with fat-free Swiss Miss hot chocolate, for example. There was a fifty-calorie pack, but certain grocery stores had twenty-calorie packs, and when I found them, I would buy every box they had. I had to rotate grocery stores a lot because the only thing stronger than my desire to stay thin was my desire to be thought of as normal by the cashiers. I would always pretend the groceries I was buying were for someone else or that I thought there was a deal. I would bring ten boxes to the counter at once and do a mediocre performance of a person who's too lazy to save money. "There's not a sale on these? Oh, well, I'm already here so I might as well just get them anyway." This was before Amazon, which lets you buy weird things in the privacy of your own home. This was back when you had to face another human being when you bought embarrassing things, back when we had to do bad improv with the cashier and cover up condoms with other products, hoping they'd scan it upside down before seeing "ribbed for her pleasure" on the box.

After a fifteen-year struggle with anorexia, I'm still not sure I even know how to describe it. Well, maybe I'll start by saying it wasn't a real struggle until I got into my twenties. My eating disorder was my best friend until I decided that I wanted to stop and simply couldn't. By the time I moved to Los Angeles, as I tried to control my need to control, the pendulum swung to the opposite extreme. My brain convinced my hands and mouth to start binge-ing instead of restricting, but I never purged or threw up my food. I'm truly not sure why, since I had the neurological makeup and perfect childhood to make me a red-hot candidate for bulimia. Maybe I wasn't ambitious enough, or maybe I was too much of a masochist, because the aftermath of bingeing meant extreme stom-ach pain and countless hours at the gym. This was a perfect justi-fication for my need to isolate. If I threw up my food, that would mean I'd actually have time to see people and function in society, which was my nightmare.

If the idea of binge-eating didn't make you jealous enough of my life, the weirder part is that I started doing it in my sleep. My body and brain were so bifurcated, so at war, that when I fell asleep, my body would take over and seek the nutrients it needed. Clearly my subconscious didn't trust me to provide myself with food anymore, so like a puppet master, it started getting the job done without me. I know sleep eating sounds funny in theory, but it's actually pretty terrifying to wake up every morning with the taste of barbecue sauce in your mouth and have it smeared all over your face. Many mornings I'd look in the mirror and think I was covered in dried blood, wondering for a second if I had been stabbed in the night before realizing I had gone nuts on straw-berry jelly in my sleep.

Every morning I felt like the dude from *Memento*, trying to piece together what happened. From what I could make of the fo-rensics, apparently I would get up three A.M. and ravage anything in the kitchen with calories. The next morning I'd wake up sur-rounded by wrappers in my bed; sometimes I was even sticky from whatever weird sauce I blindly poured down my throat. Sometimes I had painful cuts on my gums and the inside of my cheeks from whatever I had been jamming into my face at four

A.M. After I got out of bed, I'd slowly walk into the kitchen, dreading the carnage I'd find. It all felt very cinematic, like I was in a horror movie and had just walked in on a grisly crime scene. But what I found was often way weirder than a dead body. I'd walk into a scene that looked like a bomb had gone off in a grocery store and created an apocalyptic graveyard of chicken carcasses and broken jelly jars. I was used to walking on eggshells, but walking on broken glass was a new one.

To further complicate my disorder, I faced another interesting development around this time. My parents stopped giving me money. I was given money only if I was in total crisis, e.g. my perpetually worn-down brakes and dried-fruit-induced cavities. Other than that, I was on my own.

I was able to scrape together some money by selling my clothes at vintage resale stores and being a subject for focus groups. For every product ever sold, companies do market research using focus groups. They basically ask desperate broke strangers to sit in a circle and talk about what they like and dislike about the product. The company paid fifty dollars cash on the day the group met and it was always around two in the afternoon, so you can imagine the types of people these groups attracted. And if you can't, it was mostly drug addicts desperately needing cash, like, five days ago.

I was desperate for money, but the problem with me is that I'm also a type A codependent perfectionist, so I also truly wanted to help improve the products we were testing. I specifically remember a Neutrogena facial scrub brush. I was sitting in a circle of meth addicts who needed fifty dollars and needed it fast. They were saying whatever they had to say to get the discussion over with, but I kept raising my hand and pitching ideas for how to make the brush more compact, sanitary, and utilitarian. It's actually secretly my dream to be an inventor, so I rattled off a bunch of what I thought were very good ideas: "What if it was also an eyebrow brush on the other side? What if it can shave your mustache but then shape your brows, too? And it could also be a pen!" I'm not sure if you've ever been nonverbally threatened by a desperate drug addict, but I don't recommend it. Knowing how emotionally dyslexic I was back then, I probably mistook these homicidal glares as flirting.

The point is, for about two years I didn't have more than eighty dollars in my bank account, which meant no more fancy Swiss Miss, poison potato chips, or dried mangoes. Once I was broke, I realized that having an eating disorder was actually kind of a luxury. Now I was starving because I had to be, not because I wanted to be. This ended up exacerbating my disease because it helped justify my food restriction and gave me a real reason to eat nothing. My brain now reasoned that starving myself was saving money. "I ate only five hundred calories today, I'm so frugal! Take that, Suze Orman!" I found the most cost-effective food to eat on a tight budget was, not shockingly, jerky. You name the jerky, I've binged on it. Turkey, beef, jalapeño beef, salmon, jalapeño salmon. As long as it was filled with the maximum amount of preservatives and antibiotics, it was in my body.

I started choosing "safe" foods that were hard to chew and would never go bad. I basically started grocery shopping the way most people shop for tires. The more durable and long-lasting, the better. I used to buy protein bars in bulk, hoping to ration them out for the week, but of course given the midnight bouts with bingeing, I'd wake up in my bed under a blanket of the half-eaten protein bars I had eaten in an evening stupor. As the food I was eating got less edible, my stomach got less tolerant. After eating four or five of these basically indigestible protein bars in one sitting, I'd wake up in a state of rigor mortis, paralyzed by stomach pain. I'd have to lie in a fetal position for most of the day, full of regret, Red #5, and methylgubane. I just made that last word up, but knowing our food industry these days, it's probably a real ingredient.

This feels like the right time to mention that, at this point, I was so off the grid from what was actually logical, that I wasn't really eating food conducive to being thin, especially when you consider the quantities that I was consuming. By the time I got to bingeing on protein bars, I was easily eating four thousand calories a day. At this point, my disorder had evolved into something less about restricting food and more about self-sabotaging in a way that got me stuck in a shame cycle that justified my extreme isolation. After I had eaten so many calories, my entire day consisted of making my stomach hurt and then needing to go to the gym for hours to burn it all off. My addiction being such a full-time job meant that I didn't have to deal with reality, people, or, God forbid, intimacy with anyone.

Since I spent so much of my adolescence preoccupied with this eating madness, I of course hadn't developed the social skills to have good friendships, but when I met Dori and Jenny the first year I was in L.A., they were so awesome that I was determined not to let my insane food restrictions and dark secrets mess it up. This was a struggle, given that I sometimes spent days in bed or at the gym. I would frequently cancel plans in a cryptic way, and when I did show up, I'd kill the vibe by not ordering food or by asking the waiter what was in every dish and if they could make me steamed vegetables with no oil. These days the most annoying people take photos of their food to post on social media, but ten years ago it was me, the person firing off a litany of questions to the waiter about salad dressing and begging them to make a delicious dish taste awful.

Dori and Jenny were the only people who really saw me eat anything. They never attacked or accused because perhaps somehow they knew that eating disorders just grow stronger when someone tries to fix them. That said, they would occasionally ask leading questions or gently drop nutrition information à la "Did you know that eating fat actually makes you feel full longer?" I know them well enough now to know that they're way too smart and interesting to waste time talking about what makes someone feel full, so clearly they were doing it just to try and help me the only way they knew how.

One time Jenny was at my apartment off Sunset Boulevard. It was full of cockroaches and I saw rats on two different occasions, but it was within walking distance of The Comedy Store and that's all I cared about. I saw at least two or three cockroaches a day; the only good news is that I didn't have to worry about them going near my food due to how inedible it was. They never dared come near my cabinets. If your food is so full of chemicals that not even cockroaches will eat it, you need to regroup.

One day Jenny was over and for some reason ended up in my kitchen. I don't remember why or how, but I remember her opening a cabinet. When she saw the food on display, she gasped. Her face went pale. Mind you, even when she's not horrified, Jenny is already very pale. She has gorgeous alabaster skin and looks like an angelic doll a girl would have had on her dresser in the 1950s or that a creepy man would have on his dresser now. But after she took a good hard look at what I was putting in my body, her relentless smile finally fell to deep concern.

"Oh my god," she uttered.

She didn't make a joke or laugh it off. She just looked very sad for me. I don't know what it was about that moment, but for some reason it woke me up. Maybe I realized that I was hurting people I loved with my behavior, or worse, disappointing them, which was a threat to my perfectionism. Maybe I was ready to change, maybe Jenny is my guardian angel and shone a divine light on me. Or maybe I was just tired.

What's interesting to me is that Jenny isn't a doctor or a therapist or a documentary. When you live in an alternative delusional reality, facts sound like fiction, so if people tell you the truth, it doesn't really help much; it just kind of makes you want to get away from the person telling it to you. I must have subconsciously known on some level that I was killing myself; the point is, I didn't acknowledge that reality. Today denial is without a doubt my greatest fear in life because I know how powerful and insidious it is. It's made me do terrible things to my body and has even been the fuel on the fire of wars, genocides, racism, and trends like drawn-on eyebrows and shiny clear bra straps that almost draw more attention than normal opaque ones. Denial is dangerous. Make sure you don't have it.

Jenny's face that day was the first step in shattering my denial. Something shifted in me that day. This moment also collided with the point in my stand-up career when I was starting to go on tour, opening for comics like Steve Byrne and Bobby Lee, and my lack of energy was starting to sabotage my dreams. I had to be on a plane at six A.M. and had to perform at eight and ten at night. My immune system was so weak that I was always run-down and constantly sick. I was finally getting what I wanted in life, but I was too dizzy and lethargic to enjoy it. Since I was tired of being tired, I finally experimented with trying a carb here or there, and it was incredible how much energy they gave me. Eating a piece of bread would literally feel like I had just snorted a line of cocaine. When I was about twenty-three, I finally ate a whole bagel, and I was like Bradley Cooper in that movie *Limitless*, bouncing off the walls, super focused, able to get through the day without a headache or a low-blood-sugar nap. One day I ate a bowl of cereal with 2 percent milk and I wrote an entire TV pilot script in eight hours. Once I saw how productive I could be on calories, I was sold. Food was my new secret weapon. And even crazier, after a couple of weeks during which I ate real food in sane quantities, my hairbrush no longer looked like Chewbacca.

Maybe it was unhealthy for Jenny's reaction and work goals to be what helped me slay this thing; maybe I was trading one unhealthy obsession with another, but whatever it was, it was better than being a walking zombie full of sodium benzoate. It doesn't really matter what the catalyst was; the important thing was that Jenny's reaction to the "food" in my cabinets made me want to get help.

When I first decided to talk to Vera about my eating disorder, I was stunned when she told me my issue had very little to do with actual food. I thought that statement was odd, given food was pretty much all I thought about. Moreover, the disorder was, as I've already said, more about feeling like I had a modicum of control in a hectic environment than being thin. As long as I was eating something fat- and sugar-free, everything was okay. Well, everything except my liver.

Turns out my eating disorder was also about having incredibly low self-esteem, which may not be a surprise to you guys, but for me it was straight-up breaking news. When I first heard that I had low self-esteem, I was flabbergasted. Shocked, I tell you. Downright stunned. Everyone always told me I was so "strong" and "confident." I found out that many people, including myself, conflate being loud and talking a lot with having self-esteem. However, I've learned that the loudness of your voice is not an indicator of your feelings of self-worth. In my case, the two are actually antithetical: The louder I'm talking, the less faith I have that someone is actually listening. I became loud because as a kid I didn't feel heard, so I developed the habit of overcompensating and talking as if I'm always hailing a taxi. Once Vera explained this to me, it all made a lot of sense, given the paradigm I was living by was that my external appearance was more valuable than my health. Of course this assumes anyone even finds an emaciated girl with thinning hair attractive, which I certainly don't. My disease distorted my reality to the point that I lost the plot on why I was even starving myself in the first place. It went from a logical way to get attention as a kid to a mindless habit to an insidious disease that cost me a lot in dental bills and God knows how much in bone density.

Vera had me do some "inner child work." I heard people talk about their inner child, but to me it sounded creepy and perverted. I came to therapy to learn how to act like an adult, so why are we talking about being children? This sounds—I don't know—kinda childish? I learned the key to being an adult may just be honoring the young part of yourself—your basic emotional needs, insecurities, and the mental conditioning that was done at a young age. Through connecting to your inner child, which you can call whatever you want if *inner child* weirds you out: your source, your gut, your inner fetus . . . I really don't care. Through this connection you honor the defense mechanisms you developed as a kid in order to survive your family system and start to deactivate them. Essentially, you start to parent yourself the way you wished you had been parented: with patience, sensitivity, forgiveness, and butter.

Vera gave me an exercise to do where you write to your inner child and ask him/her a question. If you're struggling for an answer to something or if you aren't sure about what to do in a situation, you write out a question in your dominant hand (you) and write the response with your nondominant hand (your inner child). Initially I thought the whole idea was ridiculous and probably for narcissistic pedophiles. I hardly respond to e-mails, so how was I going to make time to sit down and write a letter to some needy imaginary kid?

I resisted doing this exercise for a very long time, but one day I was overwhelmed with anxiety and frustration and was all out of ideas on how to soothe myself. Eating wasn't working, not eating wasn't working, texting guys wasn't working, working wasn't working. Weed wasn't even working, so you know it was bad.

I figured if I did the stupid exercise, I could at least end up writing some jokes about how ridiculous the whole thing was. I wrote a couple questions out with my right hand. The first one was pretty passive-aggressive: "What do you want to eat?" I switched to my left hand as Vera instructed me to do. Look, I'm not big on ruminating about the metaphysical because I'm still trying to figure out the physical, but something I can only describe as magical happened akin to what people are apparently experiencing when they use a Ouija board: A force flowed through my left hand and it started moving the pen across the page. My left hand scribbled "peanut butter smiles."

I knew it! Ridiculous and stupid. This whole thing was a pointless sham.

I stared at the oblique, strange handwriting. It looked like the writing of a child who was trying to get down a grocery list during an earthquake. As I started knocking stand-up material around in my head, suddenly I got a pang in my stomach and my chest got warm. My eyes welled up. I suddenly remembered that when I was a kid, my dad and I used to spread peanut butter on pieces of bread and draw smiley faces in the peanut butter. Then we'd fill the smiles and eyes with honey from one of those honey bear squeeze jars that always has a shockingly sticky cap. I had completely forgotten about this until now, but clearly it was at the top of my subconscious mind. This little girl was right there, so present in me, and I had been ignoring her this whole time. The only thing that ended up being funny about the situation was that I was using a Hustler store pen, which felt very lascivious, so from then on, I used colored pencils when I did the exercise.

It's above my pay grade to explain why tapping into the five-year-old version of yourself actually makes you act more like an adult, but it's been a game changer for me. Since developing a connection with my inner child, I keep a photo of myself at five years old on my phone in a folder called "get better." In that folder I have all sorts of meditations and screen grabs of things that basically remind me to stop being crazy. Honestly, I'm way more afraid of hackers getting this folder than my nude photos, given it's chock-full of screen-grabbed inspirational quotes like "don't ask for a light load, ask for a strong back." When I'm tempted to abuse myself, criticize myself, or date a stupid idiot who has a tinted phone screen, I go into the folder, look at the photo of myself as a kid, and try to make the decision that's best for Child Whitney, since Adult Whitney always seems to go for the most masochistic, expensive, and intestine-ravaging choice.

Since I've nurtured my relationship with Child Whitney my life looks very different. I treat myself with respect, I have more dignity, I eat at a table instead of in the car, I wear bras without wires in them, and my house is essentially a dog kennel. The more mature I get, the more my child runs the show. I eat when I'm hungry and I buy food that actually comes from the dirt, not from some factory in China. If I can't pronounce all the ingredients, I try not to put it in my mouth, but if I do, I don't beat myself up either because that would be counterproductive. I wouldn't yell at a child if she ate something indulgent every now and then, so I don't yell at myself if I'm craving something that isn't kale. A doctor once told me that stressing about eating something unhealthy re-

leases cortisol in the brain, which can actually be just as bad for you if not worse than the chemicals in whatever food you're eating. If you're stuck in an airport and your only options are neon-yellow pizzas or candy from Hudson News, you might as well eat the crap and enjoy it so you're at least not compounding the damage by shaming yourself. I mean, please don't eat neon food every day, and in general don't take nutrition advice from a comedian.

Coming to terms with the fact that my mind is being steered by a five-year-old peanut butter addict has also helped me to be more patient with other people's behavior. When someone's acting a fool, I remind myself what Vera says: "We're all five." If someone is angry, I respond the way I would respond to a child having a tantrum: "Do you want something to eat? Do you want to lie down for a minute?" Sometimes this makes people angrier because they think I'm mocking or patronizing them, but for the most part they're, like, "Yeah, I'd love something to eat, actually." In my experience, about half of all conflicts are a result of low blood sugar. You're mad at someone? Have a banana. I've never met a piece of phallic fruit that couldn't fix petulance.

Looking back on my war with food, I know now that with all my eating demons, I wanted my body to have the equilibrium on the outside I didn't know how to attain on the inside. Having grown up learning that appearance was everything, I thought if I was perfect externally, my internal state might have a shot. Now that my insides are acceptably copacetic most of the time, my outsides are no longer a priority. I accept the limitations of being human and the dysmorphia that comes with living in the time of ubiquitous models, pervasive Photoshop, and Cate Blanchett's face.

I hope, if anything, in addition to humiliating myself with this chapter, I can maybe make a dent in removing the stigma of body dysmorphia. Usually when a girl is too thin, works out a lot, or wears too much makeup, we tend to roll our eyes and label her as shallow, dumb, or narcissistic. And look, she may be those things, but in my experience, usually that kind of behavior is coming from a place of tremendous pain and deep insecurity. When I'm feeling judgmental about other people's choices, it helps to remember that the engine of these behaviors can be a deep fear and disconnection from oneself. I try to remember that nobody wants to have an eating disorder; nobody aspires to that. Nobody wants to hate her own body. Nobody wants to feel like they can't leave the house without makeup. I didn't write "reading nutrition information on boxes for half an hour a day" on my vision board. It wasn't my dream in life to spend half of it obsessing over how many calories are in fuckin' mangoes.

Today, when things get hectic in my life and I feel like I'm losing control, my brain still wants to get weird with food. If my flight is delayed by three hours, I sometimes think it's a good idea to eat only pretzels at the airport instead of an actual lunch. If my schedule is insanely packed, I find myself thinking it's a good idea to drink nothing but coffee and chew gum all day. But I can usually course-correct pretty quickly because I now know how to prioritize that little girl who just wants to be loved and fed. If I just keep treating myself as if I'm parenting a five-year-old, what I should be doing becomes very clear: I have to eat fat, drink water, and avoid reading mean Twitter @replies.

If you glean nothing else from this chapter, the other good news about my overcoming an eating disorder and putting some weight on is that it makes you look about ten years younger. People keep asking me if I've gotten a facelift and I'm, like, "Nope, just got that extra side of guac." If it takes vanity to cure your insecurity, so be it.

So, I wouldn't go so far as to say I'm completely fixed forever, but for the most part I'm fine, you guys.

THE BOOBS CHAPTER

As a kid, I don't remember being much into toys, but I do remember seeing my mom's bras around the house, which were always way more fun for me to play with than My Little Ponys. That said, there was something very morose about these bras. They had giant wires and shiny stretchy lace fabric that went all the way up to the shoulder and not one, not two, but *three* clasps in the back. It looked less like a bra and more like a harness used for bungee jumping. I was always desperate to make the adults in the house laugh, so I used to put Mom's bras on and dance around. I'm now ashamed at how juvenile and corny that bit was, but for a six-year-old, it was pretty cutting-edge.

My education about breasts was an episode of *Who's the Boss?* where Tony Danza had to buy Alyssa Milano a bra. God, I miss the days when a sitcom title could be a rhetorical question. Anyway, the first breasts I ever saw in person that weren't mine belonged to Barbie. So when later I first saw my mom's boobs, I was horrified by how mushy and pendulous they were and that they had two giant moles on them. I later found out these "moles" were nipples and Barbie was the deformed gimp—not my mother. But as I said earlier, I was never too into Barbie. I didn't even enjoy putting Barbies in microwaves because the aftermath always made my Hot Pockets taste like synthetic chemical-y plastic, and I preferred them to taste like synthetic chemical-y meat and cheese. I hated Barbie's hard nubby boobs. They seemed so stoic and aloof. They were impossible to play with. They were like the mean girls in middle school who refused to hang out with you. I was more of a Rainbow Brite kind of kid anyway. She was cute but not distractingly sexual. And she had already achieved my dream of having a talking horse.

In terms of other kinds of entertainment, we weren't a big Disney family. I remember watching *The Little Mermaid* and *Snow White* and being very underwhelmed by the whole princess rigmarole. They all seemed whiny and victimish to me, always waiting around to be saved by a handsome white blond guy Hitler would have jerked off to. The princesses always needed men to rescue them even though they seemed to be perfectly fine in their fancy castles and cottages. I felt like they had amazing lives and fake problems. Snow White was living the ultimate fantasy with seven hilarious dwarves who were obsessed with her, but she let some lame Ken doll come along and ruin it. As far as I was concerned she was an ingrate.

I didn't watch a ton of cartoons, but in retrospect, it's clear that I gravitated toward the more androgynous characters. I loved the Smurfs, Alvin and the Chipmunks, and my all-time favorite, albeit short-lived, Animaniacs. Betty Boop always annoyed me: her over-the-top femininity felt forced and desperate. Maybe I was projecting because I myself felt forced and desperate to be feminine. Or maybe I was just pissed because I secretly wanted to be her. Despite her obvious charms, Betty Boop wasn't for me. Even as a kid I knew there was something dark about a sexy cartoon. To this day I don't understand why animators would make people want to have intercourse with pixels. That said, I had a pretty serious fascination with Jessica Rabbit. She was more self-possessed, with ample side-eye and an attitude like she would cut a bitch if they acted a fool. Even though her ankles were drawn in a way that made them look broken from her high heels, I saw her as powerful instead of just a sex object. She somehow exuded control of her objectification, even though I'll bet she was being drawn on a piece of paper by a man who was into that weird porn where people have sex through a pizza.

I also liked that Jessica Rabbit was a grown woman, unlike Boop, who infantilized herself with impish sounds and childish mannerisms. Conversely, Jessica Rabbit seemed very bored of sex. Regardless of my psychoanalysis of them, they inculcated me with one very crucial fact: Boobs mattered. Every story they were in was about men getting hit by cars or their jaws dropping when they walked by, anything to get a glimpse of their impossibly perky breasts. Men were literally dying to see them. My hippocampus took note.

My theory that boobs were the ticket to happiness was confirmed when my dad married his third (I think) wife when I was (I think) ten. I was not thrilled when my dad started bringing his new girlfriend around the house, but I was fascinated by her ethos and body. She drove a tomato-red Mercedes-Benz 450 convertible. I had to Google the model just now, so don't think I all of a sudden know about cars. I don't. But this one is burned into my memory because of how sexy it was. It's the one that has a cherubic front and an almost cartoonish body, just like hers. Her waist was tiny and she was impossibly tan. Not that you would have noticed any of this, given how distractingly bulbous her breasts were. She was part pretty alien, part Dolly Parton. But as a kid, I saw her as a real live Jessica Rabbit.

Since I basically thought she was my cartoon hero in the flesh, let's just call her Jessica. Jessica was the most confident woman I had ever met. At the time I didn't understand the concept of having confidence, I just thought she was the bitch trying to replace my mom and ruin my life. By the time Jessica came around, my older sister had started developing boobs. My sister is beautiful and blond, so between her, Jessica, and my mom, I was constantly surrounded by buxom blond women who got a lot of attention. Not sure if my genetics had just taken a couple years off or if my pituitary gland had mono, because I was flat-chested to the point of a possible inversion. I also had a knee condition that made me limp and unable to cross my legs or walk in a ladylike way. Later in life I learned that it's a pretty common condition called Osgood-Schlatter disease. It's caused by a growth spurt and probably GMOs or some shit we eat in mass quantity our government refuses to acknowledge or do research on.

At around nine, I developed a nubby bump poking out from beneath my right kneecap. The universe was being particularly cruel because it looked exactly like that hard nubby Barbie boob I always resented as a child. After all, they do say you become what you hate. Worse than having my nemesis's chest on my leg was the fact that this bump was filled with nerves, so every time I hit it on something, which was often, I could only find solace by screaming for hours in a fetal position in the school nurse's office. To boot, it would cause a giant black-and-green bruise, which made it look like I had a moldy knee. I was never able to wear a skirt or, even more heartbreakingly, a skort. For a couple years I went to a school requiring a uniform that involved a plaid dress, so I had to wear opaque tights underneath. I looked like a gimpy Wednesday Addams. A slut for symmetry, I developed the personality to match.

When I was eleven, the shit hit the fan in my nuclear family and my mom sent me to Roanoke, Virginia, to live with two of my aunts. They had all my favorite things: horses, dogs, and boobs. According to some online test where I spat in a tube, I am of Irish-Welsh mutt descent, but strangely my aunts are olive-skinned with perfect teeth, big lips, and even bigger boobs. The more time I spent with them, the more entitled I felt to a body like theirs. I counted the days when my DNA would take the stage and turn me into the kind of girl that cartoon men would get hit by cars just to get a glimpse of.

Unlike everyone in my family, I went through puberty oddly late. When I was twelve, I remember walking into my bedroom in Roanoke and finding a giant plastic box-shaped bag filled with maxi-pads. These were more like diapers than maxi-pads, the ones that look like an inflated safety vest, only made of layers upon layers of perfumed, bleached cotton with tiny roses emblazoned on them. The maxi-pads had a giant sticker on the bottom so they could attach to your underwear, and when you wore them with tight pants, they augmented your pelvis with a very conspicuous gender-neutral hump, like that weird thong situation sumo wrestlers wear on their undercarriage. I wanted to look like a Barbie, but these made me have the pelvis of a Ken doll.

I stacked all the pads in my bathroom, placing them one on top of another like I was playing a game of Tetris. The saddest part of the giant Jenga game of maxi-pads I made is that I didn't even need them yet. The stack sat there for what seemed like forever. I was so ashamed of not having my period yet that I did what any insecure tween who didn't get enough eye contact as a baby would do: I pretended I did. I peeled off the sticker coating of the pads, attached them to my giant Jockey underwear, and wore the colossal pads every day to the chagrin of my inner thighs, which retaliated with many an angry rash.

More devastating, my breasts were also still not cooperating. My legs were growing, my feet were growing, my Osgood-Schlatter bump was growing, my anxiety was growing, but my boobs were not. Turns out they were more scared to go out into the world than I was. To make matters weirder, I think my nipples were growing. But not my actual breasts. Well, that's not true. One of them was growing. But not the other. I looked like Barbie if someone had second thoughts and bailed halfway through microwaving her.

I compensated for the sternum disparity by becoming a master illusionist, by crafting a bra layering system that made it seem as if I had a modicum of a figure. I saved money for months to order one of the bras from the Victoria's Secret catalogue. It was forest-green satin with giant wide straps and a tiny bow between the cups. I am not sure why of all the colors I could choose, I picked the one chosen by the Girl Scouts of America and Shrek's wife.

The first layer was a bra that clasped in the back, a wireless sort of training bra, which served as my base. Then I cut a padded bra in half and put just the one cup on the flatter side of my sternum to even out the situation. Then I had another bra over that, with a clasp in the front, pulling it all together. I topped off this morass of fabric and wires with a sports bra that I pulled over my head to mush all the layers into what could from forty feet away look like an actual chest of a human girl, although up close, it looked like an octopus was trying to get out of a trash bag, so I tried not to get too close to anyone.

I actually wore this bra combo for a couple years, very satisfied by the attention my handiwork got me from teenage boys, even given the incredibly low bar they set once their bodies had been kidnapped by testosterone. I had zero guilt about my ruse because, after all, it was a secret between me and Victoria.

That summer I went to Florida with my sister and father. The weeks leading up to the trip, I was terrified about what I was going to wear to the beach. I was able to make my fabricated chest symmetrical under a shirt, but that was on dry land. I'd have had to be David Blaine to make my boobs look somewhat realistic in a bathing suit with water involved. Fortunately I didn't end up having to go into the water to watch my Franken-chest float away into the sea, but I did have something equally as traumatizing happen: I hooked up with a lacrosse player.

My sister and I were always up to no good, and one night we snuck into the lobby of a neighboring hotel, where some lacrosse teams were staying for a tournament or whatever lacrosse players play in. I don't know how it happened exactly, since I drank four

Amaretto sours, but I ended up making out with one of the lacrosse bros on the beach. By this point I had already lost my virginity, but not in a way that prepared me for making out with anyone.

I know you're going to think I'm making this up, and sometimes I even think I am, but I lost my virginity in the Virgin Islands. I know, too on the nose. I was on a cruise with my dad and Jessica. They were by the pool most of the time, and this activity was out of the question for me given my jerry-rigged sternum padding situation, so I wandered off and ended up losing my virginity to some guy from Schenectady, New York. The main headline is that while it happened I was so focused on keeping my triple bra contraption on that I didn't pay attention to anything else that was happening. Now that I actually know what sex entails, I am shocked that this boy was able to keep an erection despite the lumpy bandage-like contraption around my chest. All I did was lie there and intensely pray it didn't fall off. I was so still and quiet that I would not be surprised if this guy was a necrophiliac.

When I made out with the lacrosse player on the beach, I also worked very hard to keep my array of bras on and in place, much to this poor boy's confusion. Every time he would put his hands near my chest, I would move them away, borderline swatting at him with a Kung Fu chopping motion. His deep need to see under my bras was yet another reminder that boobs are very, very important. By this point, I wasn't even sure I would have been able to take them off if I had tried, given how intertwined they had all become, but I also couldn't take the chance that he'd see my stunted log jam of a sternum.

A year or so later I found myself on the floor of a trailer in Ocean City, Maryland, making out with a guy who was way less patient with my makeshift breasts. And yes, I'm going to blow by the whole "floor of a trailer" piece. There's not much to say about it besides that I make *strong choices*, people. Trust me, I wish hooking up with guys on beer- and blood-stained carpets was anomalous back then, but since I wasn't really introduced to the concept of dignity until like twelve years later, let's just say I had a lot of rug burn on my lower back for a couple weeks following many a spring break.

The Maryland guy was older and somewhat experienced, so he was able to unclasp one bra with one hand. I remember thinking he must be a magician or something because it took me three or four tries with two hands and I did it every day. I now know he was probably just promiscuous and that I'm very lucky he didn't give me herpes or whatever the hip STD was back then. I thought he should be my boyfriend, so decided it was worth taking my muddle of bras off and back then I thought nudity was a surefire way to make someone love you. I took one off, then another, then another. I was like one of those Russian nesting dolls, but with way deader eyes.

Once all the layers came off, I remember him looking at my chest quizzically. His face had a mixture of confusion and sympathy, basically every emotion except arousal. I was of course mortified but also slightly validated that someone else saw the same thing I saw. Something was wrong. He avoided my boob altogether for the remaining three hours of our drunken, seemingly endless, completely unenjoyable hookup. I didn't get a boyfriend out of it, but I did get even more insecure about my Picasso-y chest.

By the time I turned fourteen, I was getting impatient. I wanted my symmetrical boobs and I wanted them now. Getting good grades and being funny was getting exhausting, and I wanted the free attention from my dad that my stepmother Jessica got so effortlessly.

The major curveball within this incongruence of curves was that, as you know if you read the last chapter, this was around when my eating disorder decided to hijack my brain. If you didn't read the last chapter, this paragraph is going to be deeply baffling. The eating disorder therapist told me that not eating would cause my breast tissue to stop growing, but my eating disorder told me she was a lying, cunning psycho who was dead set on sabotaging my happiness, so I didn't listen. Given how little protein I was eating, my long-awaited period had stopped, and so did the lopsided growth of my chest. This is pretty obvious, but if you don't eat, breast tissue can't grow, and since breasts have fatty tissue in them, when you lose weight, they are often the first to go. As you know, I didn't get a handle on eating again until my mid-twenties, so essentially my eating disorder smashed my dreams of a perfect chest.

When I was about nineteen, I moved to L.A. and promptly fell madly in love with a guy. Let me rephrase that: I became magnetically attracted to a man who perfectly re-created my childhood circumstances, but I was conditioned to think that was "love at first sight." This was before I had any addiction or codependence therapy, so I basically moved in with anyone who reminded me of my dad. This guy was nomadic, randomly flying from L.A. to New York, keeping me in a state of paralyzing anxiety that I thought could only be true love. You now know that this was me in the glory days of my codependence, which was taking hold and distorting my reality like a funhouse mirror in desperate need of Windex.

I became very, very preoccupied with let's call him Mark. Where he was, what he was doing, what he wasn't doing, what I could do to make him do what I wanted him to do . . . I didn't yet know that other people weren't responsible for my emotional needs, so I exhausted myself with high expectations and emotional perfectionism. After reading *Getting the Love You Want* by Harville Hendrix, easily my least favorite title of my most favorite book, I realized that Mark had all the negative qualities of my primary caretakers, which is part of why I was so magnetically attracted to him. He triggered my comfort zone of emotions: uncertainty, anxiety, self-doubt. These feelings gave me the drug I could never get enough of: adrenaline. It made me feel alive, awake, and like I was in a sexy action movie. Because of my tendency to emotionally time travel, my subconscious mind concluded that getting him to love me would heal all my old, bleeding invisible wounds. I know what you're thinking—back in my twenties, I was a real catch.

Mark often had lunch with one of his platonic girlfriends, of whom I was insanely jealous but pretended not to be, desperate to come off as the "cool girl." I mean, she *ate lunch*. *Who eats lunch?* They hung out and I pretended not to care. Long story longer, I ended up flying to New York to see him for the Christmas holiday. And by *see him*, I mean check up on and micromanage his behavior because I had old abandonment fear coming up and which made me unable to breathe. One day Mark was out working and I was left alone in his apartment. Now, let me just remind you about the mis-wired neural pathways I had back then before I admit the terrible decisions I made that night: I had seen adultery growing up, I was in the haze of my codependence and addictive behaviors, and I was also very, very hungry. I would never do this today, but kids . . . I went through his computer. I managed to guess his password, which is shocking, given that today I forget my own password easily twice a week.

I found nothing. Mostly just trying-too-hard photos of me I had sent him in the hopes of making him think I didn't try too hard. This was before I knew my angles and how to put makeup on, so the photos looked more like I had been taken hostage by a high school yearbook photographer. After sleuthing for a while, I was ready to give up on finding something incriminating that would give me a hit of my beloved drug, adrenaline, until I had the very insane but also straight-up brilliant idea to go into his trash folder. I know, I'm a sick, sick genius. When I opened it, a cornucopia of photos of breasts appeared before me as if a pimp had made a Power-Point presentation. This trash folder had almost as many boobs as the Instagram "discover" page. My heart sank. So did my stomach and lungs and liver and uterus. This is of course a rough situation for any girl, but I think my body took it as an opportunity to release a bunch of old repressed pain I had never processed, so the floodgates of emotion opened with a bang. As I cried, I felt a deep pain in my bones, like twenty ghosts were beating me up.

When Mark came home, I lost my mind on the poor guy. Girl, I was Interrupted. The worst part of me going apeshit on him is that as much as I loved being the victim and stewing in my glorious self-righteous indignation, it turns out that I was crazy, but not crazy enough to check the *date* the photos were taken. Turns out, the photos were from years before we had even met. I probably should have known given the orange iMac G3 desktop computer in the background of the nudies, but this was way before I developed a relationship with the concept of logic.

That day I learned the hard way that a quick double tap shows you the date a picture was taken, but the real takeaway from this mess was that the photos only heightened my paranoia about my unacceptable body, given that they were of nothing but boobs. Looking back with a modicum of clarity, I can now say they were actually really beautiful, but that was the problem. Her breasts were gorgeous, perky, symmetrical, and—dare I say it?—effortless. I know that's a weird adjective to use when describing breasts, but for my whole life thus far, my boobs were a full-time job to manage: the hiding, the manipulating, the leveling, the resenting, the squishing. I just wanted my boobs to be easy.

After this incident, I became even more obsessed with breasts, or maybe more specifically, my lack of symmetrical ones. I hope this admission doesn't get me slapped with multiple lawsuits, but I was so into comparing myself to other women that when I went to the gym I started ogling women's breasts while furiously working out on the elliptical. They're everywhere! And they're all so unique and bouncy! This was the closest I will probably ever be to understanding what it's like to be a man, and guys, please hear me when I say this: I am so sorry for your plight. I had no idea. Being transfixed by boobs is exhausting.

And yes, I often pondered if this traumatic incident suddenly made me reject men and "become" a lesbian or something. But that's not really how neurology or being gay works. I wish it had been that simple; in fact, it's always been a dream of mine to be a lesbian, but I guess the universe didn't want that for me. It wanted me to live a life of redundant fighting about fighting and a revolving door of stubbly testicles.

My self-loathing was exacerbated by every perfect set of breasts I saw. One of my favorite quotes is from an inspirational speaker named Iyanla Vanzant: "Comparison is an act of violence against the self." That quote hit me right in the solar plexus. If comparison is a form of violence against yourself, me, myself, and I were in a nuclear war.

One day after a dentist appointment, I was walking through Beverly Hills, looking for my car, which I swear isn't as boring as it sounds, given that in my twenties, parking my car always became a psychological thriller. I never remembered where it was and always put too little money in the meter, so every time I parked, I would basically go into debt. This was way before I understood that spending three extra minutes to do something right could save you an hour and eighty dollars in the long run. I had not yet subscribed to a slogan I now live by from the Navy SEALs: "Slow is smooth and smooth is fast." Ironic enough, when I was twenty-five, finding my car an hour after I parked it was a job cut out only for SEAL Team Six.

So I was desperately speed-walking around Beverly Hills, looking for my car as if I were five and lost my mother at the mall. My heart was racing, my bank account bracing. I walked past all the fancy stores, luminescent and wasteful, blinded by the relentless L.A. sun. Every time I walk around Beverly Hills, I'm consumed by both wonder and disgust. It feels like I'm finally in the streets of Oz that I so badly wanted to skip down as a kid, but now that I'm here, it's ultimately just a bunch of stuff I can't afford behind glass I can't break. Given my proclivity to become enamored with unavailable people and things, Rodeo Drive is my Narnia. I temporarily stopped looking for my car and became hypnotized by the resplendent windows of Fendi, Gucci, and Prada. This was in 2008, when Gucci had a season of glam western-inspired clothing, which is my kryptonite, given it's pretty much my dream in life to be confident enough to dress like a rhinestone cowgirl.

My fantasy came to an abrupt halt when an employee appeared from behind a mannequin and started undressing it. Rather violently, if I may say so myself. It's probably not healthy to anthropomorphize a mannequin, but I was truly worried about it. Her. Anyway, seconds later I was face-to-face with the emaciated mannequin, toe-to-toe with her cubist head and vacant eyes. After a moment I realized that I was essentially looking at myself. Maybe that's why I assigned human qualities to her, because it was like looking in a mirror. Only the mannequin had perfect, symmetrical breasts, with tiny white nipples, of course. I looked at her face. She looked oddly proud. I can't say it sat well with me that an inanimate, expressionless body made of fiberglass looked happier than I was. I suddenly noticed in the reflection that my head fit perfectly on the mannequin's body, and all my features were superimposed over hers. I saw a vision of what it would be like to have symmetrical breasts. For a fleeting moment, I felt perfect.

I kept walking, brain on fire about how I would get those mannequin boobs onto my sternum. As I perused the other store windows, I came across a small door in between the luxury brand behemoths. Something—maybe the lack of luster—drew me to it. This door was the ugly duckling in the Emerald City that is Beverly Hills. On it was a litany of doctors' names in faded gold letters: cosmetic dentistry, rhinoplasty, veneers. And there it was: breast reconstruction. I had fantasized many times before about getting one small implant to even things out, but it went against everything I believed in. I wanted to be a role model, a paragon of self-acceptance. I wanted to be the person I needed when I was a kid, so a procedure to alter my appearance was always out of the question. There is no way I was going to let someone hack into my body to mold me into society's impossible physical ideal. Also, I didn't have money, so I couldn't really afford to believe anything else.

I opened the door and walked down a long hallway. I came across the door for the doctor who did breast reconstruction: it was a very underwhelming door. I had somewhat of an out-of-body experience when I went into the office. My survivalist brain took over and dragged me to the reception desk, where I asked for an appointment with the doctor. She was incredibly nice, which I found shocking. I assumed she'd judge me, throw tomatoes at me, laugh at me, accuse me of being insecure and shallow, tell me I was contributing to a harmful social construct—all the things I was accusing myself of in my head. This was before I knew that we assume everyone sees us the way we see ourselves. I was disgusted with myself, so I figured she would be disgusted with me, too. The only judgment she expressed was when I pulled out my sad check card, which you could tell before swiping it wasn't gonna go through.

I managed to convince her to let me pay for the appointment when I returned. I had just booked a job for an online talk show that paid way more than I had ever made, so I was finally able to afford things like gas and brand-name birth control. I never thought the day would come when I could actually pronounce the name of my birth control, but here I was, living the American dream.

A month later, I met with the breast reconstruction doctor. He was comically late, which I found shocking given that the people signing up to see him were probably up against enough emotional stress, but if I've learned anything in life, it's that the lower your expectations are of people, the happier you'll be. The doctor burst into the room and fired off very personal questions while struggling to write things down with a pen that was out of ink and seemed to have been so for a while now. He did that thing where you put the pen to your tongue to try to, you know, moisten it up. This, for whatever reason, for me is the equivalent of nails on a chalkboard, so I am shocked I didn't puke on him. The good/bad news is that I had not eaten lunch due to my eating disorder, so the only reason I didn't is because there really wasn't anything available to throw up.

To make matters worse, the doctor had a white crust like smegma in the corners of his mouth that frantically danced around like wet cobwebs while he talked. I was trying to will him with my mind to wipe his mouth off, but it seemed like he had literally no idea it was there. How could a man responsible for aesthetic perfection be so oblivious to such a visual disaster? This was yet another red flag on yet another man I chose to ignore.

I was wearing one of those paper-thin gowns, which went perfectly with my paper-thin self-esteem. The doctor—let's call him Dr. Smegma—summoned a nurse to come into the room to supervise our appointment. Once she came in, he asked me to open my gown. I assume this was to avoid any kind of malpractice lawsuits, but I felt way more uncomfortable with the female chaperone there staring at us. The situation just made me think of scenarios I never would have considered had she not come in. Why does my doctor need a babysitter? That can't be a good sign. I guess this is a common practice, but it just ended up feeling like an awkward, half-assed threesome. When I took the gown off, he took in my chest.

"Oh, you have scoliosis," he said with an equal mix of nonchalance and arrogance.

"I'm sorry?" I said.

He bugged his veiny eyes out at me. "You didn't know that?"

His face told me it was very weird that I didn't know by now that my spine was essentially in the shape of the lightning bolt emoji. I was so embarrassed that I pretended that I misheard him and totally knew that my spine was trying to run away from my neck.

I couldn't really process the information I was getting, mostly because I was so distracted by the manner in which I was getting it—in a cold room, with two strangers, while being overcharged. Doctors need to come up with a more genteel way of throwing out their diagnoses. I wish they would do their evaluation, then just let me go home. An hour or so later I'd check my e-mail and find a charming Paperless Post, yellow paisley print background with cherubic bluebirds holding a ribbon that reads: "Hey! you have scoliosis! Now you can freak out and cry in the privacy of your own home!"

The doctor didn't notice my obvious confusion and got more intense from there: "Scoliosis is why your breasts are asymmetrical. Were you anorexic?"

I uttered a bunch of mumbles that eventually added up to a yes. He explained that if I hadn't eaten enough fat and protein during puberty, breast tissue couldn't grow, and that the damage can be irreversible. Even if you're genetically predisposed to have breasts that fit your frame, they won't come in. Basically they were stunted, and since one had developed first, they just kinda froze where they were. This obviously makes a ton of sense, but when I was twelve and my eating disorder took over, making sense wasn't really a part of my repertoire.

Dr. Smegma took a couple of X-rays, which confirmed that my spine was in the shape of a menorah. I felt a combination of devastation and relief: devastated that I had this condition, yet relieved that someone validated my paranoia that something was wrong. Basically my shoddy tits were a combo of malnourishment and trash genetics, not the demons in my head.

Dr. Smegma handed me a big binder of photos of women's before-and-after pictures. It reminded me of those Trapper Keepers I had in middle school that had chubby unicorns on them and shockingly noisy Velcro flaps. It felt weird that in such a serious adult situation I was thinking about such innocent times in middle school. I flipped through the photos jealously. The breasts all looked very fake to me, but at least they were symmetrical.

At least they didn't look like those fake boobs that look like grapefruits topped with alligator eyes, but I still insisted that whatever had to happen, it had to be natural-looking.

"I don't want them bigger. Just even. I'm a comedian, so I can't look ridiculous. Please don't make me look like a cartoon."

I noticed that in the "after" photos, the women's breasts were always more plump and even, but I mostly noticed that the women also seemed to be sucking in their stomachs. Maybe I was projecting, but from that I deduced that now that these women had fixed their breasts, suddenly they were worried about their waistline, as if corrective surgery was like a game of whack-a-mole: Once you knock out one insecurity, another one pops up. The notion certainly didn't stop me from scheduling surgery for the following week.

Couple things: If a surgeon is available within the next week, do not go to that surgeon. If you have cancer or something that needs to be operated on immediately, obviously don't take my stupid advice. I was too young to know that it's alarming when a surgeon's schedule is wide open. You want your surgeon to be booked solid, but to have a last-minute cancellation or to be nice enough to squeeze you in between the innumerable surgeries he has. The next red flag is that the surgery was by the *airport*. Going to the airport not stressful enough for you? How about we add an invasive surgery you're ambivalent about to your trip!

I was terrified to tell my boyfriend at the time that I was planning on getting my breasts "reconstructed." That word was so dehumanizing, I felt like I was an old apartment building that had asbestos. I practiced what I would say and how I would say it over and over, terrified he would judge me, abandon me, hate me, lose respect for me. Again, I thought he would see me the way I saw myself. I mustered all the courage I had and dissociated just enough to get the words out of my mouth. I remember exactly what I said because I practiced it so many times.

"So, I know this sounds insane, and I totally don't have to do it and I can totally cancel it or reschedule it or whatever, but my whole life I've been so insecure about my chest that I was thinking about getting it fixed. It's just like one thingy that would balance them out, but I totally don't have to if you don't want me to."

"Cool! I'll drive you!"

"Oh." I was taken aback by how supportive of the idea he was. I mean, it's not a mind-bending shock that a guy would be into the idea of better breasts on his girlfriend, but I was constantly surprised at how comfortable everyone was with my paying a stranger with white funk on his mouth to maim my body in order to conform to the standard of beauty, or even to my pathological perfectionism. Maybe subconsciously I wanted someone to stop me, to talk some sense into me, to make me take my own advice about accepting your body. After all, in my first stand-up special I said verbatim: "Love your body, don't get breast implants." Didn't anyone care that I was being an insecure hypocrite? Or maybe they all just knew way before I did that people always tend to become what they despise.

I spent the next couple of days lying to people about where I was going to be the next few weeks, since I was going to have to stay in bed for a while. This was before my handle on codependence, so I had a completely maxed-out schedule full of things I had absolutely no interest in doing. Otherwise, I looked forward to how all my problems would be solved, and now that I was going to have a new boob that matched my old boob, I was going to be able to eat whatever I wanted given I was under the impression that this surgery would immediately cure my body image issues. I planned out all the delicious things I was going to eat that my deformity previously held me back from having. Things that, presurgery, I had to refuse or pretend I was allergic to. Funnel cakes! Cadbury Creme Eggs! Shake 'n Bake! Do they even make that product anymore? Chicken getting magically crispy in a bag? It doesn't matter. I'd find it on eBay if I had to!

The day of the surgery I was terrified. They told me the night before not to eat. No problem. Not eating was sort of my thing. That morning, I found myself in yet another paper-thin gown, freezing cold. I thought about how much warmer I was going to be once I could finally put on weight since given body would be evened out. Dr. Smegma came in late with a bunch of papers for me to sign, all thicker than the gown I was wearing. I didn't read any of it.

I woke up a week later covered in bandages. Chock-full of pain-killers, I walked around the house like a drunk mummy, unable to lift my arms above my rib cage. A couple weeks after that, when I was able to take the dressing off and unveil my now-symmetrical chest, I was thrilled. I could not wait for all my insecurities and fears to finally dissipate into thin air upon the unveiling of the sternum I deserved. A sternum that didn't make people look con-fused or concerned. I of course couldn't wait two weeks, so I sneaked a peek early. I discovered that my gimpy boob, the little boob that could was indeed on the same equator as my other one, but when I lifted and flexed my arm, there was a small divot run-ning from my nipple to the outside of the breast tissue.

What. The. Fuck.

I frantically picked up the phone like a *T. rex* and called the doc-tor's office. Dr. Smegma wasn't there. I called an hour later. He was out. Called that afternoon—he's busy. All of a sudden, the doctor was totally MIA. I know unavailability is basically my favorite qual-ity in a boyfriend, but not in a doctor. I couldn't track him down for three days. He finally gave me a time to come see him, and when I told him my concern, he explained that he had to cut through some muscle because of how janky my spine is. He said it in a much more erudite way than that, but he seemed pretty at peace with filleting my chest muscle and leaving a ghastly canyon where breast tissue was supposed to be. My boobs were now even more asymmetrical than before.

I didn't stand up for myself or challenge Dr. Smegma. I figured on some level that I deserved it. That's what I get for being so insecure and reckless. I could hardly afford the procedure, much less to sue this guy. I guess I could have written a Yelp review or something, but I was too in denial to acknowledge how big of a disaster this was and I was on too many muscle relaxers to remember how to spell "Yelp."

I spent the next couple years just as ashamed of my divot as I had been of my uniboob, essentially replacing one insecurity with another insecurity. I still had sex with the lights off, still had to spend most of sex trying to manipulate and hide my chest. Having sex with me must have been akin to having sex with a mime because I always had my hands up, trying to distract the guy, bobbing and weaving to cover up my sternum. I was like Madonna in the "Vogue" video, constantly doing spastic origami with my hands. I'm very certain that one guy I dated was convinced I was epileptic.

Cut to a couple of years later, thanks to my therapy for codependence, I gained the courage and ability to trust other humans. I finally confided to one of my girlfriends about my predicament. She effortlessly quipped, "Oh, that's an easy fix. I have the best guy." She wasn't shocked, grossed out, or even judgmental. After talking to a couple of other people I trusted, I found out that one of my friends had a reduction, another a lift after having a baby, and another a similar reconstruction to mine. Almost everyone I talked to had either done it or considered it, and I realized that in not having looked into getting mine fixed, I might even have been in the minority. Again, I started realizing the only person in my life who was horrified by my body rectification was me.

A friend of mine with a similar chest issue had so little shame about it that she inspired me to go to another doctor to get the fix fixed. She sent me to a real surgeon who actually had a website and whose office validated parking. When I went to meet him, someone led me into a private room that smelled like flowers and showed me where the bathroom was. It didn't even require a key. I felt like I was the queen of Versailles. His binder of before-

and-after photos looked like gorgeous wedding albums, not teen-
agers' school supplies from a swap meet.

When this surgeon came in, he was tan, with broad shoulders,
and not a lick of crust on his face. He looked me in the eye and
wrote notes with a pen that worked the first time it hit the paper.

I came in hot. "Where do you do your surgeries?"

Confounded, he responded. "Downstairs."

"When is the soonest you could do it?"

He winced. "I'm booked out for a couple months, but I am
sure someone will have to reschedule." Ah, a busy surgeon with
an office very far away from the airport. I was in the right
place. I removed my paper gown with aplomb and revealed my
chest.

"Jesus, he cut right through your muscle." The expression on
his face was that of disgust laced with compassion. "What was the
surgeon's name?"

I couldn't believe I didn't know the answer. I guess my brain
had blocked out the entire experience, including Dr. Smegma's
name.

"You have scoliosis."

"I know."

He explained how to reconstruct the reconstruction. I don't remember anything he said, but I trusted him.

After he did the procedure, Dr. Actual Doctor told me he was
able to minimize the damage, but not fix it entirely. This should
probably have been disappointing, but I was too sick of the whole
debacle to be anything but okay with it.

Today I accept my chest, but not because it's symmetrical or
better or any of that. The truth is, if I was twenty-five with the
boobs I have now, I'm sure I'd hate them for some other reason my
brain invents to re-create the cycle of feeling like I'm broken. Before I had self-esteem, I could find a flaw in anything related to
myself and used any excuse I could find to beat myself up. I'm
sure I would have found issues with even the most gorgeous

naturals: "Yuck! They're *too* pale and way too round! I mean, a C cup? C is the universal sign for *average*!"

What ultimately made me accept and like my body was the tremendous amount of work I did on my brain. Trust me, I wish the shortcuts had worked, but they just didn't. Being thin didn't work. Eating thirty cookies at a time didn't work. Being on TV didn't work. Symmetrical boobs didn't work. Boyfriends didn't work. Work didn't work. Money didn't work. I mean, it can really help sometimes, but it doesn't fix low self-worth. If actual worth and self-worth were synonymous, #lambolife would not be a hashtag on social media.

Before I did work on my insides, self-acceptance felt like a mythical utopian ideal. All over Instagram and pop culture we see memes that say "love yourself" and "accept who you are" in flowery font. Great. But how? If reading a quote on Instagram or listening to a Justin Bieber song could change your neurology about how you actually see yourself, every rehab would instantly go out of business. The same way a quote about getting in shape can't actually get you in shape, self-esteem is a muscle you actually have to build. *But how?*

The first thing I did was get older. It really helps.

Another thing that's helped in building my self-esteem has been surrounding myself with people who aren't assholes. This may sound obvious, but until pretty recently I had a lot of people in my life who didn't treat me with respect. That's of course because I didn't treat myself with respect, so it became a vicious circle, given a very complex phenomenon I'd like to reduce to "monkey see, monkey do." We take cues from others on how we should feel about ourselves, so when the people around me are mean, I tend to imitate them. Negative people are very sneaky. They're like a Taylor Swift song: the first couple times you hear it, you want to leave the room, but after four or five times, I'm dancing like a white girl with sciatica.

People's opinion of you rubs off on you. It sounds so simple: Be friends with people who accept you for who you are and don't make you feel scared or insecure or as though you have to constantly work for their approval. I've probably said this a couple times in this book, but in case you're anything like me and read books like a spaz by skimming through chapters, love is not earned. I'll repeat that: *Love is not earned.* To quote Sia, "I know I've heard that to let your feelings show / Is the only way to make friendships grow." If you can't be vulnerable with your pals, they gotta go. If I had just been able to admit my dilemma to someone ten years earlier because I had safe, nonjudgmental friendships, I probably would have saved a lot of time, money, pain, and perverted hallucinations from coming out of anesthesia that involve Tom Hardy.

Anyway, so why would I write this chapter? Why would I tell you guys my deepest, darkest, most embarrassing secret? Why would I admit to being a hypocrite? Why would I give out information that's going to invite so many nasty tweets and countless emotionally abusive Instagram comments? Something that's going to get me so many awkward backhanded compliments from strangers in airports? Because I have shame about it. And I learned that the engine of codependent, self-abusive, maladaptive, and addictive behaviors is exactly that. Shame. But shame can be mitigated or released in a shockingly simple way: by talking about it. The badass psychiatrist Phil Stutz said something on Marc Maron's podcast that I'll never forget, which is that when we admit something shameful, it loses its power and it allows grace to enter the room.

So here I am, telling you the most shameful thing I hold on to so I can drop my sword, put the boxing gloves down, and accept my relentless humanity so I can get on with living my life. The only panacea I've found for negative thoughts is to admit my negative thoughts. I'm sure painkillers and wine work too, but probably not for long, and they're way more expensive. It's pretty much my main goal in life not to have to go to get my emotional needs met at BevMo!.

To quote a real authority on shame who knows way more than

I do, Brené Brown said: "Where perfectionism exists, shame is always lurking." In order to heal my crippling perfectionism, I had to release the shame by talking about it. You know when you've drunk too much or get food poisoning, and you actually feel relieved after you puke? Puking feels terrible, but you're grateful to not have that garbage in your body anymore? Maybe that is a terrible image for the chapter following one about eating disorders, but it's the most accurate metaphor I can think of besides popping a zit, which is too gross for me to even think about. Sorry, now you're thinking about it.

When I was trying to figure out whether or not I should write this chapter, I devoured Brené Brown's quotes. I came across one from her book *The Gifts of Imperfection*: "Authenticity is a collection of choices we have to make every day. It's about the choice to show up and be real. The choice to be honest. The choice to let our true selves be seen." As I told more and more people, I realized that (a) they didn't really care because everyone is too busy dealing with their own emotional problems to care about my emotional problems and (b) most had struggled with similar issues and felt relieved and inspired that I could be vulnerable about mine. When this happened, my fear of judgment lost its power over me. Maybe the road to being a decent role model wasn't about being emotionally perfect, maybe it was about finding the courage to admit that I wasn't.

I've finally surrendered to the body I have, self-inflicted wounds and all. Today I'm in a place where I can have sex without contorting my body like I'm playing a sad game of Twister. I figure if a guy is turned off by whatever naked asymmetry I have, he's in his own struggle with his body and maybe his attraction to ones that have a penis attached to them.

Ultimately, as Stockholm syndrome-y as it sounds, I'm grateful that I went through this fiasco. I didn't want to spend my life looking at stunted breast tissue. I didn't want to spend the rest of my life being reminded of my eating disorder every time I took my shirt off. I wanted to be free of that obsession and see what it would be like not to be in an adversarial relationship with my body. Oddly, I like my scars. They look like little smiley faces. Of course they're shaped that way for medical reasons, not my mental health goals, but there's something poetic about seeing little smiles every time I look at my chest and am tempted to critique it.

Also, when I was nervously asking the second surgeon about what would happen if he cut into the scars I already had, he said, "Even better. Scar tissue is stronger than regular tissue." This made me want to cry when I heard it. I felt like going through all this made me weak. Turns out, when we make mistakes and glue ourselves back together, we end up being way stronger than we were before.

I don't feel sexier or anything now, and on some level I still replaced one insecurity with another. Instead of worrying that my boobs are weirdly shaped and crooked, I now worry people will think I'm shallow and dumb for having had corrective surgery. That said, if I broke my ankle, I'd go get it fixed, so I know that if anything in my body or brain is broken, that also deserves to get fixed, regardless of how society glamorizes, sexualizes, or minimizes it.

The whole boob debacle did make me think a lot not only about my own shame, but also about why we shame others for doing things that may seem superficial but are likely rooted in real pain or suffering. I no longer look at women who get a nose job or whatever corrective surgery as self-absorbed narcissists. I see them as victims of cripplingly low self-worth. I'm sure there are shallow people who get work done for a mess of unsavory reasons, but expanding my brain to consider the kaleidoscope of pathos that could motivate someone to do such a thing has given me a tremendous amount of compassion. The same way trying to help someone who has an eating disorder can make the disorder worse, shaming insecure people just exacerbates their insecurity. It's like one big emotional rat king.

It's healthy that we're all having a public conversation about the damage being done by online bullying and trolls, but I don't hear enough talk about how we bully ourselves. As rough as what some people write about me in comments sections online is, none of it is as mean as the things my inner voices say about me. Trolls, this is not a challenge; I'm just trying to make a point here. If other people bully me, that's a reflection on them and something I can choose not to internalize, but if I'm beating myself up, that's on me.

So, here I am, releasing my shame so I don't have to carry it around until it turns into another weird addictive behavior like sniffing glue or obsessively ordering clothes I can't afford online and then frantically returning them. And, look, if you have judgments about my past and my choices, it's all good. Turns out, with or without your approval, I'll be just fine.

THE HEADACHE CHAPTER

My head has hurt for as long as I can remember. As a kid I recall being at school, looking at corny posters on the walls with cartoon birds holding up vocabulary words, and being frustrated that I couldn't read the words I could so easily spell the day before. I remember having to sit in the car at Disneyland with Mickey Mouse ears over my eyes because the sun was so painful to look at. My parents argued outside the car, trying to figure out if they would go on with the day at the most magical place on earth or go home because of me. Maybe that was the genesis of my paralyzing guilt.

"I'm totally fine! We can stay!" I yelled, each utterance exacerbating the pounding in my skull. It tore me up that my headaches caused other people to miss out on a day of fun and spinning teacups. The only good news is that now that I'm an adult and have some perspective, I know if my parents weren't fighting about me, they'd have been fighting about something else, so maybe I did everyone a favor by giving them something tangible to argue about.

I spent a tremendous amount of time in the nurse's office in middle school. Very frequently for my swollen knee and head lice, but also for my incessant headaches. Up until I was about twelve, headaches were my biggest, well, headache. My parents didn't spend a lot of time going to doctors, and I didn't think to question that approach. Like a lot of families headed by parents raised by men who served in various wars, my family had a white-knuckle philosophy toward pain. Buck up, man up, grow some balls. So I learned how to do two of those three things.

My first encounter with medical specialists came once I hit puberty. I developed a problem that couldn't be ignored: I had acne. Unlike headaches, which were in my head, hard to describe, misunderstood by others, and easily dismissed, my acne was on my face and needed no explanation. I had deep, cystic zits that I could feel on the bones of my jaw and forehead weeks before they made their way to the surface to annihilate my self-esteem. When I would feel one coming on, I was consumed with dread, knowing I'd have to spend the next three weeks trying to manage, hide, and emotionally abuse the zit into submission. Once the pimple became red and bulbous, I could not for the life of me keep my hands off it, so I'd pop it, and by pop it, I mean dig into the swollen area with my grubby press-on nails well before it was ready, sometimes cutting into the skin and of course making it much worse than it ever would have been. I'd then make that even worse by caking drugstore concealer into it, filling the hole I left with overpriced chemicals, alcohol, and oil the way most people would put caulk into a wall.

Sometimes I had to sleep as if I were in a casket, looking straight up at the ceiling, because putting my face on a pillow was too painful. At around fourteen I discovered the Molotov cocktail of skin creams, Retin-A. It's a topical ointment that dries your skin out with alarming speed and intensity. Seriously, I think it's much better suited to remove graffiti from buildings or poison your enemies than to be applied to human skin. To save my life I couldn't comprehend moderation, so I would obsessively apply it throughout the day, even though the prescription said to use it only twice a day and the number to call poison control was on the side of the box. I was so obsessed that I'd set my alarm to wake myself up in the middle of the night to apply it. Of course this insane behavior just made it look like a blind person had repeatedly put cigarettes out on my chin, but that didn't stop me. Covering these with makeup was trickier because my skin was flaking off, so I had to develop a system: First I'd put beige lip gloss all over the charred spot as a way to sort of fill in the dried crevices, then put foundation on top of that, then concealer, then powder, then bronzer. By the end of it, I looked like exactly an Entenmann's crumb cake.

The pain of bad skin managed to eclipse the pain of my headaches, so I begged my mom to take me to the dermatologist. There were about five other medical specialists I should have gone to first—a psychiatrist, a psychologist, an orthopedist, a dentist—but according to my insecure brain, those problems mattered way less than my skin. It would be another ten years before I saw a doctor for an idiopathic pain in my right foot that had bothered me ever since I was eight. Every three weeks or so, I'd feel a spastic sharp stab in the arch of my foot, so much so that I'd frantically scrunch my shoulders and punch outward around me like the drunkest person at every wedding. It's so bad that I've actually hit a couple boyfriends who were in bed with me when it happened during the night, but given the type of lad I dated back then, they were probably into it. When I was twenty-four I finally went to a podiatrist, who told me I needed insoles because of my high arches. He put my foot in a box of watery clay until it dried into the molds. He told me to come pick them up in two weeks, but when I came back to the office to get them, they sprung it on me that the orthotics would be eight hundred bucks, so naturally I pretended I left my wallet in my car, left the office, and never returned. This also happens to be the least weird thing I've done to save eight hundred dollars.

About seven years later, I was in a writers' room one day and was attacked by one of my foot spasms.

"FUCK, FUCK, FUCK, FUCK!" I screamed while falling to my knees and slamming my hand on the table. Five seconds later, the pain passed and I was back to pitching jokes. The people in the room were aghast.

"Okay, what page were we on?"

When a writer asked me what just happened, I said nonchalantly, "Oh, that's just my foot thing. You know how, like, three times a week one of your feet feels like someone is stabbing a knife into it?"

They looked at me as if I was as crazy as I actually was. I either actually thought or had convinced myself that everyone just felt a shocking amount of pain in their feet like that every now and then. The horror on their faces inspired me to get my foot X-rayed just to prove them wrong, to show them that my foot was normal. Plus, I had health insurance now, so it was time to party.

Halfway through my time in the podiatrist's office, I realized I was at the same doctor I had run out on seven years earlier when I heard the bill would be eight hundred dollars. I could tell he was trying to figure out how he knew me, so I immediately dropped into a bad southern accent, hoping it would throw him off the trail. I promise this was not conscious; it was like some automatic act of self-preservation over which I swear I had no control. I could tell he was onto my ruse, but he was too mortified for both of us to call me out. I felt like at that point, the only thing weirder than pretending to have a southern accent would be to stop pretending to have a southern accent.

I stood on the X-ray machine, trying to put pressure on my foot so it would flatten out and look normal on the scan. I don't even know if that's a thing, but this was the same logic I used to try and be heavier at the eating disorder specialist: magical thinking. When the doctor came in after the X-ray, he looked at me with a mix of shock and respect.

"You have an extra bone in your foot," he said. "Haven't you been in pain?"

Of course I had been in pain, but my migraines started so young that I had to kind of pick which pain I was going to give my attention to. As a woman, I always have a variety of pains to manage, so I often find myself prioritizing the most debilitating ones. Between migraines, cramps, my dumb knee, my hunger pangs, tooth pain from having braces, UTIs, and blisters from shoes designed by sadistic men, I had sort of gone deaf concerning which pain to listen to.

Because I had migraines so young, my tolerance for pain was very high. I often got very sick and didn't notice, just grateful it was anything but a headache. At my workaholism/codependence peak around age thirty, I was forced to go to a rheumatologist because I developed a condition called costochondritis, which is an inflammation in your cartilage where the ribs and breastbone come together. I know! Yucky! I am warning you: Do not look this up on the Internet because you will think you have it, and chances are, you don't. The causes of costochondritis are many, but my doctor told me mine was from stress and possibly from having pneumonia and not treating it quickly enough. It's the kind of thing people get if they either don't value themselves enough to go to the doctor or were alive during the Civil War. Yes, I felt a weird pain in my chest, but as you well know, I'm codependent, so if someone else had this health problem, I'd learn to fly a helicopter in order to fly them to the closest hospital, but if I had the health problem, getting it treated just seemed like a waste of time. I mean, I wouldn't want to burden a doctor with my medical problems in the middle of his busy workday.

The condition transpired after I had just come back from a stressful vacation with a boyfriend I had been fighting with for seven days. I was mentally and emotionally drained, and more in love than ever. When we landed after ten days of improvising a sequel to *The War of the Roses* in a hut by a beach, we got back and had a crazy guilt/shame spiral attachment bond, so I had a hard time leaving, even though I had to turn in the finale script of a TV show the next day. I had planned on writing it over the break

while relaxing by a pool, but there wasn't much time between crying and throwing the hotel Bible across the room. I didn't want
him to feel abandoned, which was of course me projecting *my* fear
of abandonment, so I waited until he fell asleep before going home.

I stayed up all night writing the episode. I know that because
I'm an insomniac, staying up all night to work may seem like it
makes a lot of sense for me, but oddly, working through the night
isn't my style. My insomnia is more about worrying over things I
can't control than actually being productive.

By some weird miracle, I managed to bang out a version of the
script. The next day I went into work and noticed that inhaling
was painful. Again, as a woman, I find a lot of mundane involuntary behaviors are painful for no reason at all: sitting at a desk,
having sex, having boobs, having a uterus . . . But breathing? This
was a new one. I walked into the writers' room, greeted by eight
hilarious comedy writers. King idiot, dear friend, and hilarious
person Dan Levy immediately made me laugh, and it felt like a
wrecking ball went through my chest. Laughing and inhaling felt
like I was getting stabbed by a Ninja star, so I told the writers I'd
be fine as long as they just didn't make me laugh all day. In a comedy writers' room. Where we write comedy. Where the writers are
funny. Where their job is to pitch jokes. And make people laugh.
Telling comedy writers they can't be funny is like telling white
people they can't wear plaid.

A writer pulled me aside and urged me to go to the doctor. I was
annoyed by her concern because receiving love made me very uncomfortable at the time, but this was one instance where my codependence worked to my advantage because I ended up going to
the doctor solely because I didn't want her to be mad at me or feel
rejected.

The doctor I went to referred me to a rheumatologist. I didn't
really know what that was, but the plethora of vowels in the title
made me very nervous. This specialist explained to me not only

that I had this rare condition called costochondritis, which sounded like a dorky dad joke about someone who can't stop going to Costco, but also that I had a condition called hypermobility. From what I gathered and Googled, it's a genetic bummer that results from the underwhelming DNA of Western Europeans. It causes joints to move beyond the healthy range of a joint, which you'd think just makes me super flexible and amazing in bed, but it actually couldn't be less sexy. Us hypermobility sufferers put too much pressure on our joints, which accumulates over time and eventually causes something called "noncollision injuries." You've all heard a story similar to the one where someone fifty-five or so throws his back out doing something as simple as sneezing. It's basically the bone version of the straw breaking the camel's back, except you can actually break your back, maybe not with a straw, but certainly by reaching for one.

I already feel it happening: a couple years ago I strained my neck making a point in an argument. A guy I was dating said something incredibly patronizing and I cocked my neck forward like a petulant pigeon. My head was stuck in that position for three days. I looked like that girl cocking her head who became famous as a meme and then sued Instagram and won. And who is now probably going to sue me and win. Congrats, girl.

The doctor told me that because of my hypermobility, which is actually very common and often under- and misdiagnosed, I was walking incorrectly. To find out at thirty that you don't know how to walk is very annoying information to have to process. I suck at relationships, I suck at sleeping, I suck at eating, I suck at liking myself, I suck at managing my time, and now I suck at walking? The one thing I thought I had in the bag. He said that people with hypermobility walk with their joints instead of their muscles, so the joints are absorbing all the impact the muscles should be absorbing. But I didn't really have many muscles. Once I realized that, I was struck by a miraculous revelation.

"Is this why my butt is so flat?!" I asked.

The doc was pretty stunned that this was my takeaway, given how much harm this condition can do over time, but he also affirmed my theory. Basically, yes, it was. I was walking with my ankles, knees, and hips instead of my calves, quads, and glutes, which as far as I was concerned was stopping me from having the ass of Serena Williams. Well, honestly, fifty other things are also stopping me, but this was the one I would like to blame.

"So, what do I take for it?" I asked.

"You mean, what do you *do* for it?"

"I don't follow."

Nettled but not surprised by my desire for a quick fix, Dr. Vowels told me I had to relearn how to walk. I had to go to corrective Pilates three times a week to train my body to engage my muscles and disengage my joints. Up until this point I had only been encouraged to figure out how to be engaged to a man, not how to engage my stupid core. I went to one corrective Pilates session and almost had a nervous breakdown from boredom. I never went back, but this time I did pay.

I know, you thought we were talking about my acne and now we're talking about joints and Pilates. This whole thing is an admittedly circuitous way of explaining why at fourteen, I really should have been going to other doctors, but a dermatologist was ultimately the doctor I went to because vanity always won out over health. That said, doctors couldn't even do much given my self-sabotaging impulses. It's always been hard for me to go to a dentist, dermatologist, or even therapist because I used to be way more concerned with impressing them than with getting help from them. I remember spending a hilariously long time putting makeup on to go to the dermatologist—the exact person to whom I should have been revealing rather than concealing my facial carnage. I walked in, full face of Wet n Wild with a whisper of Urban Decay eye shadow. As soon as the dermatologist saw me, he quipped,

"Oh, you're going to need to go on Accutane." In case you don't know, Accutane is a medication for acne. I was so dysmorphic that I actually thought the centimeter of viscous beige goop was rendering my pimples invisible. This guy totally shattered my denial that three-dollar foundation didn't instantly erase my flaws like a Snapchat filter.

Once I was prescribed Accutane, I finally felt I had a cure for my insecurity and fear of going outside. The doctor's office gave me a thick stack of paperwork to sign, which is never a good, well, sign. I was then told I had to get a pregnancy test in order to secure the pills. I was fourteen, wasn't it obvious that I wasn't pregnant? Don't answer that. I went to some other office to get a pregnancy test. The only sex I had really had at this point was the "sex" on the random cruise and in my head with Ethan Hawke, so I wasn't particularly nervous about being pregnant. Once this was officially confirmed, I was given a second prescription—for birth control, which you have to take simultaneously with Accutane. Not gonna lie, I found it endearing that this medication came with a chaser. It got less endearing when I found out why.

When I picked up the package for my miracle drug at the pharmacy, I expected some kind of pretty, glittery pink box, since that's usually how the pharmaceutical industry panders to females, but not this one. When I took the package out of the bag, a chill went down my spine. Accutane comes in little booklets, and on the back of each pill is a drawing of a pregnant woman with a red line through it, as if taking this drug while pregnant would cause both mother and child to immediately burst into flames. It didn't just have one picture of a pregnant woman crossed out; there was one on every little pill satchel, so there's like thirty crossed-out pregnant ladies. It was as if the pharmaceutical company hired Damien Hirst to design its packaging.

I also saw somewhere in the warnings that you can't donate blood while you're taking the medication. That one just felt mean.

I had never given blood before, but I still felt robbed that I couldn't if I wanted to. It felt rude to tell someone that they can't help other people because they're too full of poison. Also, if my blood is too dangerous to put in someone else's body, shouldn't I maybe not have it in my body? Or maybe somebody should be donating blood to me while I'm consuming this venomous toxin? I got that feeling you have when you get an X-ray and the nurse quickly scurries out of the room to avoid the radiation behind what seems to be bulletproof glass, while you just sit there like a moron getting zapped by it.

The crossed-out dead babies vibe on the packaging should have been a red flag. I mean, the package is literally all red, so it even looked like a tiny cardboard red flag. It was very red, but so was my face, and I couldn't stand looking at it anymore. I took one of the pills, then started casually perusing the pamphlet of side effects. Usually side effects can fit on the side of the bottle or your laptop screen when you Google them, but this one had so many, it needed its own publishing company. I was new to medication at that point, so I naively read all the side effects, as if they had any bearing on whether or not I'd take the drug. It was sort of like reading a service agreement before clicking "agree." You'd never have any decent apps if you actually read all the fine print.

The side effects of this drug are borderline violent: joint pain, bone pain, back pain, drowsiness, blurred vision, nervousness, dizziness, headaches, sleep problems, and crying spells. That said, these were all problems I had had before I started taking Accutane, so I figured it might actually be good to finally have an excuse for them.

But there were some that were harder to stomach. Rectal bleeding, for example. Ah, well, I reasoned, I guess I'd rather have a bloody ass than a bloody face.

Hearing loss was also on the list of side effects. That one's pretty alarming now, but back then I figured that most of what I heard at fourteen was either the word "no" or stuff about $y = mx + b$, so losing my hearing might actually be a welcome relief.

Another one that didn't faze me was "changes in your fingernails and toenails." I had already lost a toenail from running too much, and if my fingernails got jacked up, I figured it was nothing my signature mid-nineties French manicure couldn't obscure. I basically justified taking the medication by figuring out how to hide any of the impending side effects or rationalizing that I already lived with half of them.

I was told that my skin would get dry for a couple of months, which was already happening due to my scorched earth approach to facial imperfections, but nobody prepared me for the giant sheets of skin that started to fall off my face during school. I'd scratch my face during class and skin would flake off like pasty Post-it notes. I was so embarrassed that I would surreptitiously put them in my pocket, carrying around pieces of my molting face in my pants.

After I had been taking the medication for a month, my headaches got worse and so did my skin. With Accutane it's one of those "it gets worse before it gets better" deals. For some reason, I feel like you only hear this adage in the medical industry. You never hear a waiter say, "The spaghetti tastes like actual shit at first, but just keep chewing and I promise it will grow on you . . ." or a diet product about which they promise that "after you gain fifty pounds, you'll be thin as a rail!" It just feels like if it gets worse before it gets better, the product isn't ready and they should maybe circle back to the drawing board and let us know when it's actually ready for public consumption. When I brought this to my dermatologist's attention, he said, "Look, doctors do the best we can with the information we have." I guess this is why doctors call what they do a "practice" and not "the championships."

After a couple months on Accutane, my skin eventually got a

little better, but by the time I was fifteen, my insomnia was getting worse due to a myriad of maladaptive behaviors. I drank diet soda pretty much all day long like an idiot, began to severely restrict calories, and my perfectionism over schoolwork started possessing my brain. One thing I thought was odd about my house as a teenager was that our medicine cabinet always had way more stuff in it than our refrigerator. I deduced from this that Band-Aids, metaphorical and actual, were a better solution than preventive action. Don't eat, just take vitamins. Don't support your immune system, just take a Sudafed when your immune system collapses. You get it. Anyway, I'm not sure when I discovered NyQuil, but this revelation was like finally meeting my knight in shining armor: drug-induced sleep.

From what I can gather, the problem with taking these drugs to sleep is that they don't provide REM and delta wave sleep, so you're not getting the deep rest your brain actually needs; you're just in a short-term chemically induced coma. Also, from what we all gather, I am not a doctor, but doctors have told me this so it must be at least half true. Anyway, I was sleeping more, but my headaches were more awake than ever. They began screaming the moment I woke up instead of around the predictable noon start time. Even if I was still sleep deprived and sluggish all day, at least my headaches were up early, starting their workday with renewed vigor. I didn't think to stop taking them or address the wounds that caused insomnia, I just figured I needed better sleeping pills.

Once I was in college, I moved on to real sleepy drugs like Ambien and Sonata. After all, I was a grown-up now; it was time I waited in line and overpaid for my pills.

To put it bluntly, Ambien and I do not have good chemistry. I have great chemistry with men who are addicted to Ambien, but the pill itself and I are mortal enemies. On Ambien, I've done some very stupid things. Like, even for me in my twenties, they were stupid. Once on Ambien I e-mailed a lawyer and fired him even though he was not my lawyer.

One time in an Ambien stupor I walked to a 7-Eleven in Philadelphia at three A.M and bought an apple. This was already out of character for me because I had maxed out on apples when I was fifteen and experimenting with the most low-calorie foods I could find, subsequently losing my taste for them completely. Ambien apparently erased that trauma and I found myself buying myself a beautiful giant red apple from 7-Eleven. This apple was so good that I ate it voraciously before I even got out of the store. The next morning, I woke up thinking about this beautiful apple, so I went back to 7-Eleven to get another one for breakfast. Imagine my surprise when I walked in and saw that all the apples were wrapped tightly in thick Saran Wrap.

"Are these apples always in Saran Wrap?" I asked the cashier.

"Yes."

"Like, if there was an apple here at three A.M. last night, would it have been wrapped in Saran Wrap?"

"Yes."

"Cool."

Shortly thereafter I went to the doctor to renew my prescription, I joked that I had eaten about ten square inches of plastic wrap in the middle of the night. He looked as concerned as I had ever seen a doctor look, probably more about getting sued than my actual health. He suggested I stop taking Ambien and take something else called Sonata. This works in time-release increments of three hours, so I could take it to fall asleep and then ease into some natural sleep myself. I knew this healthy upgrade would never work for my manic brain, so I just figured I'd wake up every three hours and pop another one. (And people say women are bad at math.)

I took Sonata for a while with equally embarrassing results. One time I was on a flight to England for a job and I was flying first class for the first time. It was so fancy—the seats turned into beds, and they gave you a bag with socks, pajamas, and a duty-free catalogue of things to buy like perfume, booze, overpriced corny hooker necklaces, and already outdated electronic gadgets designed to save you thirty seconds. It was basically all I've ever asked for in life: free drinks, ample legroom, and products I couldn't afford.

It was such a long flight that they turned the lights off so everyone could sleep. Given that I couldn't sleep alone in my own bed, the prospect of sleeping with a bunch of strangers in the sky felt particularly challenging. I took my Sonata and got down to business. To the shock of my entire body, I fell asleep almost instantly. I woke up seven hours later in yummy British Airways pajamas to English flight attendants making announcements. I was thrilled that I finally got seven hours of uninterrupted deep sleep until I looked down and realized I had no recollection of dressing myself in the pajamas that were on my body. I looked to my right and saw my other clothes perfectly folded next to me.

Uh-oh.

Oh no.

The flight attendant slowly and timidly approached me, panic in her eyes. Clearly we had had a very intense night together I didn't know much about. I looked around and noticed a couple passengers also looking at me with both fear and disgust. I found out that during my "sleep" I had disrobed in front of everyone on the flight and changed into my pj's. As if that weren't mortifying enough, on my way off the plane I was presented with three bags of tiny stuffed airplanes, which apparently I had ordered in a Sonata stupor from the duty-free catalogue.

When I tried to go off Sonata, my migraines got even worse, I'm sure exacerbated by sleep deprivation and chemical withdrawal. Luckily, Lunesta came along, which was sort of positioned as the "healthy" sleeping pill, maybe because it was a mature blue color, maybe because the name sounded like a majestic white horse. Lunesta became the American Spirit cigarettes of sleeping pills, still horrible for you, but somehow cool and accepted by health-conscious people who go to Spin class and eat acai berries but can't seem to get to sleep. Probably because they're so hungry from Spinning and eating acai berries.

Don't be jealous, but by my mid-twenties, I started dating people who struggled with addiction, which was a catalyst for my having some awareness about my own addictive behavior. I went to an AA meeting with a guy I was dating and heard people talking about how their chemical dependencies started with sleeping pills, and how they panicked if they were low on pills or temporarily misplaced the bottle. To my surprise and chagrin, I related to what they were saying. I started to gain a comprehension of my own addictive DNA and realized that my pill popping could very easily evolve into something very ugly and *US Weekly*-y.

I've never been into drinking or doing recreational drugs because by a stroke of dumb luck my addiction to perfectionism and control eclipsed my desire for a hedonistic escape. My role was that of the caretaker, and I got my high of validation by caring for inebriated people. Like, literal validation—I'd get their parking ticket validated, drive them home, clean up their puke, and fall in love with them.

I realized my sleeping pill habit had gone on a little too long for my and my liver's comfort and decided I wanted to stop. I went to a doctor and told him this, but instead of helping me wean off the pills or sending me to a therapist to address whatever was keeping me up at night, he prescribed an antidepressant that had the side effect of drowsiness. This way I was on antidepressants technically, not sleeping pills. Small technicality that makes no sense now, but seemed like a genius life hack at the time. I was too desperate for a good night's sleep to process how ludicrous it was to prescribe someone a drug solely for the side effect. I did have to hand the doctor some points for creativity, though. This was something that also happened to me later when I was given a prescription for an Alzheimer's medication that apparently had a side effect of reducing headaches to treat my migraines. Again, medicine is called a "practice."

Going off sleeping pills and onto antidepressants pushed my migraines into overdrive, although by this point I couldn't really tell the difference between side effects and withdrawal symptoms. Nobody told me that you have to wean yourself off antidepressants, but that may be because I didn't ask anyone. Probably because I didn't want to know the answer. I stopped taking them cold turkey, thinking I was some kind of hero. I started having what are called "brain zaps," which is like having tiny lightning bolts hit you in your brain all day. I personally feel that if any medication causes you to feel like your brain is being electrocuted, that should sort of be the opener when it's prescribed to you. Maybe something like, "Hey, if you ever want to go off these, give us a heads-up or else you'll be twitching during conversations for three months," which would have saved me a lot of weird looks on dates.

Alas, my migraines got worse. I was getting migraines every couple days at this point, and the symptoms were escalating. When I was a kid, the headaches would feel like aimless banging, but now they had evolved into a more sophisticated migraine: My left arm would go numb; I'd lose vision in my left eye and couldn't make out words. This was getting serious. I could tolerate physical pain, but not being able to text really pissed me off.

This got especially scary once I moved to Los Angeles and had to drive a car. I didn't know the city well, which isn't necessarily indicative of my idiocy, given the city seems to have been planned out about as carefully as a Jackson Pollock painting. This was pre–Google Maps, back when us ancient fossils had to actually read street signs. I know, ridiculous.

I had a lot of really scary moments driving with a migraine and being far away from home. Before the pain really sets in, the warning my brain gives me is that I can see words, but they might as well be hieroglyphics. A couple times I had to curl up in my car and wait hours for a migraine to pass so I could figure out how to drive home. A few times I took cabs and had to have someone drive me back to my parked car the next day. I had all the behavior of a crackhead, but without the fun part of getting to do crack.

A lot of people ask me what a migraine feels like, and I still struggle with describing it. From what I gather, everyone who gets them has different experiences, but if I were to try to describe mine, I'd say it's like an incredibly intense pressure that pushes against my skull, eyes, and nose. It's like my head is in labor. I also get very nauseous, my muscles feel super sore, and my left arm goes numb. It's like being attacked by eighty birds while recovering from the worst hangover you've ever had. When the pain got physically intolerable, I'd have to go to the emergency room. I tried to do this as rarely as possible because it's comically expensive to be sick in America and I never paid my emergency room bill, so I had to alternate hospitals once I had one too many invoices in collections. And by this time, I had pieced together that the worse my credit was, the worse my headaches were.

One particularly annoying episode at the ER happened when my dad came into town to visit. At the time our relationship was strained but also incredibly important to me. As I mentioned before, my dad was very funny and endlessly charming, perhaps to a fault. We spent most of our time together acting out Chevy Chase movies and maligning businesses that we think are scams, such as organic foods, vitamins, and protein powder. The more I think about it, the more I realize that my dad wired my brain to think critically, always questioning authority and commonly embraced truths. He challenged things that other people blindly accept and take for granted, which always fascinated me. We'd go to the grocery store, and while he was perusing the fruit section, he'd open up to the whole store, asking loudly to anyone who would listen, "How do we know this is organic? *Who decides this stuff?*" I honestly have no idea if anyone else would find this funny, but it would make me laugh until my ribs hurt.

My dad was also ferociously smart and had an incredible ability to tell stories, whether they're true or not. On the first day of his visit we went to his favorite restaurant in L.A., which is known for organic meals, a perfect setup for his diatribe about the organic foods conspiracy. I laughed so hard I started crying. Through my tears I realized I couldn't read the menu. Goddamn it.

I felt a sharp pain behind my eyeball, so I knew I was going to have to go to the emergency room. When my eyeballs get involved, that means the migraine is about to spread to my arm. It also meant puke was imminent. I looked at my dad sitting across from me. His face started melting like one of Salvador Dalí's clocks.

I never admitted the extent of my migraines to my dad because I didn't want him to think I was weak or fallible in any way. Back then I conflated sickness with weakness, maybe because my family valued toughness and tenacity, and my saying I had a headache always seemed to be received as if I were being dramatic, like I was a damsel in distress and had a "case of the vapors."

After waiting a comically long time in the waiting room, because sadly ERs have become like DMVs for sick people, I finally got to see a doctor. By the time the ER doc came into the room, I was in fetal position on the sterile "bed."

He studied my chart. "Recreational drugs?" is all I heard.

"What?"

"Do you use recreational drugs?"

It took me a second to figure out what was going on. By that time in my life I had already dated multiple men who struggled with drug addiction, and I remembered that when they relapsed they would go to the hospital and pretend to have a headache, toothache, appendix pain—anything to convince the hospital to give them painkillers. It dawned on me that I had come into the ER so many times that this doctor was trying to ascertain if I was scamming him for drugs, so I started trying to convince him that I was not on drugs, which made it seem like I was on very many drugs.

"I'm not *on* drugs. I *need* drugs."

Even though I couldn't see, I could tell that he didn't believe me and he was probably right not to, because I sounded very crazy.

When I described my migraine in excruciating detail, he softened. He finally believed that I had a migraine, either because those who don't suffer from migraines could never know that much detail about them or because people on drugs don't talk about brain stems and optical nerves. Either way, it worked and the doctor agreed to jack me up with painkillers.

I remember the doctor having trouble getting the needle into my vein because I was quivering so much from the pain. To add to the list of my genetic bummers, I was also once told by a nurse that I have "rolly veins," meaning they slip out of the way when a needle gets near them, so when someone tries to inject me with a needle, it's basically like trying to pick up a bar of soap in the shower. Once the morphine was finally in my system and the pain started subsiding, I was able to focus on the frustration that was consuming me. I got hit with a wave of anger and let an aggressive hypothetical question rip: *"Jesus, what causes migraines?!"*

There was a weirdly long silence. Too long. So long that it felt like I was in the Lifetime movie version of this scene, right at the moment where the doctor was about to tell me he was in love with me. He was not in love with me. Turns out he was just trying to figure out how to answer the question.

"We don't exactly know."

My eyes bugged out of my pounding head. *"You don't know?!"*

I remember going off on some unoriginal rant about how society has put a man on the moon, yet we don't know what causes migraines.

"Well, we don't know that much about the human brain in general."

"What? *We don't?!*"

So we know how cars work, how planes work, how computers work, but we don't know how our own brains work? It blew my mind that humans had found time to invent spray butter, taxidermy, and selfie sticks, yet didn't know what caused paralyzing headaches for people. Over eleven million adults and children lie in bed and miss work and life and parenting while in excruciating pain, yet we have numerous cellulite creams? I feel that as a society we need to work on our priorities. Yes, AIDS and cancer and life-threatening diseases are way more important than migraines, but migraines should at least rank above cellulite.

I don't remember the rest of my conversation with the doctor, because he was kind enough to give me a second dose of morphine. I woke up two days later. My headache was gone and so was my dad. I was heartbroken. He had come all the way to Los Angeles to see me, and I spent the whole trip in bed, comatose. I know it seems like it's not that big of a deal, that I could just see him next time—at the holidays, at my birthday, whenever—but that's not really how our family works. We don't have a set commitment to see each other on holidays and every time I see my family, there's a sense of urgency to repair the damage from the past and make up for lost time. That very day I decided I was going to stop missing out on so much of my life and figure out how to prevent migraines. If I missed out on a whole weekend with my dad, who is to say migraines wouldn't put me in a blackout on my wedding day or my baby's birth? I mean, I'd be thrilled to be knocked out on drugs when I give birth, but because my body is tearing in half, not because I have a stupid migraine.

Over the next seven years I spent countless hours and dollars on migraine specialists. I finally made some progress when a neurologist in Philadelphia helped me to differentiate between two separate conditions I had, so I was able to zone in on what was actually a migraine and what wasn't. Turns out, not all of my headaches are technically migraines because I also have a separate condition that causes auditory hallucinations. It's called—wait for it—exploding head syndrome. From what I gather, this condition was discovered pretty recently, so I guess by the time they figured it out, all the elegant, scientific-sounding terms had been taken, so doctors were just, like, "I dunno . . . Screw it, let's just call it exploding head syndrome."

To me, *exploding head syndrome* sounds more like a description of a migraine than a diagnosis of a whole different condition. So what is the difference? Well, migraines for me are a random ambush that can happen at any time of day, indiscriminate of what I planned to do that day and how important I think my time is. My exploding head episodes only happen when I'm falling asleep. When I start to doze off, I'll hear impossibly loud banging noises and feel like a chain saw is splitting my cerebellum in half. It isn't pain per se; it's more of an internal reverberation that makes me feel as if I'm in an MRI machine, where you have to weather those impossibly loud and jarring banging noises. Side note: Hey, tech dorks, can we put less time and energy into 3-D video games and sex dolls and more time into getting X-ray machines that don't cause emotional damage while scanning for physical damage? Thanks so much.

I always figured the banging in my head was night terrors because that seems like something I would have. I just figured I had them during the day, too. I brought this up to the neurologist in case it was a migraine symptom, and she asked how long I had been experiencing the banging sensations in my head while falling asleep.

"Since I was, like, five?"

"And you're now twenty-five?" she asked, half incredulous, half annoyed.

"Yeah, so twenty years, I guess."

I felt more old than alarmed. "This is pretty common, I'd think," I said.

She looked bewildered that I was making up statistics. "This condition affects only about 10 percent of the population."

I hated that I was wrong, but hearing that made me feel kind of special.

Being able to differentiate between my exploding head and my migraines—aka my imploding head—helped me to figure out how to better treat them. The first step in diagnosing something is not confusing it with something else, obviously. I thought maybe lack of sleep was the culprit, but when I would fall asleep, my head would feel like a building was collapsing on it, so I couldn't get a consistent variable to isolate. The doctor gave me an herbal supplement called butterbur root. I know, it sounds ridiculous, but apparently it has an anti-inflammatory effect. I took this for a couple years, and whether it was psychosomatic, a placebo effect, or it actually worked, my migraines did start to wane. It was the closest thing to a miracle I'd experienced since I discovered someone figured out how to make Greek yogurt popsicles.

A couple of years later I read that butterbur root, much like the men in my life at the time, was associated with serious safety concerns. While flipping through *Neurology Times* one day I read, "Butterbur extract has been shown to contain pyrrolizidine alkaloids (PAs), a toxic substance that causes hepatoxicity in humans and has been shown to be mutagenic and carcinogenic in animal studies." *Cool.*

So there went that solution. Once I started working and having employees, my fear of getting a migraine was almost as debilitating as the migraine itself. When I was making a TV show, if I had gotten a migraine, it would paralyze the production and cost hundreds of thousands of dollars. I had some hope because a couple of new medications had come out that you could take when you felt a migraine coming on to at least truncate the progress of it. Every time I couldn't read a word in a script, I'd take one to prevent a headache. Sometimes I was just an idiot and had misspelled the word, but most of the time it was a harbinger of a migraine.

By the time I was twenty-eight, the headaches were as frequent and as intense as I can remember. I called my doctor, crying, mostly because of how hard it was to get a doctor on an actual phone, but also because I felt like a hole was being drilled into my skull on a daily basis, which I needed like a hole in the head.

"I've been doing what you said, alternating the medications every other day when I take them."

"Oh, you're not supposed to take them more than twice a week, or else they *cause* migraines," she said casually.

I wish you could have seen my face when I heard this information. I looked like Munch's *The Scream* remixed with the face of a basketball coach when a player misses a free throw. The medication preventing the ailment causes the ailment? This is when I finally figured out that I had to stop listening to dismissive, busy doctors. I realized that most of the pills that had been prescribed for me in my lifetime solved one problem but caused numerous other ones.

Since the Band-Aid approach of fixing migraines after they came on didn't work, I decided to really get to the bottom of what was causing them, so I had to figure out what my triggers were. I wanted to break the cycle of my family's empty refrigerator/full medicine cabinet logic and start preventing these attacks. Modern medicine had failed me time and time again, and to keep resorting to pills would be the definition of insanity: "doing the same thing over and over again and expecting a different result." Some say Einstein said that, some say it was Mark Twain, but for me to keep checking online who actually said it would be, well, insanity.

I decided to go on a sort of *Eat Pray Love* tour of doctors, but it was more like a *Pay Pray Pay* situation, given I was throwing a ton of money at this journey and was running on faith alone to get me through it. I was throwing shit against the wall, but at least I wasn't banging my head against it, because banging my head against a shit-covered wall finally stopped being appealing.

The first non-pharmacological thing I did was get allergy tested.

I'm not sure why I had never done this before, especially given that my mom was very allergic to bees. I also knew some kids at school who always had an EpiPen because a bee sting could be fatal. That whole idea just terrified me—that one of the tiniest organisms on Earth could kill what is presumably its most advanced and intelligent one solely with its butt. They just poke their deadly tush into someone's arm and that person's life is over? Literally my worst nightmare is that I have an enemy that's less than a centimeter big and can fly.

Getting allergy tested is very annoying. If you aren't already aware, they stick about a billion (thirty) tiny pins in you with whatever they're testing for on the tip to see if your skin gets inflamed. Ironically, getting tested for allergies, and even a bee allergy, very much mimics getting stung by a swarm of bees: They put all the needles in your back and wait to see which ones leave red bumps. If a red bump appears, you're allergic. Turns out that I'm allergic to *needles*. Not sure why redness is the big indicator, given all needles make all skin red. The whole thing made no sense to me, but I was desperate. Turns out I'm not allergic to bees, but that I am very allergic to dust. The bad news is that dust is literally everywhere; the good news is that I finally had motivation to use a vacuum.

I pulled up all the carpets in my house and was on my hands and knees, cleaning constantly to remove every speck of dust from my house. I was like Cinderella, but without the happy ending.

Next stop was my sinuses. I went to an ear, nose, and throat doctor. He told me my sinuses were swollen, which could cause pressure in the head, therefore causing migraines. I had never heard about putting needles in your head before, but to me, it seemed like more of a plot twist in a horror movie than a medical solution. He pulled a syringe out, and as he moved it toward my face, my primal brain took over. I'm not an anthropologist or a neurologist, but my guess is that primates aren't wired to be cool about some guy moving toward our faces with what is essentially a sharp metal weapon. I had to use all the self-control I had not to instinctively punch him in the throat. It took a while for me to overcome my violent impulses, but thankfully he had a weird photo of Madonna from the nineties in his office that she had signed. Inspecting her handwriting and fantasizing about a celebrity autograph forgery business enabled me to dissociate long enough to get through the needle going into my head via my nostril.

To add insult to injury of realizing my dream forgery business was illegal, the ENT told me I had a deviated septum.

"Do you have trouble sleeping?" he prodded encouragingly.

Of course I did, but I had ninety-nine problems that kept me up at night, and my deviated septum felt like it hovered around number fifty-six.

"When did you break your nose?" he asked.

I thought long and hard, unable to recall a pivotal moment in my life. Had I broken my nose while on sleeping pills and completely forgotten about it? I started brainstorming out loud things that could have broken it: basketball, laying facedown in tanning beds, a couple blackout drunk nights in my early twenties? He looked disgusted and bored while I recounted a litany of terrible choices.

I finally realized he was giving me surreptitious permission to get a nose job. He pointed out that my nostrils are uneven and that my nose was very crooked. If you took into consideration my cripplingly low self-worth, you might think that this would be a slam dunk for rhinoplasty, but my nose was actually one of the only things I didn't mind about myself. It worked, it had character, it was sturdy. I had never even had a nosebleed. I pierced my nose when I was twelve, and when I took the nose ring out three months later, the skin healed up like a champ, whereas most noses would have had an unsightly hole in them forever. My nose was resilient, and I appreciated that.

My tour of doctors continued. I started collecting more information about my triggers, such as that certain perfumes and too much light at certain angles cause migraines. So if you see me in public wearing sunglasses and looking at the floor, I'm not avoiding you, I'm avoiding a migraine. And if I hug you, then immediately run away from you, it's because you're wearing Charlie Girl or some perfume that could knock me out for three days.

Straining your eyes can be a headache trigger, so I got my vision checked. Sure enough, I needed glasses for distance. I also started wearing a mouth guard at night because grinding my teeth in my sleep was causing tension in my jaw muscles, which releases lactic acid, which can throw off your neurochemistry. All of these were solutions and valid triggers, but even though I was controlling the amount of light I saw and the amount of dust and perfume I inhaled, and fixed my vision, sleep, hormones, and sinus swelling, I was still getting headaches.

Eventually, I threw up a Hail Mary and decided to meet with one more doctor at UCLA who has a great reputation for helping migraine sufferers. This doctor explained to me how migraines actually work in a way that finally made sense to me. To paraphrase, she explained gently, "the migraine brains are simply more sensitive to outside stimuli than other people's brains are. They don't like any kind of chemical change, and they need routine and consistency. Wake up the same time every day, drink coffee the same time every day, eat consistently at the same time, go to bed the same time every night." Finally, an excuse to be a robot.

She talked about the brain as if it were a toddler that had to be nurtured, not a villain that had to be slayed. It made me wonder why we treat our bodies like something outside ourselves when it's actually what we inhabit. It's not attacking us, it's where we live. I fought my pain with synthetic chemicals, never bothering to understand how everything worked or what it actually needed. I was trying to Windex shards of glass instead of protecting the window from being broken in the first place.

Meeting this UCLA doctor was the beginning of my journey to educating myself about neurochemicals, what triggers them to be released and what they do to our brains. I'm pretty horrified that we're taught so little about how our body's engine works. Why did I spend a year doing stoichiometry in chemistry class, which I've never used in my life, but I didn't know what cortisol does? When we stress out, our body releases cortisol, which sabotages our sleep, suppresses the immune system, and ages us. It *ages us*, you guys. If someone told me fifteen years ago that stress would make me look older, I would have taken a very different approach to life. I certainly wouldn't have been stuck in the tragic irony of stressing out to pay for facials that were supposed to make me look younger.

I learned that what triggered migraines was actually the stress I experienced while trying to cure them. I'm so conditioned to do more, to try harder, to overwork, that my brain would never stop hurting unless I rewired it and changed my approach altogether. The obsession with work was passed down from generation to generation in my family: My grandfather juggled owning a candy store and a coal mine, and refused to stop working until the day he died. My father inherited that work ethic. I remember waking up at two A.M. and going into the kitchen for a snack and seeing my dad wide awake, working at the kitchen table. He always carried around a yellow legal pad no matter where we went so he could work anytime, anywhere. We all of course have to work for money and meaning in our lives, but seeing a blueprint that glorified constant hustle, I confused work with my worth.

Looking back at all the headaches I had endured, I actually feel like they weren't trying to hurt me; I feel like they were actually trying to help me. My brain stem was trying to tell me something, whether it was to slow down, take a nap, stop taking a pill, cancel my plans, break up with someone, not eat something, eat something, stop trying so hard to impress someone, drink water, get off my phone, do literally anything but what I was doing. Because my instinct was always to do more, in order to solve this problem, I basically had to stop trying so hard to solve this problem.

Since I had no synapses dedicated to this skill of doing less, what ultimately helped me overcome migraines was the inner child work I've told you about. And if you missed the eating disorder chapter, don't worry, inner child work isn't in violation of any child labor laws, it's essentially connecting with your inner child.

Once I finally started to acquiesce to the needs of my inner child, my headaches lessened. As you may have noticed, kids don't know or really care about what adults have on their schedules. They aren't interested in how much money you make or how late you're running for a meeting. They have not yet subscribed to our rat-race, hamster-wheel culture of self-abandonment. They don't yet know that *needy* is a pejorative word, so when kids have to pee, they say they have to pee; when they're hungry, they say they're hungry. They have not yet learned to suppress their needs to impress people or pretend they're fine because they've been brainwashed to believe that being needless is a sign of strength. They don't walk on eggshells to be liked, so connecting with my inner child helped me redevelop the muscle of anticipating and addressing my own needs instead of worrying about someone else's. This may all seem pretty obvious, but before inner-child work, I literally used to hold pee in for hours or skip eating if I felt either would inconvenience someone or slow down my work. Now that I have connected with my inner child, I don't constantly feel like I'm in labor about to birth one.

Child Whitney has become my compass, and my headaches have become the strict parents I needed but never had. When I've overcommitted myself, date a guy who causes me anxiety, or pound Chinese food made almost entirely of chemicals and MSG, my headaches appear to scold me and steer me in another direction. It's as if Google Maps had a feature where your phone electrocuted you whenever you got off on the wrong exit.

Maybe you don't get headaches, but maybe your body talks to you in other ways. Maybe you get back pain, cold sores, anxiety. Something you think is idiopathic may actually be your inner child tugging on your shirt asking you to investigate or to slow down and make a different choice. Maybe your stomach hurts; maybe you're sad and don't know why; maybe you yell at people; maybe you can't stop masturbating; maybe you dabble in Scientology. Whatever shape your pain takes, I hope you can see it as your body trying to communicate with you, perhaps to the point of rendering you immobile to force you to take it seriously.

Although at first I viewed my headaches as preventing me from living a full life, I now truly think my headaches protected me from far worse ramifications of my bad ideas. A lot of the time migraines kept me from engaging in unhealthy behavior. They made me go home and sleep when my instinct was to work until three A.M.; they guided me into a dark room instead of letting me hang out with a dark person. Because hangovers yielded migraines, my headaches also steered me away from alcohol, which is truly a gift given how addictive my personality is. Without migraines God knows what I'd be doing, what weirdo I would have married in Vegas, what unlucky kids I'd be badly parenting. Without headaches I'd probably be a full-blown hot mess, instead of the half-blown one I am now.

The search for a migraine cure taught me a lot of things I never would have learned otherwise. I learned about the workings of our brain, neurochemicals, and allergies. My migraines led me to do a lot of things that otherwise wouldn't have occurred to me. Without trying to fix my brain, I never would have gotten my vision checked, for example. And thank God I did get contacts, because without them I'd still be oblivious to my unibrow and wearing foundation countless shades darker than my actual skin tone.

In order to heal my headaches, I had to stop thinking in terms of what I had to do; instead I had to start thinking in terms of what I had to stop doing. I was so programmed to do more, to try harder, to force solutions, and to go to the pharmacy for solutions that I didn't even think of what I could eliminate instead of what I could add. Doing this made my life way more boring, but my headaches abated and so did the number of pill bottles that fell out of my purse on first dates.

My headaches also taught me a valuable lesson about my reaction to pain. It gives me chills now to think that my response to pain was to toughen up, then normalize it. I was so used to hearing "calm down," "relax," and "everything is fine" that I ended up believing it and doubting my own reality. I internalized my parents' and their parents' white-knuckle philosophy of ignoring pain. I'm not qualified to psychoanalyze what exactly happened to make me feel shame for suffering, but my reaction to having pain was embarrassment. I also didn't want to feed the stereotype of women not being as tough as men, so I never wanted to show distress, and as an adult I wanted so badly to be low-maintenance, easy, and cool. But there's nothing cool about being five thousand dollars in debt to an emergency room or puking out of a car on the freeway.

I shudder when I think about how quickly and easily I normalize pain, both physical and emotional. My headaches ended up becoming akin to what happens when you need to beat a lie detector test: Lying is stressful to the body, and the polygraph machine picks up on that by measuring your racing pulse, sweaty palms, dry mouth. Basically everything happening in your body when you take your hair extensions out to reveal your actual hair, or lack thereof, to a guy. The trick to beating the lie detector machine is not to become a better liar, but to become worse at telling the truth. That's what it means to normalize an unacceptable situation. Also, criminals, you're welcome for the hot tip.

Normalizing is how to beat a lie detector test, but not how to

win at life, although these days going numb and martyring ourselves seems to have become the norm.

I'm not sure when having a high tolerance for pain became impressive or cool, but it's neither. Pain is important information,
and I can't imagine there's any pain that's by accident. I'm not
talking about the pain people are born with or the horrible diseases that make people needlessly suffer. And the fact that I need
to qualify that is another example of normalizing pain! So often
my inner monologue tells me to "stop complaining. It's not like
you have leukemia. Some people have real problems, you dummy
ingrate!" Yes, there are people in way more pain than some of us,
but that doesn't mean we should ignore our own.

This trend of minimizing and even glorifying pain—emotional
or physical—has got to stop. Nefarious adages we throw around
like "no pain, no gain" are so deeply imbedded into our psyches
that sometimes it doesn't even occur to us that pain is your body's
form of giving you a warning. It's our body telling us to "stop doing that and get out of there, ya goof." And yes, I realize pain may
yield results with exercising, but anything past sore muscles is not
okay to ignore.

I think it's time we all reject the glamorization of tolerating
pain. High heels, waist trainers, CrossFit, staying in painful
relationships—these are all very masochistic. Yes, I know relationships technically take work, but I have a job, and unless a relationship is putting money into my 401(k), I can't make working on it
my main priority.

Recently it's become cool to brag about how little sleep you got,
how hard you work, how many pills you take, how often you've
been sick. It seems the easier our lives are made by modern technology, the more people need to make up struggles for themselves.
As recently as eighty years ago, and still today in many Third
World countries, people really were sick pretty much all the time,
and now that we finally have the means to be healthy, people seem

to want to brag about being sick. I blame people who regram that stupid quote "What doesn't kill you makes you stronger." Whoever said that is either very stupid or had awesome painkillers. Also, it seems the only people who throw that quote around have not had anything come close to killing them, besides maybe me. This glorification of pain perpetuates the idea that our bodies are a machine we need to test, as opposed to a super fragile bag of skin full of important-as-shit organs.

From now on, I'm not going to minimize my pain. I will be loud about my discomfort. People might think I'm dramatic or annoying, but that's okay, because you know what else is annoying? Feeling like someone is stabbing you in the brain all day. I will ignore the voices in my head telling me to "toughen up" and "calm down." I'll ask for help. And if the help sucks, I'll ask someone else. I will not settle for help that is dismissive and unfocused. If someone casually throws pills at me instead of a long-term solution, then I'll get down to business with a negative Yelp review.

Messing with neurochemistry is not a joke, people. This whole trend of giving anyone who walks into a doctor's office antidepressants when that person isn't clinically depressed is as crazy as getting tattoo lip liner. I'm not saying antidepressants don't save millions of lives. I know many people who got their sanity, joy, and humanity back with the help of antidepressants; they're a miracle for people who suffer from depression, but to take them if you're not clinically depressed can distance you from the actual solution to your issue. For people who aren't depressed, these pills can exacerbate the problem and pile on self-defeating side effects, which is what happened to me. Taking drugs when it's not medically necessary is like putting diesel fuel in a gas car, which I have also done. I don't recommend doing either.

Dismissing people, especially women, who have complicated ailments with pills is an age-old tradition and one that I think we should all challenge. As I watch one of my dear family members battle antibiotic resistance and many people I love grapple with various pill dependencies, I worry about what mindlessly taking pills does to our, well, mind.

My pain management aside, I've hit my limit in losing valuable people's productivity and time to the side effects of unnecessary antidepressants, painkillers, and various avoidable sicknesses. I've seen friends lose their sparkle, their passion, motivation, and even sanity. How can we live our dreams if we can't even dream because we're in chemically induced stupors? Maybe freedom is as easy as not bottling it up and not relying on bottles.

I love technology and science as much as the next person, but it shouldn't replace common sense and our body's natural system of checks and balances. Before we had MRI machines and X-rays, we had a brilliantly designed nervous system telling us what worked and what didn't quicker than the fastest Starbucks Wi-Fi.

Let's make it sexy to say "ouch." Let's make it cool to say "uncle." Let's make it cool to say "I need help." Don't calm down. Don't relax. Gals, there's no honor in being a "good girl" anymore. And guys, don't "man up" or "suck it up." In general, stay away from anything up, including uppers, because, well, what goes up must come down.

Don't say you're okay when you're not; don't say you're fine. I mean, I'm fine, but you don't have to be.

THE PIT BULL CHAPTER

It's always annoyed me that dogs are a "man's best friend," but diamonds are a "girl's best friend." This seems incredibly unfair. Men get awesome super cute pups and we get tiny sharp stones that just make people think we're superficial and that we have to give back in a break-up? Diamonds have been a way better friend to men than they've been to women; they're a great way to get laid and make an argument go away. To women, they've often been a substitute for actual love or a thing we have to worry might fall into a drain while we're washing our hands. Honestly, if a man was to propose to me, I'd way rather he be holding a dog than a diamond ring that I'm just gonna misplace or end up putting on eBay.

I'd pick dogs over diamonds as my best friend any day. Growing up, I lived on a farm for a couple of years with eight and a half dogs and six horses, and they became my family. I don't need to sell anyone on how awesome dogs are, but I do feel the need to defend the breed I tend to spend the most time with: pit bulls. At the time I'm writing this I have three pit bulls, but by the time this comes out, I'm sure you will have already seen me on the show *Hoarders* with way more.

I never cease to be heartbroken by some people's visceral reaction to pit bulls. One time my FedEx guy came to my door, and when he saw one of my dogs through the window, he dropped my package and ran to his truck, yelling "No pit bull!" He has a body like a brioche, so it was actually kind of funny to watch him run, but when I really processed it, I couldn't believe someone could have such an intrinsically terrified reaction to an animal that's well-trained, behind glass and a gate, and sleeps in bed with a girl who uses three-pound weights in Spin class.

Did he really think my dog was going to maul him to death? I mean, this guy had actual terror in his eyes of a dog who gets, like, 10K likes on Instagram based on his sweet face alone.

Look, I'm not saying be an ignorant moron. Having a respectful fear of animals with sharp teeth is always wise. I'm circumspect around every new dog I come across. If you ever see me meet a dog for the first time, especially when I'm walking into its home, I never touch its head right away or invade its space. I hold my ground and let it decide if it wants to hang out with me. It usually does, thank God, and if it doesn't, you'll have to witness me having a pretty intense emotional meltdown, but smothering dogs you don't know is never a good idea. In addition to disregulating the dog, it also makes people think you're very lonely. I think in general we all tend to approach dogs as if they're toys; we're too aggressive and feel too entitled to their bodies. If someone I didn't know came up to me on the street and started palming my face, I'd immediately punch them in the neck and karate-chop them until they died of confusion. I try to give dogs that same respect, because for all I know, they may have an injury they need to protect or have an obtuse owner who, while trying to be "nice" to the dog, didn't train it to have discipline around strangers.

There's no doubt that pit bulls cast a larger cultural shadow in America than any other breed of dog. They're often misunderstood, misrepresented, and mistreated, but like the sexy hot vampires in teen emotional-porn movies, they're also idealized, romanticized, and pathologized. They're one of the most popular breeds in America, yet they're also outlawed in some states and shunned in others, depending on the year or even month. They're sorta like the McRib, except I'd actually let a pit bull near my mouth.

As a "type" of dog, pit bulls have always been part-breed/part-brand. I actually didn't even know until pretty recently that pit bulls aren't even a real breed. There is no true "purebred" pit bull: they're usually a mix of the American Staffordshire terrier, bull terrier, and bulldog. They're the anti-breed breed, which is part of their beauty to me. They're like the America of dogs, comprised of many different backgrounds, shapes, and sizes. Also, like America, a pit bull can be seen as, well, a bully.

To be very clear in terms of the history of pit bulls, many have absolutely been bred to fight. I'll stay away from the more gruesome details, but as early as the 1830s they were selected and bred to have large jaw muscles in their heads and a very high arousal rate, which means they can go from 0 to 60 incredibly fast. If a pit bull were a car, it would be a Porsche. I don't know that much about cars, so if there's a sports car that can accelerate faster than a Porsche, then a pit bull would be whatever car that is. I hate comparing them to sports cars because whatever car I select, it's probably driven by a man with hair plugs having a midlife crisis, but I think it's a useful metaphor nonetheless.

Because pit bulls have essentially been bred to be weapons, they can and will literally fight to the death if they're trained by a terrible person to do so or are defending their own lives. They're born with the tools and the body to be wildly successful at violence, but they aren't born with an inherent desire or need to be violent toward people. In fact, the tragic irony of their fighting heritage is that they were also selected to have an inherently low incidence of aggressiveness toward humans. Dog handlers who had to step in and pull their dogs out of the fighting pit didn't tolerate dogs that would go after people. People who run dogfights are incredibly sick and stupid, but I guess not stupid enough to put themselves in danger, so the result of it all is that breeders created one of the most tragic creatures there is: an animal with the teeth of a shark, the muscles of a lion, and the heart of a teddy bear.

Many people conflate a pit bull's behavior with the crimes of their abusers. In my experience, if dogs have any tendency toward violence, it is a direct result of human abuse, training the dog to behave in such a way so it sees no choice or having been taken from their mothers too young, which creates maladaptive behaviors. Dogs are extensions and reflections of their owners, which explains why mine are needy attention whores who live for eye contact. That said, like all animals, they're wired to survive and defend their lives, so I'm the first to say that if a pit bull—or any dog for that matter—feels threatened or has a history of abuse, I'd get out of the way very quickly and contact a professional.

Statistically, small dogs actually bite more frequently than pit bulls, but a pit bull bite is obviously going to be a bigger news headline given it will leave more damage. When a Chihuahua bites you, it's not going to do much harm unless you're made of mayonnaise. I found a dog on the street in Compton, who I think is part shih tzu, part something else—my guess is psycho albino rat. She has a deformed foot from being a product of backyard breeding and God knows what kind of trauma while living on the street, so at first when I picked her up or tried to clean her ears, she'd bite me no less than forty times in a row. She actually cut skin, whereas my pit bulls only hurt me emotionally, like when out of nowhere one of them will just get off the bed and walk into the other room, leaving me momentarily paralyzed with heartbreak.

Although I love all dogs—and especially mixed alien weirdo street mutts (honestly, the fewer legs, the better)—in the last five years or so, I've gravitated toward pit bulls because they remind me of, well, me. They have big teeth, their menacing look tends to belie their mushy insides, and they very frequently break valuable things by accident.

Pit bulls are the most abused dog in the country. Beagles and greyhounds are also horrifically abused in lab testing and racing, respectively, but bullies at the moment are the most common breed found in shelters and hence the most frequently euthanized, but then again who knows what goes unrecorded. People who run backyard dogfighting rings train the dogs to minimize their need for human contact and of course to fight other dogs to the death. Perhaps I see myself in pit bulls because I feel like I, too, was conditioned for the same things. That said, saying I'm like a pit bull is a huge insult to pit bulls. Every pit bull I've met has shown more patience and loyalty than I ever have. They also usually smell way less like a dog than I do.

I relate to the baggage bred into a pit bull's brain because I grew up watching family members battle it out, slam doors, and yell at each other about stuff I learned about from *Melrose Place*. Fighting became my comfort zone because not only was I taught by pros how to do it, but it was a kind of attention that I could understand. I wrongly thought arguing was an expression of love or that it just came with the territory of being "in love." When there wasn't some kind of conflict in my relationships, I'd get anxious, always waiting for the other shoe to drop. Considering the type of guys I dated, that shoe would be one of those weird finger sneakers that outline every toe.

In my family of origin, conflict was the primary mode of communication, followed closely by passive aggression. But the key to conflict, I learned, is never backing down from a fight. As a result, I developed a very tough exterior to protect my fragile insides, which to this day I think are made of actual Peeps. I subconsciously wanted to become the scary-looking pit bull people see walking down the street and sheepishly cross to the other side to avoid. Nobody can hurt you if they can't get close to you.

But there's no victory in being scary. In my experience, the scariest people are usually the most scared. They've learned to be intimidating as a self-defense mechanism in order to avoid being hurt. When I look back at myself in my twenties, I see a terrified girl fighting wars that had been over for twenty years. I was still living by the now-obsolete rules that had gotten me through life in one piece. I thought being intimidating was going to protect me, when in reality nothing can protect you from the harsh lessons of life. Trust me, I've tried everything from vodka to Icy Hot to ointment with weed in it, and annoyingly, the only way out is through.

As you know, I don't rescue humans anymore because I'm in therapy for codependence. Also, rescuing humans doesn't even work. It's an exhausting waste of time that just makes them hate you. Just look at Batman, he lived alone in a cave.

I've redirected that energy into rescuing animals, beings who actually need and appreciate help. I promote and follow many animal charities on social media. Social media may be the apocalyptic end of society as we know it, but it does help get dogs adopted, so it makes said apocalypse slightly less terrifying. For most people, social media is a fun diversion where they get to read inspirational quotes that are frequently attributed to the wrong person and see photos of disturbingly large butts that are a slipped disk waiting to happen. Since I follow so many animal rescue organizations, social media is not particularly fun for me. Rather, it's an emotional land mine. In between borderline racist memes and annoying photos of cappuccinos with heart-shaped foam, scrolling through always yields faces of stray, abused dogs in need of a home and often urgent surgeries. Sigh. If only people's actual hearts were as big as the ones in their Instagram cappuccinos.

One day I was on Instagram, perusing the feed of an ex-boyfriend, minding my own business, and I saw a post of an angelic pit bull behind rusty metal bars at a shelter notorious for killing dogs very quickly. He was a year-old blue pit, which are the ones that look like tiny gray baby hippos on steroids. He was set to be euthanized in two days, and his eyes seemed to tell me that he somehow knew that. My solar plexus warmed with rage. Over my dead body would I let this dog be a dead body.

I called a rescue I worked with and arranged to have someone go down and get him from the shelter. When I came home, the dog was already at my house, waiting at my front door with two people from the charity. When I saw this tiny burro, my eyes welled up. It was love at first sight. This was already better than any online date I had ever had: Not only was this guy on time but he was early, well mannered, and even cuter than his photo.

I know he technically had the genetics of a pit bull, but he looked to me to be part seal, part baby elephant, part Vin Diesel. He had a broken tail and a perma-smile lined with an unnecessary amount of teeth, and his head and neck were strapped with muscles that no dog should ever need to use.

Usually the first thing I do when I rescue a dog is rename him. Given that I rescue mostly pit bulls, they always come with some testosterone-addled, intimidating name an irresponsible, insecure person gave it that isn't particularly helpful in trying to change the stereotypes about them. Names like Butch, Gun, or Tank. I mean, to me these sound like very harmless male strippers, but I can see how this could make people more scared if they're already trepidatious about pit bulls. A dog's name makes other people feel a certain way about it, the same way human names do. Like when I hear the name Vlad, I think "scary Russian bouncer," and when I see the name Chad, I swipe left. This blue pit came with the name Fang, which made no sense given how timid and sweet he was. That name did not match his personality. Naming this dog Fang would be like naming me "wife." After spending some time with him, I decided to call him Billy.

The first thing I generally do when I meet new dogs with a dubious background of abuse is try and identify their triggers. What scares them? This helps me figure out what may have happened to them in the past and how to proceed with their training, healing, and placement into a forever home. It can be painful to watch them react negatively, but they can't progress unless I know what wounds I'm dealing with. I'll raise my hand to see if they cower, which tells me they've been hit. I'll slam doors, try to put them in a crate, throw a fake cat in front of them, anything that could help me glean what they've been through and what issues we'll have to address. I also highly recommend doing these tests with humans on the first or second date. It saves a lot of time down the line.

After testing Billy a bit, from what I could tell he hated being left alone, was very scared of people yet had severe abandonment issues, and loved food. We already had more in common than any man I'd ever dated.

I also related to how socially awkward Billy was. He wasn't really sure what to do with his balloon arrangement of a body. I later found out that this could be the result of being taken from his mother too early. Puppies should be with their mother for at least eight weeks, but often breeders take them as early as two or three weeks. When removed too early, dogs can get too clingy with their owners, have socialization issues, and even bite, because bite inhibition is learned from their siblings and mother. Puppies need to be with their moms as long as possible, unlike humans, who seem to get weirder the more time they spend with their mothers.

When I sat in a chair, Billy sat under it, always seeking the place in the room where he'd be the least vulnerable. Once he finally did warm up to me, the poor boy wasn't even sure how to show his affection. He had absolutely no practice licking humans, and every time he tried to lick me, he did it with the wrong side of his tongue. The jellyfishy underside would slime me first; then he'd chase it with the rough upper part. Getting a kiss from him was sloppier than some of the drunken make-out sessions I had with random strangers during spring break at the Cancún Señor Frog's.

Once I felt I had built some trust with Billy, I carefully introduced him to my other dogs. When Billy met my gaggle of clowns, he wasn't overly charmed by them the way I am, but he was genial. I could tell he was slightly suspicious of their innocent and unconditional kindness. Chances are, he was used to dogs that were trained to attack him, so he stared at them warily, as if he anticipated, but didn't at all want, a fight.

"And he's cynical?" I thought. I beamed with pride. I mean, this dog just went from my soul mate to my offspring. Billy was cute, sweet, and to top it off, very on brand for me.

Billy had also been neutered only a week before I met him, and it takes about month for the testosterone to subside after the surgery, so I knew he was going to have the energy of a rambunctious teenage boy, something I was used to from dating forty-something guys in L.A. Now, what's the only thing trickier than the energy and attitude of a teenage boy? A teenage boy composed entirely of muscles and bulletproof tendons, topped off with forty tiny knives embedded in his face.

In my humble opinion I concluded that Billy needed at least a month of impulse control training, which is normal for a one-year-old dog who has just been neutered and has zero discipline or socialization. As I mentioned before, pit bulls have been bred to have a high arousal rate, and it's important for their and your safety to make sure they're able to stop doing whatever they're doing when you ask them to so they don't run into traffic or jump on you when you're in a pair of overpriced white pants that are probably going to get ruined anyway, but you'd rather it not be before you even leave the house.

By day three, Billy was following me wherever I went. If I was in the shower, his nose was on the glass, ogling me. If I was in the tub, his chin was on the side of the tub. If I was on the toilet, his chin was on my feet, but only because I wouldn't let him rest his face between my knees because it felt like we were bordering on something illegal.

That evening I tried to see if Billy could make it through the night in the crate. No dice. He was screaming his head off, so I moved the crate into my bedroom so he'd be able to see me. Even less dice. I finally acquiesced and let Billy sleep in the bed just as I do any man who shows the slightest bit of neediness.

When I let Billy up on the bed, he plopped his impossibly-heavy-for-its-size block head on my chest. When I looked at a selfie of us (I mean, come on, I had to take one), I was able to see a look of relief on his face. Maybe I was projecting, but the boy finally seemed to believe that he was safe. I tried to push him off me so I could breathe, but he just bounced back, desperate for physical contact. This little dude wasn't taking any chances.

The next day I planned to dedicate some time to etiquette training with Billy. But since I myself wasn't yet trained in etiquette, I spilled coffee all over myself and the floor. The cup shattered all over my bedroom. After yelling about five iterations of the word *fuck*, I bent over to start cleaning up the mess. One of my dogs, Daisy, the one who looks like a tiny cow made out of ice cream, came over and licked my face. My dogs always know how to calm me down when I'm stressing. Pills make me gag, so dogs are like Xanax but without the almost puking part.

I had found Daisy on the street a couple months earlier, and she still had a bunch of random bald spots and scrapes, so I started

examining them and assuring her of all the things I wished someone would have assured me about when I was a kid. Side note: I'm convinced that when people talk to their dogs, they're saying things they subconsciously need to hear. You've all seen people who meet a new dog and within ten seconds are saying "I love you," a phrase it could take years to say to a human being. I can always tell a lot about someone based on what they say to their dog. My go-tos are usually "I promise I'll never leave you" and "Here's some food," two phrases I wish someone would say to me on a regular basis.

Billy came over to join in with some of his backward clumsy eel kisses. I assure you there's a ton I don't know about dog psychology, and I'm sure I make training mistakes all the time, but I do know some things about training dogs, or at least what has worked for me and my weirdo pack. It works for me to establish myself as the alpha, which means I have to act like, well, a goddamn alpha bitch. For example, I learned you walk *through* a dog, not around a dog, even if it means having to slow down and push them out of the way with your legs. This helps them understand that they're in my house, not vice versa, and that I'm the pack leader. Behaving this way was hard for me at first because I thought it was mean, but the meanest thing you can do with a dog is be unclear and submissive given they've evolved to be led by us. Otherwise they feel they have to be the leader, which makes them aggressive, territorial, stressed out, and they start to pee on stuff you care about. This basically means I have to own my space by walking around like Beyoncé, which does not come naturally to me given my genetics.

To be the alpha I also feed myself before I feed my dogs, I walk through a door before they do, look them in the eye, and so forth. I try not to be on the floor with my dogs too much because they could interpret that as my being submissive or their being equal to me. They're not equal to me. They're better than me, but they can't know that. My dogs are so submissive at this point that my being on the floor with them every now and then doesn't mess up the power dynamic. Also, I trip and fall a lot, so not ever being on the floor isn't really an option.

Even if I'm on the ground, I still enforce the alpha dynamic. If

I'm done playing on the floor with them, I push them off me and claim my space to make sure my dogs always understand boundaries. It was hard for me at first, because as you well know, it's hard for me to tolerate the discomfort of others, but unlike a lot of confusing people, dogs do very well with discipline. Anyway, I was ready to get up, so I pushed Daisy to the side. With my other hand I pushed Billy to my other side.

Then it happened. What exactly I'll never completely know, but within seconds my ear was hanging off my head.

I don't remember that much, but here's what I specifically don't remember: growling, fighting, struggling. I do remember pulling away and Billy getting stuck in my hair. I felt hairs pulling out of my head. I mean, of all the days, the one day in the past ten years I was actually wearing my hair down, it had to be this one. Billy and I were both panicking, and even though we were both bred to fight, neither one of us wanted any part of this sloppy melee. We may have been emotionally entangled, but neither of us wanted to be physically entangled.

From what I've heard, when mammals get injured, a surge of adrenaline basically turns them into superheroes. Out of nowhere I was able to stand up without using my hands. I somehow flew from my bedroom floor to my bathroom, guided by core muscles that came out of hibernation. Apparently the sight of my own blood makes me instantly capable of parkour.

What I saw in the mirror was more confounding than horrifying. My brain was obviously in denial about what had happened because I couldn't figure out why I was wearing a giant hoop earring. "I don't wear hoop earrings," I thought. It dawned on me that it wasn't an earring. It was an *ear*. *My* ear. Dangling by a thread, which I now know are technically called elastin fibers. My neck, my hands, and the right side of my face were covered with blood. It was very clear what I should do next: Call 911 and get an ambulance to come pick me up. So what did I do? Grabbed my keys and got in my car.

I drove about three miles like I was in Grand Theft Auto before I realized that driving while holding a flaccid, hemorrhaging ear was a very poor decision. I'm already a bad enough driver with both hands and ears available, so with only one of each, this move was borderline homicidal and suicidal.

I sped onto the infamous Mulholland Drive. Love the movie, hate the street. It's basically a serpentine hiking trail that's super congested because it's on the "star tours" bus route. Mulholland Drive is also a mess because it's eternally torn up and under construction, much like my personality, or on this particular day, the skin on my head.

I drove toward a construction site that had been pissing me off for weeks. Every day I had to wait for the construction worker to let me pass through the now-one-lane street. Every morning I pulled up, stopped, resented him, and forced a smile. Little did I know that the man who had been a daily annoyance for the past month was about to be my guardian angel in one of the most traumatic moments of my life.

I hadn't cried or felt any physical pain yet, but once I looked over to the construction worker and we made eye contact, I exploded in sobs. Through tears and blood I uttered a phrase that my vocal cords usually boycott: "I need help."

He didn't miss a beat. He called an ambulance and started looking through my car for things that could work as tourniquets. Luckily, he had no problem finding something, given half my wardrobe lives in the backseat of my car.

When the paramedics arrived, they asked me to show them my ear, but I couldn't. By this time I was violently shaking and my whole chest was contracting. I wasn't even sure if the ear was still attached to my head and I didn't want to find out. The three very handsome, buff paramedics finally convinced me to show it to them. Solely because they were cute and primordial biology is a filthy pervert, I finally acquiesced and pulled my hands away

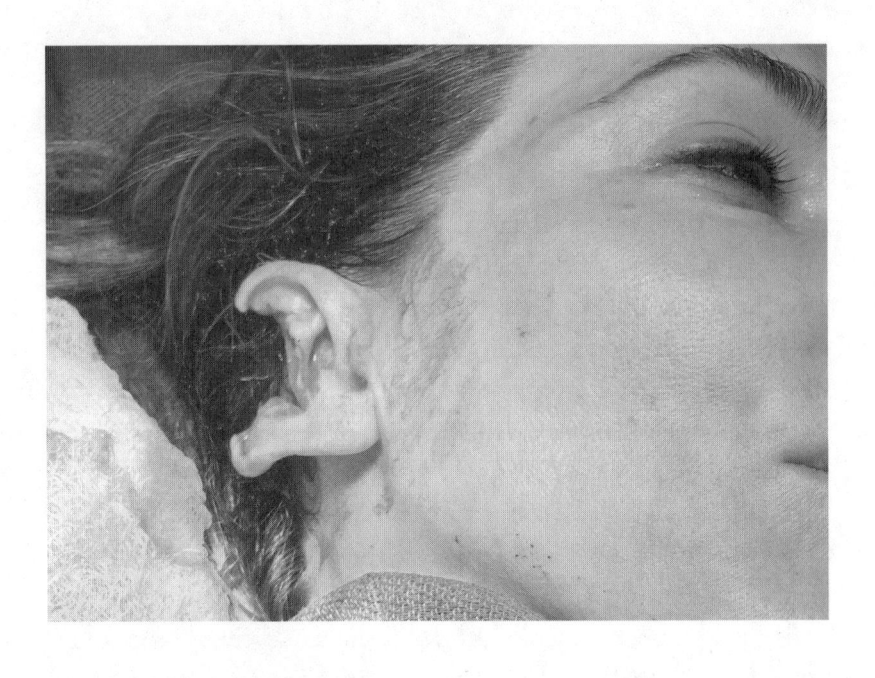

from my ear. Nothing. My hand was stuck. The blood had congealed so much that my hand was plastered to my head. The hot EMTs poured something over my hand to liquefy the blood. Once I was finally able to pry my hand away from it, they saw my "ear."

Their eye line told me that my ear was still in the same general vicinity of my head, but their winces implied that the injury was bad. I remember one of them gasping, which I concluded couldn't possibly be a good sign, given the horror paramedics are exposed to on a daily basis. Look, I believe men should be able to wince and not be shamed for it, but I have to admit that I've seen grown men wince only a couple other times in my life: when Anderson Silva's leg snapped on live TV, when "two girls one cup" was making the rounds on YouTube, and when I showed a paramedic my cartilage frappuccino of an ear. Suddenly this day was in very weird company.

I heard the sirens of an ambulance. That noise usually makes me anxious, but when the ambulance is for you, a sense of relief fills your body. Once I was in the ambulance, that relief was quickly shattered. I was strapped to a wheelchair, but was far from secure. Every time we stopped or turned, I would jolt over the chair like a crash test dummy, bracing while trying to hold my ear on. I was less than thrilled to find out that while being rushed to the ER I had to engage my core, and as far as I'm concerned, the only thing worse than missing an ear is having sore abs.

I'm not sure if paramedics are trained to make boring small talk to make sure you're coherent, but the guy in the ambulance with me was what I can only describe as aggressively casual.

"Cold out today, huh?" was his opener.

It was as if we had been married for forty years and had officially run out of things to talk about. Mind you, I was in a fetal position on a wheelchair, releasing guttural screams and erratic prayers to a couple of different gods. The most annoying part was that it wasn't even cold out. We live in L.A.; it's actually never been cold before. His small talk wasn't even based on accurate information. My guess was he was nervous about how much I was crying and his weird conversation was intended to distract me. From what I gather, it's pretty overwhelming for men to see a woman suffering, even when they cause it, and this may actually have been the least bizarre way I've ever seen a man cope with watching me cry. In the past, when men have seen me have a meltdown, they've done everything from abruptly leaving the room to start laughing to offering me money to stop. Twice I've had guys get an erection when they saw me cry. I know, primordial human nature is a nightmare.

I mustered all the strength I had to formulate a sentence, something in the vein of asking the aggressively casual paramedic if I could borrow his phone. With no irony or apology, he handed me an old LG flip phone. Look, I'm not a snob about technology. I'm basically a Luddite: I've never waited in line for a new iPhone, until very recently I thought *.com* meant *.computer*, and my current e-mail has a *number* in it. I know. Ghastly stuff. Oh, and .com stands for .commerce if you're like me and didn't know.

I never got the flip phone to work, but trying to remember phone numbers and press the impossibly tiny keys at least kept me distracted during the seemingly five-year ride to the ER. Maybe that's why they give patients a Stone Age phone, so it keeps them busy, serving as more of a Rubik's Cube than an actual communication device. The truth is, there really was nobody I could call. If I'd had a functioning smartphone, I would have bombarded a bunch of people who couldn't do much except show up and wait for other people to help me. Stressing my friends out would just stress me out more. The only people who could actually help me in this moment were complete strangers. Maybe this was a profound Buddhist lesson in nirvana or maybe it was a sign from the universe to befriend some surgeons.

We've all had horrible ER experiences, so I won't pretend like I'm the first person on the planet to be rolled into a corner in the waiting room facing the wall. The nurse had nice enough intentions and was trying to keep me hidden, but I wasn't really worried about TMZ showing up at the ER. Given how white I was from shock and how much blood I had on my face, I would have loved to have seen the headline the next day: "Marilyn Manson Rushed to ER Holding a Phone from 2006."

I leaned my forehead against the cold, Pepto-Bismol-colored wall and rocked back and forth, trying to keep myself amused by uttering "Nobody puts Baby in a corner" after Baby was aggressively put in a corner. I realized I was literally banging my head against a wall. This is something I do in a metaphorical sense very regularly, but doing it literally was a new development.

I turned the wheelchair around and a young, handsome Middle Eastern guy was sitting to my right. He looked at me intently. "What do you need?" he asked in a thick accent. I didn't know the answer, and even if I did, I don't think he could have given it to me, so I settled for "Can I borrow your phone?"

Without flinching, he gave me the phone he was using. I'm not even sure he said goodbye to the person he was talking to. When I thanked him, he looked surprised. He continued his intense eye contact with me and said, "Don't thank me. We're people. This is what we do. *We help each other.*" I remember thinking what he said would be very profound if it was in a movie. What a shame such a great moment was being wasted on real life.

I felt very guilty that I was using his phone and leaving him without one in an ER, so I kept thanking him over and over. Annoyed, he pulled another phone from his back pocket, held it up to show me he was good, and nonchalantly started using his other phone instead. He had *two phones* on him. This is the kind of moment in a writers' room that we would call "too broad," as in, it's funny but too ridiculous to ever actually happen in reality.

As I studied his phone, I was convinced I must have also had some kind of damage to my brain or eyes because I couldn't make out the characters in the little keyboard. They all looked like tiny sea monkeys. I finally realized through my trauma haze that what I was looking at were Arabic letters. I was too embarrassed to ask him to change the keyboard to English characters, so I just pretended I knew how to use it. Look, I like to think I've made a solid amount of progress around my codependence, but when shit hits the fan, I often revert to my primary mental conditioning. So here I was, lying to a stranger in an emergency room, with my ear hanging off my head, pretending to know one of the most complex languages in the world.

Before I could embarrass myself further, I finally got called in to see a doctor. I was rolled into a room with three other patients separated by paper curtains. A lovely male nurse put me in the bed and said, "The doctor will be right with you." I've been to the ER enough times to know this phrase actually means: "You're going to sit here for about an hour, so if you have a serious injury, you might as well just spend some time on WebMD and do the surgery on yourself with a car key and some chicken wire."

"You're okay, you're okay," I kept saying to myself. I was not okay, but delusion has always been my most reliable anesthetic. I had read that when animals get injured, their senses sharpen. Even though I was missing most of my ear, my hearing was the best it had ever been. I was surprised I could hear the doctor two curtains away talking quietly to a patient. The patient was describing his common head cold in excruciatingly boring detail. The doctor probably should have just diagnosed him with Munchausen syndrome and sent him home, but he sat there listening and saying "It's going around." I was so antsy to get treated that in this moment I saw the cruel irony in sick people being called "patients."

I was feeling forgotten about and invisible, so I tried to do breathing exercises Vera had taught me. You breathe in for five seconds, hold for five seconds, breathe out for five seconds; then you repeat this again and again. This calms down the amygdala, which is the part of the brain that basically tells your body to go apeshit with panic. After about twenty minutes, I deduced that the vibe in the ER was way too mellow for my taste: The nurses moseyed around and nobody seemed to be in the slightest bit of a rush. It seemed to me like once you've been working in an emergency room long enough, nothing seems like an emergency. Maybe I didn't need a doctor or a nurse; maybe I needed Shonda Rhimes to come in here and infuse everyone with the intensity of *Grey's Anatomy*.

Just as the breathing exercise started working, I heard the doctor ask the male nurse about a sports person retiring from whatever sports he does. "He's not getting traded?"

You guys, I tried very hard to be cool and wait my turn, but small talk about sports? Well, that did it.

I truly don't remember getting out of the hospital bed, but within seconds I was giving a lecture to the entire ER. I was channeling Tony Robbins meets a JV soccer coach who lives vicariously through his players. I vividly remember saying, "The lack of leadership in here is *incorrigible.*" I don't think I had ever said that word out loud in my life, and when I did, we were all pretty impressed. I followed that up with a diatribe on how poorly the ER was being run, even though I knew literally nothing about how an ER should be run. I'd be remiss if I didn't tell you that as my speech gained momentum, I started delivering it as if I was in a rap battle, and I'd be lying if I said I wasn't defaulting to an impersonation of Eminem in *8 Mile.* Maybe it was because I had to keep my hand on my ear, which felt like a rapper holding one of his headphones. Regardless, I want to be clear that I'm not proud of any of this.

"The vibe here is way too casual, folks, and I need someone to take charge of my situation. Who is responsible for getting antibiotics?"

Apparently when I've lost a good amount of blood, it seems like a good idea to use the word *folks.*

My attitude didn't land great with most of the nurses, but one cute, very competent-looking blond nurse seemed as if she was relieved that someone finally addressed the elephant in the emergency room. She also seemed to be fed up by the fact that there were eight people in a room with eight other bleeding people but no clear pecking order of who was to stop whose bleeding. She chirped "I'm on it" and left the room. I don't know her, but I was proud of her.

The ER doc wasn't impressed by my heroic speech. He rolled his tongue around in his pigment-less mouth as he sauntered over to me. He gave me that look men give women when they think we're being dramatic. I've seen this look more times than I can count. I was gonna say "a million times" but don't want to actually be dramatic.

"Ma'am, you need to calm down, *you're not gonna die.*" As if that weren't patronizing enough, he gesticulated toward me, sort of like a mini "Heil Hitler" right at my face. Now, before I tell you about the emotional carnival that followed this gesture, I'll admit that I'm still not exactly sure what *mansplaining* means, but if this wasn't it, I'm gonna need a word for whatever he had just done. He cunt-descended to me? Dr. Dick-ed me? Ego-farted on me? I guess I don't even know how to mansplain it.

I'm not sure how at sixty-something years old this man had not yet learned that the easiest way to make a woman less calm is to tell her to calm down. It was in this moment that I completely lost my shit—which come to think of it, I'm not sure I ever really had in the first place. So in that case I lost the already very lost shit. Another issue that further complicated the dynamic was that when this doctor put his hand in my face, I noticed that he was wearing a large cuff bracelet made of a mixture of coral and turquoise in a Tetris-type pattern. I was baffled that the same man who just treated me like a histrionic child also enjoys the spiritual benefits of precious New Mexican stones. Dude needs to pick a lane.

Dr. Ego continued to say things like "Relax" and "It's gonna be fine." I realized very quickly that this man had a core belief that women are irrational and overly sensitive. Everything I said was just playing into his prewritten narrative of who he assumed I was based on every woman he had ever dated. Words were obsolete because he clearly wasn't hearing what I was actually saying, so the only thing I could think to do was to take off the bandage wrapped around my head and show him my beet salad of an ear. He winced.

Once he realized I was telling the truth and that my injury wasn't a result of PMS or just from generally being a female, he got serious and left to call a plastic surgeon. By the time this happened, my friend Dori had arrived. You already know Dori, because she was one of the pals who was so patient with me around my eating-disorder madness. But allow me to give her some dimension: She's hands down one of the toughest, most competent people I know. One time she called me on a weekday, and as soon as I picked up the phone I started rambling for twenty minutes at how terribly my day was going. Traffic was crazy! There was a line at CVS! That guy I'm dating is totally being so weird! She comforted and advised me for ten minutes on my fake problems. After I felt better, I finally asked her, "So, how's your day?" She calmly replied, "Well, this morning I got hit by a car."

This girl was in the hospital recovering from having just had screws put into her knee and ankle, a pretty solid opener for a conversation and certainly a home-run excuse to interrupt someone else who's complaining about nothing, but Dori is constitutionally incapable of being selfish. Dori also happens to be from New Jersey, is incredibly flexible, has taken magician classes, and has the incredible gift of being able to pee anywhere.

Dori's arriving was what my amygdala needed because it meant I was going to be okay. If Dori is somewhere, shit is going to get handled, so my body finally got the permission to collapse into being the terrified five-year-old that I was. She was able to say with poise and grace all the eloquent things I planned on saying but ended up coming out of my mouth as "What the fuck is happening?!"

Finally, a surgeon arrived. He was very old, which was a relief. In fields like tech and computer science, the younger someone is, perhaps the more they know, but in the field of medicine, I want my doctors to look like a vintage leather couch. In tense situations, the presence of old age makes me feel safe, especially when it comes to doctors, pilots, and wine. I thought the surgeon and I were going to get along swimmingly until he started putting needles into my open lacerations without any warning. After I jolted around on the bed and yelled horrible things at him, he finally told me that he was injecting anesthesia, and that in order to get numb, you have to feel a shocking amount of pain. The ole "it gets worse before it gets better" racket. It felt like the ER version of when you unsubscribe from Pottery Barn e-mails and they *send you an e-mail* confirming you unsubscribed. Honestly, I'd feel less disrespected if a Pottery Barn employee just came to my house and slapped my nipple.

Dr. Ego had told me I was going to go to the OR, so imagine my surprise when Dr. Old As Hell started stitching up my ear right then and there, before the anesthesia had even kicked in. "What the fuck!" came out of my mouth for maybe the two hundredth time. Once he was stitching me up, my tone switched. I tend to get incredibly polite when I'm in pain and exaggerate the enunciation of words. I said, "Sir, I don't think the anesthesia has kicked in yet, because that is a shocking level of discomfort, sir!"

Dr. Old As Hell didn't respond.

"Can you please inform me before you stick a needle in my ear so I can mentally prepare myself for the excruciating pain, sir?" Nothing. He wasn't even rolling his eyes at me like most doctors do. Just zero response. This man was literally ignoring me.

Insane as it sounds, I don't think my deep panic was caused by the dog bite, the fact that I now had bloodstains all over my favorite sofa, or Dr. Old As Hell's telling me that my ear might not "take" and that I might need a prosthetic. Those things I could actually handle for some reason. My mind only kicked into a state of deep fear when I felt I wasn't being heard. The only thing more triggering to my inner child than being patronized is being straight-up ignored completely.

I continued to scream and cry as Dr. Old As Hell continued to crochet my ear without acknowledging I existed. Later that day, Dori called Dr. Old As Hell's office to ask about when I could come

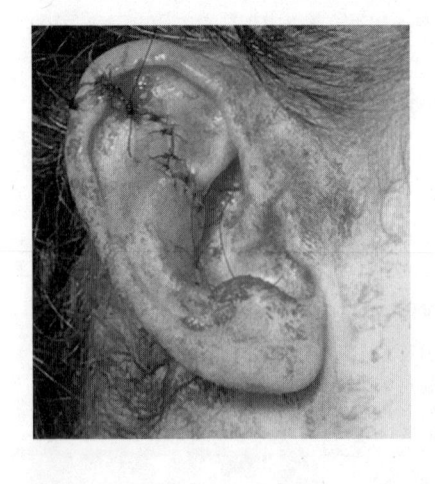

get the stitches out and the receptionist told her that Dr. Old As Hell doesn't take phone calls because he's deaf. Deaf. DEAF. Look, I love deaf people. In fact, I prefer people to be deaf given I regret everything I say moments after saying it. But, I feel like when someone introduces you to your deaf surgeon, the least they can do is maybe, I don't know, tell you he's deaf? The good news is at least it wasn't my imagination that I wasn't being heard.

So why am I telling you this story? What's the point except to gross you out and make you think I'm still very insane and have made none of the progress I swear I've made? What could the lesson possibly be?

Well, this all felt like an oddly familiar situation in my life. I urgently rescued something that needed me, took him in without acknowledging his limitations and traumatized neurology, let him get in my bed, projected a fantasy onto him of how perfect our life would be together, and it all ended in a tremendous amount of pain. I had played out this cycle before, only in romantic relationships. It also happens to be a version of the cycle of something called love addiction.

When Vera first told me that I might be dabbling in love addiction, I scoffed. "But I haven't dated anyone in like six months." I had already proven her point by protesting too much because usually the more defensive I am about something, the more true it is. I also had been counting the months, which is a pretty addict-y thing to do.

Look, I had no idea what love addiction was, and truthfully I still get very confused about it, because love addiction and the concept of true love are very easy to conflate. Regardless, I still didn't believe I had it because, well, yuck. Vera explained to me that love addiction isn't about how often you're in love, it's about what happens when you are.

She outlined to me how love addiction works—or for that matter, doesn't work. Since I'm obviously not a psychiatrist, I don't want to generalize about all love addicts because I can't speak to anyone's experience but my own, so I'll just tell you how mine specifically manifests.

When in "love," I overlook red flags and the other person's shortcomings to justify staying in the relationship. This is a form of denial that has helped me justify dating people who follow thirty porn stars on Instagram and ask me to pay off their student loans. My brain is able to instantly turn red flags into green lights by twisting the negative into a positive: "He's asking me to pay his student loans . . . I mean, look at the bright side! He went to college!"

I would glorify the person instead of accepting the reality of who they have actually shown themselves to be. I put them on a pedestal and exaggerated their good qualities and minimized their negative ones. I'd give points for things that should be categorized under baseline basic respect—for example, "He *called* me! He's such a class act!" To be clear, you don't get points for making a phone call to a person you are dating.

I tended to get in relationships with people before I actually knew them. I'd fill in the blanks with projections of what I hoped they were. I saw that as way more convenient than finding out the truth, because, well, the truth always ruins my love affair with dopamine. If I actually knew someone's low credit score or history of incarceration, it would destroy my fantasy and mess up my to-do list, on which "being in a relationship" always seemed to be number one. I avoided asking questions I didn't want to know the answers to under the guise of "it's none of my business what happened before me." Which is of course false, because if someone got herpes before me, it's my business and my business's business.

I would fall in love with someone's potential rather than with who they actually were. I'd walk in, find a guy who was smart and funny but a complete mess, and light up like a talent agent from the 1950s. I'd think to myself, "This kid's gonna be a star!" I'd take on a guy the way Michelle Pfeiffer took on the punk-ass kids from *Dangerous Minds*, seeing the best in them and pushing them to be better. And also like Michelle Pfeiffer in

Dangerous Minds, I had to teach a couple of guys how to read. Of course, this dynamic caused my relationships to feel maternal, making my partner resent me and making sex feel like incest. To add insult to injury, I basically ended up coaching a guy to be the best he can be for the next girl who came along. To anyone dating my exes, you're welcome for getting them together so you could have the perfect boyfriend. Love you, girl.

If a friend disapproved of the relationship, I'd distance myself from the friend until the relationship was over the same way that I've seen drug addicts and alcoholics push away anyone who confronts them about their using and drinking. I made excuses and tried to protect the person when friends pointed out warning signs or bad behavior. I would actually end up projecting the criticism I should have used for the guy I was with onto my good-intentioned friends. For example: "Lindsay is just really judgmental and narrow-minded." Instead of thinking clearly: "Lindsay's right, it's a total deal breaker that the guy I'm dating didn't tell me about the kid he has with another girl."

I was constantly in an adrenalized state of fear and uncertainty, but it never occurred to me to leave the relationship. I mistook the ominous anxiety in the pit in my stomach for "passion" and "butterflies." In some relationships I cried so much that I might as well have been dating an actual onion. Also, as a society can we stop confusing everyone by romanticizing that tingling feeling we get in our stomachs by calling it "butterflies"? Maybe we can use a less attractive bug that actually reflects the macabre nature of what our physiology is trying to tell us? Maybe, like, a flesh-eating maggot, or to stay on theme with this chapter, an earwig?

I chose people who made me feel anxious and insecure and re-created my childhood circumstances of getting erratic attention. I gravitated toward people who were either physically or emotionally unavailable to subconsciously ensure I was getting a constant hit from my "internal drug cabinet." Instead of heroin or cocaine, I used to be addicted to cortisol and adrenaline (which turns into dopamine! Yay!). That drove me to pick people who couldn't give me safety or stability, which caused those chemicals to go buck wild on my brain. You live in London? Yes, please. You work until three A.M., and when you are available, you're super tired, so every time we have the chance to connect, your eyes are half closed? Sure, let's move in together. One day you tell me you're in love with me, but then you disappear and go on a week-long bender on Long Island? Absolutely. You travel for four months at a time in places that have horrible cell service? Don't mind if I do marry ya.

I found myself in numerous relationships at once, out of fear that one would end or that I'd be abandoned. From what I understand, this is a classic addict move. We hoard our supply or always have a backup plan for how to get a hit of our drug. I mean, no self-respecting addict has only one drug dealer.

There are many more elements to love addiction that I could mention, but I want this book to be able to fit into your carry-on bag. Also, I'm going to keep it specific to my deal because I can't speak for anyone but myself in terms of how it manifests. At first I couldn't wrap my head around the concept of love addiction, but it really helped to use the metaphor of drug or food addiction, since I was told by people way smarter than me that it's all basically the same neurological reactions, even if we all pick different drugs. My excuses are all pretty congruous with how other addicts talk when they minimize their behavior to justify using substances: "I only do blow on the weekends"; or someone I know who just got a DUI saying, "But I'm only drinking beer now instead of whiskey"; or "But red wine is actually supposed to be good for you! So many antioxidants!" I employed those same types of rationalizations with guys who were terrible for me: "So what if he cheated before? His girlfriend was so mean to him!" "A little conflict is good for me. He calls me out on my shit!" "We're going to see each other four times a week now instead of every night" as if making a schedule would magically change a person's values.

I once heard addiction being described in a way that resonated with me to a chilling degree: "It was great for a while. Then it stopped being fun, but I didn't know how to stop." That's how I felt my romantic relationships were. They always started with Netflix and chill and ended in incriminating pix and being physically ill. I realized that after all the initial dopamine wore off in the first year, I wasn't enjoying relationships, I was enduring them.

My brain continued to fight the idea of having an addiction, which is apparently pretty typical of addictive brains, so to add insult to injury, on top of being an addict I was also unoriginal. I argued with Vera about how it's a biological imperative to want to pair up with people and breed. "Maybe it's just my biological clock . . . Without love we'd have no species. We'd be extinct!" I reasoned. I now understood why they call addiction "the disease that tells you that you don't have a disease."

My brain would play emotional Twister all day long to avoid coming to terms with this diagnosis. I blamed Disney movies, romance novels, magazines, social constructs, the Beatles. They told me all you need is love. Isn't that what life is all about? Finding a soul mate? A partner? Jerry Maguire said "You complete me," which means we're incomplete without another person, right? ALL YOU NEED IS LOVE.

"But all you need is love," I said to Vera.

It took saying that out loud to realize how unhealthy that song lyric is. The song doesn't say, "All you need is love, but when you get it, you should still put yourself first, have boundaries, and keep your social life. You also need sleep, health insurance, and of course food and water. Also, don't forget love isn't supposed to cause you anxiety or stress! And when you're in love with some-one, you should also *like* them. And get a prenup!" I have a feeling if the song were written that way it wouldn't be in the iTunes Top 100, but it would have set some more sane expectations about what we actually need. I was operating under the mentality that every-thing I did, made, and smeared on my face was in the name of current or future "love."

I can't imagine hearing that you're an addict or that you have a "disease" is ever fun, but once it sunk in for me, I actually felt a huge sense of relief and freedom. Since addiction isn't a choice, it made me feel way better about my ridiculous behavior in the past. Running from guy to guy, thinking a breakup was the end of the world, staring at my phone—it was all part of a neural wiring sys-tem that science could explain. I didn't actually believe that post-ing a photo of me having fun on social media would make an ex appreciate me more, my disease just tricked me into thinking it would. Whew.

Again, how does this relate to Billy and my ear, which now looks like a melted candle? Well, I don't want to anthropomorphize Billy too much because comparing him to a human is actually pretty degrading. Dogs are way cooler than people, but what I did with him was a microcosmic version of what I tended to do in rela-tionships. Vera told me that love addicts tend to confuse love with pity, or in my case, a pitty. They also get into intense relationships with people they can "rescue." Yup. As soon as I saw Billy suffer-ing in a photo on Instagram, there was no turning back. My brain tells me that I'm the only person who can understand someone, save someone, that they *need me*. To be fair, Billy actually did need someone, because he's voiceless, but other humans don't need me unless they're dying of blood loss during the apocalypse and I am the only person left on earth with their blood type.

The more people warned me that Billy was dangerous, the more I wanted to protect him. Similarly, when people warned me about guys, it only made me want to commit to the guy more because I now had skin in the game in the form of my ego. In the past, any time I heard something negative about a guy I was dating, it strangely bonded me to him. We developed our "it's us against the world" type of relationship where we adhered to each other based on the delusion that nobody understood us. I wanted that Romeo and Juliet/Eminem and Kim Mathers type of love. And yes, I realize this is the second time I've referenced Eminem in this chapter, which actually makes a lot of sense since he's at the top of the list of people with whom I'd like to be in an addictive relationship. I'm clearly also addicted to referencing him.

When I was a kid, I read *Romeo and Juliet*. I know Shakespeare is amazing and all, but I am very confused about why schools think it's a good idea for kids to read this play while still formulating a blueprint about how relationships should look. But I guess for me the damage had already been done, because I remember reading that they committed suicide and thinking it was an excellent solution to their problem. As a teenager, I watched *Sid and Nancy* and thought it was the most romantic movie I'd ever seen. This is not a healthy reaction to either of these stories.

I was an expert at ignoring negative information about romantic prospects. I used to see a red flag, and if it wasn't congruous with my plans to date someone, I'd just paint it white. And Martha Stewart ain't got nothin' on me when it comes to redecorating reality, especially wallpapering over the writing on the wall.

Once I got Billy, I overlooked all the red flags that warned me to take things slow: he had a year's worth of history I knew nothing about; he was untrained; he had a mouth full of tiny razors. I gave him credit for things he shouldn't get credit for—for example, "He was so good with my dogs!" Like a guy calling you on the phone, this is something to file under THINGS YOU DON'T GET POINTS FOR. I did the same thing with men. I constantly gave points to men for things that should be filed under "the least you can do." My girlfriends forced smiles when I announced, "He didn't yell at me for checking luggage! Isn't he amazing!?" Having a low bar is a lovely place to be for a while because everything that happens is a dazzling delight. Every day is like a surprise party. He didn't cheat on me today? He's *the one*. He's not addicted to gang-bang porn? My knight in shining armor!

The engine of my addictive behavior for sure involved an adrenaline addiction, but also an intense fear of abandonment. I didn't see the madness in this fearful thinking until one day Vera realized what was going on and dropped a bomb on me: "Adults can't be abandoned, Whitney. You have a car. You have a house. Adults can only abandon themselves."

Bang. Tweet it, blog it. Retweet it, screen-grab it.

A big part of addiction involves managing your supply. This means that basically you go apeshit when your "supply" is threatened. Managing my supply manifested itself in some really sad and expensive ways: not traveling too far from home and/or going with the guy I was dating wherever he went. I mean, he did invite me, I didn't just follow him like a crazy stalker, but I often found myself sitting alone in a hotel room watching cat videos when I could have been way happier sitting alone in *my* room watching cat videos. I spent countless parties and weddings distracted and paranoid, on my phone, getting my hits of the guy I was dating instead of enjoying the present company. I remember spending an entire bachelorette party buried in my phone texting with my drug of choice when I could have been having way more fun doing actual drugs with my friends.

When love addiction takes hold, my world gets very small. When Billy came into my life, he became my primary focus. I sent my other dogs to be boarded so I could focus solely on him and make him feel special. I was so worried about him feeling alone that I rushed home from work early to see him, speeding through stoplights, texting and driving, weaving in and out of cars. If active alcoholics drink and drive, perhaps love addicts text and drive. This is the behavior driven by the engine of an addictive brain: when in order to get our perceived emotional needs met, we put our physical selves in danger.

After working with Vera, I now understand love should not be urgent or stressful. It should not make my life harder, and I should not be risking my health or safety when I'm in a relationship. If I can't keep my priorities straight when I'm with a person, I'm gonna have to face it, I'm addicted to love.

Love addiction is about being addicted to a person and all the neurochemicals being with that person triggers, and before I had a game plan to manage it, I can't even describe how scary it was. *Obsession* is a word that's thrown around a lot about things like froyo, binge-worthy TV shows, and a perfume I wore in the nineties, but when you have an addictive brain, obsession can be crippling. And my addiction doesn't discriminate; it doesn't have standards or good taste. In fact, usually the more damaging the person in my life is, the stronger my addiction can be. The stronger the heroin, the higher a person's tolerance can get and the more addicted they become. I never got addicted to a relationship with a nice college grad who did charity work because that was too safe; it wouldn't provide the adrenaline that fed my addiction. I never particularly liked or respected any of the relationships I was addicted to, yet my brain told me I couldn't live without them. One guy was a clinical narcissist with a cocaine habit, one was a night-club promoter, one was super into drag racing . . . so the truth is, I'd probably have died *with them*.

A week or so after the incident, I took Billy to get an aggression test from Brandon McMillan, a very badass dog trainer and animal behaviorist, to find out if Billy had aggression issues that were insurmountable. I was terrified. If it had not been for the painkillers I was taking for my ear, I never could have handled the anxiety of possibly finding out that he attacked me on purpose. To ascertain if Billy was aggressive, I watched Brandon do a series of exercises to test Billy. With a foam arm contraption, Brandon put Billy in situations where even nonaggressive dogs would have retaliated, cornering him against a wall, causing him stress on purpose to see if he would react in a maladaptive way. Billy didn't bite or even growl, even when his life seemed to be at stake. I beamed with pride. Turns out he wasn't inherently violent, he just had the tricky combination of no impulse control and big giant teeth, which I can relate to. I was relieved to learn that he wasn't the asshole, I was. The good news is I wasn't totally delusional about Billy, but per usual, I was delusional about who to let into my bed on the first night we met.

Since the Billy debacle, I've learned a lot about what happened that day and why. A lot of it was my fault. I know now that I should never have let him in the bed with me or lie on top of me all night because that's actually a dominant behavior that I conflated with us being soul mates. It was selfish of me to cave in and allow adorable selfie-worthy behavior to eclipse what was best for Billy and our relationship. What he needed was discipline and clear boundaries. I got so swept up in "loving" him that I forgot to actually love him. This was not fair to Billy because it set him up to fail. He had no training or coping mechanisms yet, so he made an honest mistake. The problem is that when small dogs make mistakes, you might get a scratch on your ankle, but when pit bulls make mistakes, you end up looking like a cubist painting.

When I saw his sweet face and learned that he was abused, I threw all logic and reason out the window. I felt entitled to the happiness Disney movies promised me as a kid. I wanted love to conquer all, I wanted love to be blind, I wanted us to be soul mates, everything Céline Dion said on the *Titanic* soundtrack. As Carrie Bradshaw said in the finale of *Sex and the City*, which was later plagiarized by a *Bachelor* contestant and now me, "I'm looking for love. Real love. Ridiculous, inconvenient, consuming can't-live-without-each-other love." I wanted to be Carrie and I wanted Billy to be Mr. Big.

Billy wasn't Mr. Big, but he did become my teacher. It took losing an ear for me to learn to take it slow with people, friends, work relationships, house hunting, hair color decisions, and the animals I bring into my home.

Today I try to take people at face value instead of projecting my hopes and dreams onto them. I no longer believe people change unless they're working their asses off to change. And someone saying they want change doesn't count. Downloading an app of daily meditations does not count as changing either. Someone saying they want to do work or intend to do work doesn't count as actual work. Me doing work for them does not count as them doing work. If these adages had only been in a fortune cookie when I was sixteen, I would have saved a lot of time and money in two A.M. cab rides to weird neighborhoods and getting into fights about Facebook comments. I no longer think my "love" can change someone's neurology or value system, which is huge progress given I truly used to think that a well-written Valentine's Day card outlining how much I love someone was going to do in one day what psychotherapy can hardly do in ten years.

Of course, being a pit bull myself and also having had very little impulse control training, I ran right at Billy a thousand miles an hour. I didn't want him to live in fear for another minute, I wanted him to have the love he deserved. In doing so, I forgot a crucial thing: The kind of love I wanted to give him was not the kind of love he actually needed at that stage in our relationship. He wanted hugs and kisses and constant affection that would never end, but what he needed was a careful kind of love, a methodical love that would make him feel safe by providing safety and structure, not one that would implode from impossibly high expectations and enmeshment. As I write this, I'm realizing that I'm not even sure what the definition of love is or should be. Unlike Forrest Gump, I may not know what love is, but I certainly know what it isn't: It isn't urgent, it isn't stressful, it isn't about pity. I don't think that to love someone else you should have to abandon yourself. I should probably write things like "Love is about loving yourself first" or

"You have to be in a relationship with yourself before you can be with someone else," but I'm not a motivational speaker or an expert on love and I don't want this book to read like an annoying Pinterest feed.

I learned a lot the day I had my ear bitten off. I learned that cartilage doesn't heal the same way bones do. I learned that we should all memorize at least three people's phone numbers and I learned to never underestimate a cute blond nurse even though porn has conditioned us to. I learned that blood hardens like nail polish, and that my blood tastes like sweet-and-sour soup. One of the most important things I learned is that sometimes we file very unhealthy behaviors under the term *love*. I feel really lucky to have learned this in a dramatic enough way for me to pay attention, but not so bad that I couldn't live to tell about it. If it hadn't been for Billy, who woke me up and inspired me to rethink my behavior in relationships, I'd probably be married to some sicko and trying to raise a kid my baby daddy named after himself.

When I think back on that surreal moment, I really do feel lucky. Given all the other ways it could have gone, I have to admit that the way it all turned out is something of a miracle. And for those of you who still think pit bulls are inherently bad or that he did indeed attack me, I promise you that if he truly wanted to kill me, he could have done so in an instant. If you take a look at the alligator jaw that dog was born with, it's hard to imagine how he did as little damage as he did. If he had nibbled anywhere else on my face, I'd look like spaghetti Bolognese.

As you may know, a dog's mouth is his "hands," so perhaps he was grabbing me by the ear the way a strict mother would to teach me what I needed to learn. I'm not looking at the event as a near miss to put in the rearview mirror. I want to hold on to what happened as an important reminder to slow down in relationships instead of diving in headfirst, without knowing if there's any water in the pool. The goal for me now is to slow down and play things by ear. Sorry, I couldn't help myself.

The scar on my ear is still prominent, and it didn't totally attach symmetrically at the top, but I like it this way. I mean, ears are incredibly weird, so now mine is just weird in a different way. Even if I look like half a Hobbit, it's a lesson that'll always be right there when I need it. Today all I have to do is look in the mirror and be reminded how quickly I can end up sabotaging myself if I get into an addictive relationship.

My wonky ear reminds me on a daily basis not to confuse love with sympathy or rescuing someone with intimacy. I no longer let myself get emotionally attached to people who confuse me, deplete me, or pose a danger to me. Although danger is the ultimate aphrodisiac for me, such behavior is a negative contribution to my future. As Vera says, "If you're attracted to someone, that's a red flag." So if I'm too magnetically attracted to a person, that probably means something else is going on, like I'm getting adrenaline from their craziness, which means I may not get to date them, the same way I don't get to eat pizza for every meal or buy every pair of vintage cowboy boots I see online at two A.M.

My Van Gogh ear is a gift from Billy. Every day it'll remind me to meet others the way they are, not how I want them to be. It'll remind me to practice a patient love, a love where boundaries, self-respect, and self-love come first. Most of all, it will remind me to be humble. Especially on bad hair days when my hair is up in a bun.

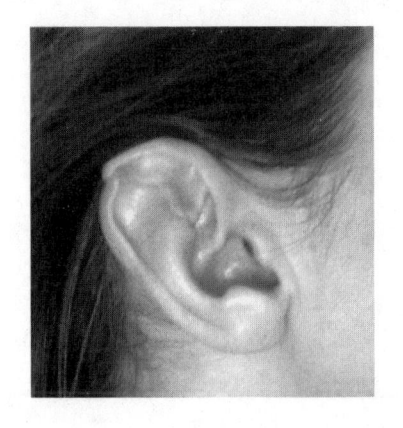

See? My ear is totally fine.

THE MIDDLE EAST CHAPTER

According to *The Guardian* newspaper, I'm the first woman comedian to do stand-up in the Middle East. I have no idea if that's true. I'd Google it, but I'm too afraid I'll be put on a watch list or something. Plus, if *The Guardian* says it's true, that's between them and their fact checkers.

That said, there's no way it's true. I've met tons of Persian women in Beverly Hills, and they're hilarious. Plus, the Sphinx was a female, and she told the world's best riddle 4,500 years ago, which I think caused people to die if they didn't answer it correctly. So like all great comedians, she killed.

If I'm the first woman to perform stand-up in the Middle East, that would be very cool, but a dubious honor because I would have liked for a Middle Eastern woman to have been the first woman to do stand-up in the Middle East. Maybe that just wasn't in the cards. Although I'm flattered, it pisses me off that Middle Eastern women wouldn't have had that opportunity. Look, there's a lot of heavy, third-rail emotion swirling around everything Middle Eastern and I'm not going to pretend to be any kind of authority on it, but what I do know is that all my life I've been drawn to things that make me uncomfortable—and not just karaoke, eye contact, and Spanx.

Like any uncomfortable topic, the Middle East is a very important and flammable one. There have been many comprehensive books about the layers of complexities of female identity in the Arab world. I haven't read them and this isn't one of them, but I do have a friend named Ahmed Ahmed, a comedian who organizes comedy tours all over the Middle East, and he asked if I wanted to go to Dubai and Lebanon with them. He warned me that female stand-ups weren't really a thing in the Middle East, although from what I knew, females were treated exactly like they were, well, things. He couldn't guarantee my act would be well received, but I jumped at the chance because at the time I wasn't being received particularly well in a lot of places in America either. I probably should have been scared, but I was doing shows in parking lots in downtown L.A. at the time, so nothing really scared me anymore.

Like any American, I had heard plenty of stories in the news about sexism and misogyny in the Arab world—reports about girls being deprived of their basic freedoms and education, and of grown women in Saudi Arabia being banned from driving. Everybody I knew was obsessed with that particular injustice, the not-being-allowed-to-drive thing—that was like the final straw for people in L.A. In America the idea of women not being allowed to drive is, of course, outrageous. Instead of being unable to drive, we just get constantly made fun of and meme'd for being bad at it.

I figured that this trip could be an opportunity to help out with all of this. Perhaps I could go to the Middle East and use stand-up as a way to show men that women could be in control without breaking things, be slightly masculine without the world collapsing, and have an opinion without anything catching on fire. For the women, maybe I could be a role model. By doing stand-up, I could show them how to, maybe even literally, stand up for themselves. Perhaps I could inspire them to fight their oppression and live their dreams. I saw myself as Liam Neeson, jumping into action to smuggle these people out of the Stone Age. I may not have had Liam Neeson's very specific set of skills, given that my abilities didn't involve masterfully killing people, but they did involve telling *Cosmo* magazine and Myspace jokes. Be nice. It was 2007.

I'm already terrible at packing for trips, but packing to go to the Middle East was particularly challenging. I usually pack for every possible catastrophic scenario. I'm the person who packs an umbrella to go to the desert and sunscreen to go to Scotland. But packing for the Middle East was slightly more daunting because the catastrophes didn't live only in my paranoid head. It seemed like dangerous things really did happen there. I made about twelve copies of my passport and packed a comical amount of lip balm, but I wasn't sure what clothing to pack, since women expressing themselves over there didn't seem like a big hit. From what I gathered, women had to cover up most of their bodies, but I also gathered that it was incredibly hot, so I was confused about what to pack. I settled on everything I owned.

My experience in the Middle East started the moment we boarded Emirates Airlines. The plane was very modern, and the flight attendants were tall, beautiful, and impeccably dressed, like the central casting Pan Am stewardesses in that Leonardo DiCaprio movie. Perfect skin, perfect bodies, perfect lipstick, not one flyaway hair on their heads despite constantly flying. That said, I was perplexed by the color choice of their bespoke lady suits. *Beige.* Possibly the most neutral color available. I had never seen a flight attendant in beige, and wondered why anyone would pick such a noncolor that doesn't look good on anyone except maybe Viola Davis. A color that flatters no one, but also offends no one. Interesting. Right off the bat I got the message: Don't offend anyone. Just fit in. Be beige.

Luckily I was seated next to Sebastian Maniscalco, another comedian on the tour. Sebastian became my lifelong friend despite having to sit next to me for the duration of a fourteen-hour flight. I fumbled with the TV, trying to take a selfie with the map-screen thingie, and when the world map came up to show us where we were flying, I made the big mistake of asking him "Are we going over Hawaii?"

I'm not sure why I even asked that. I had always wanted to go to Hawaii, and maybe flying over it would have been sufficient for me at that point. Sebastian seemed more disgusted than shocked by my question. He couldn't understand how a person could get on a plane and not know which direction they were flying. I was a very lost person at that point in my life, so the direction of the Middle East from L.A. wasn't even in the top ten directions I needed to focus on.

After fourteen hours of watching prison documentaries, we finally landed. The pilot said that we were in Dubai, but from above it looked way more like a three-dimensional Candy Land. I had never seen anything like it, not even in video games, not even in my dreams, not even on LSD. It was glittery and glossy and colorful—as if a bunch of five-year-olds were given a billion dollars and used giant fancy silverware to build a city. It's like a Disney movie, but with a dark, unsettling undercurrent. Malice in Wonderland, perhaps.

The most fascinating part of Dubai is the bipolar nature of it: It's both modern and old world, ancient and futuristic at the same time, everything colliding in a frenzy of hypocritical mixed messages. Giant indoor ski slopes have been built next to thousand-year-old mosques. It kind of felt like the city version of your ninety-year-old grandma getting brand-new breast implants.

At the bottom of a new hotel under construction, I saw a plethora of Rolls-Royces, but at the top of the building, emaciated, sweating laborers worked in the scalding sun for minuscule pay. The juxtaposition of old and new, high and low, rich and poor made Dubai seem to me like the city version of a girl wearing a miniskirt with Ugg boots. This city just refuses to pick a lane.

Although the extreme wealth and caste system was upsetting, it wasn't why I was there. I had to stay focused on the treatment of women. But how would I find them and rescue them if they were all holed up, unable to drive or read? Do I embark on a door-to-door deal like the Mormons? Or maybe like a Mary Kay saleslady, since the Middle East seems pretty set in terms of having committed to a religion? Should I hand out flyers letting everyone know that I had landed and was ready to inspire them? I guess I was just going to have to really "lean in" and scale the walls of the tyrannical domiciles to find which women needed rescuing. Look, nobody said being a hero was going to be easy.

Imagine my surprise when we got to the hotel and everywhere I looked there were women, but not the type of women I expected to see. I thought they'd all be in opaque flowing garb, covering everything but their hollow eyes, floating around like cartoon ghosts. Instead, I saw women in—gasp—jeans, short shorts, belly-baring tops, strappy sandals. I was very confused. This was *not* the Middle East I signed up to save! I went to the pool of my hotel and women were in *bathing suits*! Some of them didn't even seem to be wearing sunscreen, much less a hijab. I thought I was going to have to help these women fight oppression by giving them permission to remove their garb, but every woman I saw made me turn into a mom and want to cover them up.

I was quickly informed that my hotel and the area I was staying was filled with mostly tourists and high-class prostitutes, so I wasn't getting a real sample of what the Middle East was really like. Hanging there was like eating spaghetti from the Olive Garden and saying you're Italian, so I was gonna have to venture out of the westernized bubble I was staying in to actively seek the women I needed to rescue. After all, Liam Neeson didn't just mosey on over to France and bump into his daughter's captors at the Auntie Anne's Pretzel stand at Charles de Gaulle. He had to seek her out. Oppressed women weren't going to be in my hotel lobby waiting for me. I was going to have to track them down, so I decided to go where all sad, oppressed people who don't work or drive usually hang out: the mall.

The mall was the most mall-y mall I've ever been to. The mall in Dubai makes the Mall of America look like one Lego. It's kind of like an airport with shops you'd actually want to shop at. The moment I got there, I found exactly what I was looking for. Well, the two things I was looking for. I found bootleg designer purses, but more importantly, I found women in hijabs and even some in burkas.

If you don't know the difference, don't worry, neither did I back then, and to be fair, I probably still don't. What I gather from my Middle Eastern friends and Wikipedia is that the hijab looks like a headscarf that covers the head and ears, but not necessarily the face, whereas the burka covers women completely. There's also something called a niqab, which is essentially a remix of both: a burka that leaves the eye area clear. There are other incarnations of these, like a shayla, a khimar, and a chador, but I don't know enough about this to tell you the real difference, and frankly, I'm worried the Internet doesn't know either, especially since I've gotten two Google alerts in the past five years giving me breaking news that I died.

Seeing the burkas in person was a real bummer. And not like the buying-a-jumpsuit-online, then getting-it-in-the-mail-and-realizing-only-JLo-could-successfully-wear-it kind of bummer. It was more of the heartbreak variety of bummer. I had only seen burkas in horrific post–9/11 news footage and seeing them in person sent chills down my spine.

They looked nothing like what I thought they would. Maybe it's the tragic romantic in me, but for some reason I expected them to at least be kind of pretty, made of diaphanous fabrics, gorgeous colors, and ornate beaded designs. I guess my naive brain assumed that women must have agreed to this uniform because it was undeniably luxurious and—I don't know—somehow worth it. I also thought, wrongly of course, that everything in the Middle East was beautiful, comprised of silks, golds, and unicorn dreams. My ignorance isn't surprising given the extent of my experience with the Middle East included watching parts of *Lawrence of Arabia* and dozing off while my niece watched *Aladdin*.

Imagine my surprise when I discovered that most of the burkas and hijabs were made of cheap-looking fabrics, as if the whole thing was more a synthetic formality than a sacred ritual rooted in traditional beliefs. I didn't understand how such an ancient cultural norm could have such an ersatz incarnation. I guess I assumed, or at least hoped, they were still using intricate handmade fabrics that were threaded during the time the beliefs actually came about. But no, no. Most of the burkas and hijabs I saw were made of a cheap black fabric, which to me felt like it added insult to injury.

These women are made to wear these fabrics 24/7 and the fabric isn't even soft? For me, that was the straw that broke the camel's back. Another thing I expected to see based on movies but didn't get to see: a camel! The Middle East really needs to work on its PR.

I know this is starting to sound shallow, but what I'm trying to say is that the hijabs were especially jarring to me because they looked *so modern*. So . . . made in China. I guess the root of my confusion was that in this day and age, hijabs and burkas were still being manufactured. I figured, or at least hoped, that the women were still using leftover ones from when subjugating women was more universal. But no, they were still churning out new ones. It dawned on me that there was a factory that had many machines churning these things out. It blew my mind that a bunch of people go to work every day and their job is to make new batches of these oppressive garments. America still has corset factories or whatever, but they're more for strippers and spicing up fading marriages, not because women are still required to wear them. I guess I was under the assumption that women having to cover themselves was being phased out, a tradition for the older generation, like VHS tapes or Quaaludes.

Even if younger girls were wearing them, I assumed theirs were passed on from generations before them, and that maybe there was something poignant or ceremonial about wearing your grandmother's garments. Maybe that was part of why they wore them, for posterity, I rationalized. I'm not sure if I'm making sense, but it was just hard for me to process that *new* burkas were being made, that this wasn't an obsolete trend that was on the way out. These weren't like ephemeral jelly bracelets or stone-washed overall shorts. These getups were here to stay.

My theory was confirmed by the kiosks in the mall that sold hijabs. In America kiosks sell dream catchers; in Dubai they sold nightmares: cheap, tacky fabric that women are forced to wear because they're thought of as inferior. As if that weren't bad enough, they have to *go to a mall* to get one. As if being oppressed isn't bad enough, they had to drive around and look for parking? There was no ceremony, no passing down the fabrics with harps playing and light hitting the gorgeous skin of the women receiving them? It was much less cinematic. They just grabbed some hijabs on sale between buying socks and picking up toilet paper.

I didn't know how or what to feel, but from what I could tell, I was, per usual, in a state of total hypocrisy: insulted by the lack of respect toward a symbol I disdained. If these women had to be confined and hidden in these fabrics, they should at least be pretty, special, and breathable, I thought. I was, very obviously, missing the point.

I had a momentary crack in my self-righteousness long enough to realize that I was staring at these women very creepily. I looked them up and down as if they couldn't see me. I was outraged by how they were treated as subhuman, yet there I was, objectifying them as if I was watching them on a TV screen.

They stared back at me, unflinching. It seems as if they felt my judgmental gaze and were determined to let me know that they were just as judgmental about me. This is before I traveled the world enough to know that many people around the world disdain Americans and our values, just like how I had a preconceived disdain for theirs. The women in hijabs and I ogled one another with the same wonder and patronizing compassion in our eyes. I got into a few staring matches with a couple different women, but each time I was always the one who got nervous, always the first to look away, pretending I got a call on a cell phone that didn't even have international service. These women may have been oppressed, but they certainly weren't shy.

I was taken aback by this whole situation because I was anticipating that the women would be meek, scared, beaten down. I thought they'd be mere shells of themselves given they had been treated like they were worthless for so long that maybe they finally started believing it. But it felt to me like they knew I was making that assumption and were trying to tell me with their eyes that my assumption was wrong. They didn't want me to pity them. The older women intimidated me too much for me to approach them, but I came across a group of younger girls sitting on a bench, laughing gregariously. Since I'm constitutionally unable to mind my own business, I was dying to ask them a million questions. They all had their heads covered with hijabs, but paired them with very fashion-forward, youthful outfits. Some even seemed to be intentionally coordinated, as if they had numerous hijabs so they could mix and match them with various outfits. I found it particularly, well, ironic that a couple of them paired their headscarf with a tiny tank top and Daisy Dukes. This felt like it should be offensive—pairing what seemed to be sacred tradition of muting sexuality with a modern expression of aggressive sexuality—but, again, this country refused to pick a lane. Regardless, I was very confused. Were they allowed to show skin or not? My brain couldn't compute what kind of oppression I was dealing with.

The girls looked about twenty-five, but when I mentally removed all the makeup from the faces of those who were actually revealing their faces, I deduced that they were probably closer to twenty-one. They were cracking jokes, taking selfies, and texting. They seemed *so American,* I thought. But then I realized that having that thought is *so American.* The point is, these were young, impressionable women. Our girls. Our world's future. Being oppressed and abused, being forced to cover their heads and faces with scarves. They must be saved, I thought. And who better to save them than an American girl with some dick jokes and eight grand in credit card debt?

I wanted them to know that nothing that was put in their heads was true. They could go to school, marry whomever they wanted, and have kids when they were forty—that is, if they even wanted kids at all. Did they know they could be anything they wanted in life? That they could run the world? I took a deep breath and sauntered over to the girls in headscarves, with my head covered in nothing but a bad dye job.

"Excuse me? Can I ask you a question?" I asked, speaking too loudly, enunciating every syllable. I'm not sure if it's a uniquely American thing to assume that saying a language loudly makes someone immediately learn it, but that's what I did. As if that wasn't embarrassing enough, they spoke flawless English.

The girl who responded first had her face almost completely covered by a hijab. She was breathing heavily, which I could tell from the fabric fluttering around her mouth. It was surprising to me that the girl who was the most covered up was also the most confident in responding to me. Did the covering of the face act as a sort of shield? Did it oddly empower them because of their anonymity, the way the Internet does for trolls? My head was swirling with guesses about what happens to someone's personality when their physicality and identity are removed from the equation.

"So, I can ask you a question?" I asked again.

She responded with a simple and powerful "yes."

She didn't say "Sure." She said *yes*. If someone asked me if they could talk to me, I would say "Sure," a more apologetic affirmation, which half the time means "I want to say no but I'm too worried you'll be mad." This girl said yes. With the one word I had heard her say, she was already more direct and self-possessed than I have ever been.

I responded with some version of "I'm just curious if wearing headscarves makes you feel oppressed at all?"

They laughed. A lot. Now I was the one being looked at as if I was from the Dark Ages.

I remember what one of the girls said verbatim: "We are not oppressed. We see American women as oppressed. You're judged by your appearance, the women get plastic surgery, everyone has an eating disorder. We aren't judged on our looks."

Damn. That's not how I thought that was gonna go down.

Before we process how wrong and reductive I was about the Middle East, let's address how wrong and reductive this girl was about America. Although we seemed like total opposites, we did have one thing in common: We both had no clue what the other person's life was like. I mean, yes, I personally had corrective surgery and an eating disorder and am judged by my appearance on a daily basis. In fact I'm often lambasted for it, so the girl was on to something, but not all American women go through that, right? RIGHT?

The girls, seemingly all at once, explained to me that they didn't feel subjugated by their traditional garb. They very assertively stated that they were relieved that they didn't have to obsess about their hair or makeup, even though the ones whose faces I could see were wearing some makeup. When I timidly pointed that out, they explained that if they didn't want to wear makeup or didn't have time to put it on, they'd choose a headscarf that covered more of their face. If they wanted to wear makeup, they'd cover less. I wasn't sure if this was a traumatized person's rationalization for their oppression or a genius life hack, but regardless they felt that they didn't have to spend time and money trying to mirror a socially constructed ideal of beauty. They could if they wanted to, but were not bound to it. Suddenly my face not being covered by a scarf was actually frustrating because I really wanted to hide my confusion.

Although I'm horrified by the way women are institutionally treated in conservative parts of the Middle East, I was able to see the point being made here. Whether they were trying to convince me or convince themselves, I could see how hijabs could be self-empowering if it helped them remove the obsession with being physically perfect. It made me think about how I couldn't leave the house without concealer under my eyes, how I had wasted days of my life trying to glue on false eyelashes, applying and reapplying liquid eyeliner because it's impossible to get straight, and lasering every hair off my body. I'm ashamed to say I've looked into tattoo eyebrow filling more than once.

Even if I go in my backyard alone, I have to put stuff on my face. If I don't put on sunscreen, I'll look like a basketball by three P.M. The tradition of women covering themselves is obviously rooted in oppressive sexist lunacy, but these girls were making it work for them, perhaps reclaiming it in a powerful feminist way. Then again, maybe they were rationalizing something abusive. I don't know which was actually happening, but regardless, it made me think: Being able to cover my face with something other than a handful of expensive chemicals did sound pretty nice.

Even though the girls threw a little shade my way, they seemed grateful that I was at least asking about their situation instead of digging my heels into my assumptions. At least I was a smart enough American to know I was a stupid American.

The girls retaliated with many questions of their own, which was also surprising to me. I'm not sure why, after ten minutes of talking to confident, opinionated women, I was still shocked by the fact that Middle Eastern women are confident and opinionated, but my brain was clearly very resistant to updating its paradigm. Maybe it was jet lag, maybe it was arrogance, maybe it was self-preservation rooted in the tribal need to malign the "other," but my brain just could not trust that what they were saying was true. The girls asked if I ever felt obligated by the constant scrutiny that Western culture put on my body, my face, my appearance. I responded the only way I knew how: I lied and pretended the answer was no.

They saw through my bullshit immediately. As I said, the fabric over their eyes was very poorly made, so they could easily see that my face was full of doubt.

I guess I just wanted the answer to be no so badly. I wanted to be a feminist role model coming in from the utopian West to save the day with my shining example of bravery and self-acceptance. But to my surprise and chagrin, I wasn't a good example. I was wearing Invisalign orthodontics over a set of teeth that had already had braces for two years, and *clear* ones at that. Even at twelve years old, when it was socially acceptable to have a row of chompers covered in cumbersome metal and colored rubber bands, I was so insecure that I begged for clear braces. And by clear I mean whatever color of the food I just ate was.

I saw no irony in accusing these girls of wearing something oppressive whilst I was strapped into a bra with metal wires rubbing against my ribs—ribs that were showing, since I was constantly dieting. I conveniently left out the constant exfoliating, teasing, dyeing, tanning, bronzing, eye shadowing, plucking, threading, shaving, steaming, cortisone-shot-ting, derma-roller-ing, pore shrinking, cuticle cutting, teeth whitening, dry shampooing, lip-liner-ing, eyelash-extension-ing, Spinning, squatting, juicing, and airbrushing photos.

After all, I was indeed wearing my own version of traditional obscuring garb, just Western-style. I had spent time and money getting my hair the right color and the right texture. I had spent years finding the lip stain that made me look like I wasn't a corpse. Every morning I put foundation on my face to cover up my flaws and minimize my pores. I was spraying my face with self-tanner on a daily basis, and I got painful weekly facials to make my skin look younger. These girls were hitting a nerve. Suddenly, I had hijab envy.

I thought the hijab was designed to make women invisible. But these women were telling me they felt more confident in their individualism and their personalities because they weren't constantly being scrutinized on their looks.

Brain explode.

Now, let me take a moment to say that I'm not trying to trivialize a garment that has been so degrading to so many women. I'm fully aware that these girls could have been completely delusional, been brainwashed to think such things, have had Stockholm syndrome, or have been lying to me or to themselves. They could also have been the only four girls in the Middle East who felt this way. I'm not an anthropologist or sociologist; at the end of the day I might just be an alarmist who sounds like a chauvinist.

The Middle Eastern girls I met may not have had schooling or equality, but they sure as hell had self-esteem. Could it be that although they were victims, taking your looks out of the equation could breed higher self-worth, even if you're in an archaic culture that victimizes you? How could these girls be more confident and self-assured than I was? I mean, after all, I'm American, confidence is supposed to be my thing.

I want to blame the business I'm in for my self-consciousness and insecurity, but unfortunately I can't. This physical obsession thing started way before I had ever done television. I shudder to think that my experience is probably fairly typical of most American girls: worrying about what to wear, how to tone up, how shimmery my eyes should be. My brain started doing something it hates doing: math. I put it together that I spent an hour a day on my appearance, times 365 days a year . . . 365 hours a year?

That's more than fifteen days. A year.

If I live until I'm eighty, that's 160-plus weeks of my life spent putting expensive creamy poison on my face.

I thought about all the other things I could do with that time. I could learn a language, travel the world, open a ranch for rescue animals, build a school in Africa—not that I could afford to do any of those things, but still. I was embarrassed at the amount of time I spent on my outer self, especially when my inner self was such a mess. I'm sure this is pretty standard behavior of anyone in their twenties, but with this new clarity, my priorities just felt wrong. It all felt like an institutionalized and expensive pressure and a distraction from life. In college I read *The Beauty Myth* by Naomi Wolf, which addressed a lot of these issues in a much more sophisticated way than I'm doing now, but I remember reading about how the obsession with physical perfection keeps women subjugated. I'm sure men's obsession with their appearance does the same for them, but I'm not really an expert in that department because I have a no-bathroom-sharing rule when I'm dating someone. Anyway, the book blew my mind, but I didn't have the self-awareness yet to think it applied to me. Now that I was in the Middle East, having an epiphany about my own preoccupation with appearance, I was finally ready to process it all. How could girls get ahead and accomplish their goals if their focus on physical appearance causes them to have seven less hours a week than men do? The whole thing made me sick.

Once I got back to my hotel, I had a vivid image of myself on my deathbed. I imagined what I'd be thinking as I took my last breaths. I don't know how I was dying, but I didn't look that old in my vision, which means I either think I'm gonna die young or that I'm going to get many a facelift. Anyway, I'm lying there dying. I wasn't on my deathbed thinking "I can't believe I wasted so much time on friendships! I just wished I had spent more time curling my eyelashes!" I doubt any woman on her deathbed said, "I just wished I had worn more blush! I can't believe I wasted all that stupid quality time with my dumb children!" Chances are, I'm going to look back and wish I spent more time with people I love, trying to make an impact on the world, and eating fondue.

My conversation with the girls at the mall has haunted me for years, but for that day, their self-possessed vibe gave me more confidence about going onstage in front of a Middle Eastern crowd. I had to perform in front of a couple thousand Middle Easterners in just a few hours, and I was grateful that I no longer had the irrational fear that I would get stoned by someone in the audience, even though I was so nervous that I was secretly hoping someone would find me some weed and get me the other kind of stoned.

When I go to a foreign country to perform, or even to various states in America, I'll write some specific jokes to cater to that area. People are paying money to see my show, and I feel it's only fair that I address anything I find ridiculous about their hometown. I thought about doing this for Dubai but ultimately decided not to, not only because I was completely confounded by the culture, but also because I felt I shouldn't pander to them or try to endear them to me; I should just bring my liberated brand of comedy to them to show how we progressive people get down. I would be fearless and strong, demonstrating that women could be badasses, too. Also, if I'm gonna be honest, I was also terrified of offending them or pronouncing a word wrong.

I was having trouble balancing my desire to show them how self-actualized I was with the fact that I was at a complete loss over what to wear. I tried to find the middle ground in between maintaining my identity but also respecting their norms. As much as I resented them, I knew I had to cover my body, but I wanted to do it on my terms. I thought about wearing a giant pink Snuggie, which honestly I'm always looking for an excuse to make my permanent uniform onstage anyway, but it was way too hot. Apparently, I was really into subversive statements mocking and satirizing oppressive culture as long as it didn't involve my having to sweat.

Then I thought maybe I'd wear jeans and a T-shirt—classic Americana—but that felt slightly passive-aggressive, and I much prefer being actively aggressive. I considered a dress with heels, thus looking as traditionally feminine as possible as an F-you to their suppression of femininity. The problem with that is I have literally never worn a dress, much less heels, onstage, and I figured rolling my ankle while performing would not be conducive to showing the Middle East how strong women could be.

I also considered dressing very sexy, the opposite of how traditional women dress there. Maybe that would make the point that women can be smart, strong, and sexual all at the same time, but I also wanted the women to see me as their ally. I didn't want them to think I was trying to outshine them or steal their man or something, which, frankly, maybe I would have done, given how into mean guys I was at that time in my life. Pre-therapy, a sexist Middle Eastern dude actually would have been the ultimate aphrodisiac.

I settled on bell-bottom jeans that have never been in style, New Balance sneakers, and a black slightly bedazzled blazer. I figured it was androgynous, neutral, and respectable. "Be beige." Blazers mean power, pants mean business, sneakers mean freedom and comfort. The perfect message to send, I thought. What I didn't realize is that the message I was actually sending was: In order to be respected as a woman, dress like a man. I wanted my outfit to hide my femininity, for my gender to be invisible. I'm not sure if I accomplished that, but I did accomplish looking like a sexually confused teenage boy from the seventies. Maybe this was the closest thing to a burka we had in America: dressing like a man with a full face of makeup on.

Two comics went onstage ahead of me and both did very well. Both were also men. They may have been dressed less like men than I was, but they were men nonetheless. Now, I've never been one to get nervous before I go onstage, even the first time I ever did stand-up, mostly because adrenaline and fear are sort of my comfort zone. But on this night, not only did I feel fear, I also felt pressure. Pressure to be funny of course, but also to be an example. I felt I was carrying the weight of the world on my shoulders. I felt like maybe I had to represent America, to represent women, to represent freedom. I felt like maybe if I just nailed this, all the women in the audience might reject their circumstances, wake up, and leave their oppressors. They'd see that life could be different and that they were capable of doing whatever they set their minds to! They, too, could tell dick jokes at night to strangers if they wanted to!

The other obstacle that I was facing, besides an ancient patriar-chy, was that the show was in an outdoor venue. I'm sure that the idea of doing comedy outside sounds super fun to noncomedians, but the truth is that outdoor venues are a mess because the laughs tend to dissipate into the sky instead of bouncing off walls and ceilings. So for this show all I had to rely on were my emotional walls and the glass ceiling.

I couldn't believe it was my turn to go up. I guess time flies when you're having fear. I remember being brought up with a glowing, super complimentary intro that was probably intended to get the audience on my side, but it ended up just making me feel more pressure.

Everyone asks if being a female in comedy (in America) is hard, and I never have a good answer because I feel like everyone has a hard job. It's hard to be a male and a female in any career be-cause working sucks sometimes. I shudder when I think about what accountants must have to do all day. I can barely remember my cell phone passcode, much less be able to sit at a desk and add all day. Every job blows. I'm just grateful that mine doesn't involve blow jobs.

That said, the one thing that does nettle me is when being a fe-male is the focus of my intro—that is to say, "You're going to love this next comedian, she's a *lady*!" or "Are you guys ready for a *girl comic*?" as if to warn the audience that a female is coming on, so if they need to go make a call or take a bathroom break, now's the time. I know this isn't malicious, but pointing out that I'm a girl before I get onstage always seems a little odd, since nobody ever makes intros like that for any other career. No customer service rep warns you, "I'm sending an insurance adjuster over to survey the property. Just a heads-up, it's a lady!" No hostess at a restau-rant says, "Your server will be right with you. It's a guy! Enjoy!" And even within the comedy world, we also don't specify any-thing else about the comedian besides gender. No show host ever says, "This next comedian is black!" or "Next up is a homosexual comedian. Keep it going for the gay guy!"

"Keep it going for Whitney Cummings!"

Oof.

I had always been made fun of for my last name, but this was the first time I ever worried it could actually be illegal to say it out loud.

Once I got onstage, I scanned the crowd for what I was up against. I saw a mixture of men and women, some dressed in traditional garb, some not—again shattering my idea of the homogeneous backward population of the Middle East. I had envisioned that all the women would be in burkas and after my set they'd all rise up, rip off their oppressive garb, and storm into the sunset with me, prancing toward liberty. Nope. It was way messier and more complicated than that. First of all, the sun had already set, and second, every woman was in a different incarnation of the garb, if in the garb at all. Panicked by this curveball, I locked onto one girl who seemed particularly supportive and decided to just do my whole show for her.

I started by addressing my unfortunate last name and made a joke that referenced the base of it, which is, sadly for me as a teenager, *cum*.

I held my breath, ready for the onslaught of boos, gasps, tomatoes. There was a slight beat of silence, then something very weird happened. The audience laughed. Hard. I'll never know what lay within that beat of silence. Maybe it was a language barrier or a collective moment of wondering if they were allowed to think it was funny, but that was all the encouragement I needed to go another twenty minutes yelling about boobs and vaginas to an area of the world known for covering those very things up.

These laughs didn't sound like the laughs in America. They felt like they were coming from a deeper place. They were a special kind of laugh that felt like repression desperately aching to be released. The laughs were like the Middle East itself—half very new, half very old.

When I finally got comfortable, I was able to look at other people in the crowd besides the girl I locked onto, and I saw something I didn't expect to see. The men were also laughing. They weren't mad, threatened, offended, or scared. Turns out I was the only one guilty of all of those things.

And yes, for the haters reading this (hi! and thanks! and sorry!), I do realize the people at this show in no way represented the entirety of the Middle Eastern culture. I was performing for a very specific and small sample of people. The kind of person who would come to a comedy show is already going to be way more modern and tolerant. I realize that the hostile misogynistic weirdos, the conservative fundamentalists, and the very oppressed women who weren't allowed to leave the house wouldn't even know about the show, much less buy a ticket. That said, it still felt like a win that in the Middle East a woman could go onstage and yell into a microphone about squirting.

That night, people showed me photos of myself onstage, and although I probably should have been beaming with pride, when I looked at the photos all I could see were the bags under my eyes. "I'll use the money I made from the tour to buy some de-puffing eye cream," I thought. Ugh, the girls at the mall were right.

The next day we were off to Lebanon, a place I knew even less about than Dubai. No amount of Googling prepared me for how beautiful it was. It looked more like the Middle East that was in my head before I saw Dubai. It was rustic and majestic, like the pre-loaded screensaver that comes with your computer. Beirut was of course very developed, but the cosmopolitan mass of glass buildings was surrounded by rugged mountains and ancient mosques. The water that lined the city was an opaque emerald green, whereas Dubai's water was an impossibly clear blue. Beirut had more grit, more edge, and more women in headscarves.

After the Dubai show, I was feeling safer and more confident about the whole being-a-woman thing. I also felt safe because I got to wander around the city with Tom Papa, one of the funniest people I know. Male comedians aren't known for being the toughest people in the world, but at least I had someone with the charm and wit to talk us out of any trouble we could get into. He and I saw everything from abject poverty to annoying tourists to the biggest Fendi store I've ever seen. I couldn't really pin this place down either, which was very annoying. My black-and-white brain saw only gray, my least favorite color.

Tom and I stumbled upon a gorgeous old mosque called the Mohammad Al-Amin Mosque. The spoils of modernity aggressively compete for your attention in Beirut: the billboards, the ads, the stores, the sales, the music, the fountains. Despite all the gorgeous things in your purview, this mosque effortlessly draws your eye with an eerily quiet ability to hypnotize you. I can't quite figure out why it's so arresting. Buildings are of course immobile, but this mosque feels especially still. Maybe it's the odd combination of gold and turquoise; maybe it's the stones it's comprised of, which are of course beige.

Tom and I decided to go in. I had no idea if you needed some kind of ID or wristband or club card or something, but to my surprise, it seemed to be open to everyone, even obnoxious Americans like us. Having just done stand-up in front of a bunch of Middle Easterners who accepted me, I felt pretty invincible, so I sauntered into that mosque like it was my bitch.

When we entered, Tom and I marveled at the shocking beauty of the inside. It's actually sort of unfathomable how gorgeous this place is. The domed ceilings are decorated with an infinitesimal number of colorful, painfully symmetrical tiles. I wondered, how can a country with such perfect tiles have such imperfect beliefs? A dangerously large chandelier hung from the ceiling. I thought about how gorgeous it would be if the thing just crashed to the ground in slow motion, but it didn't seem like chaos was something that could happen in a place this serene. It was so impossibly quiet. I've spent my fair share of time in churches, and even when they're supposed to be quiet, you hear feet rustling and people breathing. Not here. This place was dead silent. It was so quiet that I could hear the voices in my head, which is never good news given how grumpy my inner monologue was back then. I responded to the whole experience as any predictable twenty-six-year-old tourist would: I pulled my camera out to take a billion selfies.

Suddenly I heard a woman yelling. Screaming, in fact.

I instinctively crouched over, covering my head with my hands. I guess because I had been in Lebanon for a day and had seen so many buildings with bullet holes in them, my monkey brain assumed it was a bomb or that the gargantuan chandelier finally gave up. Out of the corner of my eye, I saw a woman in a hijab running toward me. She begged me in Arabic to do something, but I didn't know what. Did she need me to rescue her? To protect her from an abusive man? Was she coming to me for help? Did she need me to bring her back to America so she could live her best life? Ooh! Did she want a photo with me?

Tom and I finally realized that this woman was desperate for me to cover my head with a hijab. I looked around and realized I was the only woman in the mosque without a headscarf on. According to the alarmed expression on this woman's face, this was a big mistake.

Clearly there was a misunderstanding, I thought. I tried to clear it up by speaking clearly and loudly: "I'm American! I'm not Muslim!"

The woman looked at me like I was insane. I mean, I *was* insane back then, but she didn't know that. She dragged me to the entrance, and rather forcefully I may add. Another stereotype debunked: In addition to Muslim women not being mentally weak, they're not physically weak either.

Once we were in the lobby area, she ran into a room and came back holding up a black hijab. My heart sank. Not only because it was made of the cheap black fabric I found so depressing, but to put it on felt like a betrayal of women, progress, and everything I believed in.

On top of that, this ritual just felt arbitrary to me. It was okay to take photos and videos in the mosque with the most modern technology, and post them on Facebook with dumb emojis? That wasn't demeaning to the culture, but for a woman's head to be exposed was? I couldn't understand why my side part and pony-tail was upsetting to this religion. I mean, I may have had the least insulting appearance there given some of the tourists were wearing cargo shorts paired with Teva sandals. One guy was wearing a Hard Rock Hotel T-shirt. As far as I'm concerned, the male tourists were the ones that should have had to cover themselves. It didn't make sense to me that Crocs with socks are okay but my forehead is where they drew the line.

I quickly realized this wasn't about logic, reason, or justice. It was about tradition and my chromosomes. I was a girl and this was the deal.

I thought about refusing to put it on. Maybe I would resist and make some news headlines that got into the papers, then to women who weren't allowed to leave their homes. The only problem is I was thinking about all these brave heretical ideas as I forced a smile and wrapped the hijab around my head.

I don't know what's to blame for me succumbing so quickly to the tradition; maybe it was being shamed, maybe it was my co-dependence, maybe it was my aversion to conflict, maybe it was mirror neurons. I couldn't begin to understand the intricacies of being a woman in the Middle East, but my motivation for acquiescing was ultimately that I just wanted to be respectful of the woman begging me to put it on. She had probably endured so much of her life being disrespected that I didn't want to be yet another person dismissing her existence. Maybe I was wrong to think that way. Maybe the most respectful thing I could have done for her was to refuse and set an example, showing her that she, too, could refuse to put it on if she wanted to.

For the first couple minutes, the hajib felt very weird. It was itchy, I was tripping over it, I couldn't get to my pockets with ease,

and black is not a flattering color on me. I'm so pale and awkward that I looked like the Grim Reaper with a knee injury.

Now, the scariest part of all this was not that the lady screamed at me, or that I almost tripped over the cloak-like contraption numerous times. The scariest part was that after about ten minutes, I totally forgot I was even wearing it. It went from annoying and cumbersome to weightless, even comfortable.

That night we did the show for Beirut. Perhaps as a mini revolt against having to wear the hijab that day, I wore a short-sleeved button-down, revealing my forearms with aplomb. However, that night I felt less victorious. I felt like a phony. Earlier that day I had acquiesced to covering myself with an oppressive symbol of misogyny, and that night I was onstage, talking about how strong and empowered I was.

The shows went well, and again I was surprised that the same country that hours earlier made me cover up in a mosque was the same country that found it hilarious that I was talking about balls. The whole dichotomy was exhausting. I needed this region to just make up its mind already: Were they sexist or not?!

I left the next day without saving anyone. All I had were some stories I didn't know what to make of yet and some trying-too-hard photos of myself trying to look cute in front of old jaunty fountains.

A couple years later I did a network TV show and had the same impulse to use my platform to set an example for women. I wanted to create complicated female characters that challenged their circumstances and didn't conform to what society wanted them to be. I wanted them to find strength in vulnerability without depicting them as overly needy and sensitive. But if they were overly needy and sensitive, the guy was tolerant and understanding of it, instead of exhausted and annoyed by it, which is a stereotype I feel is sexist toward men. Trust me, women can be exhausted and annoyed by needy women too. I tried to make a show in which the gender roles were reversed, where the guy (played by Chris D'Elia) wanted to get married, and the girl (played by yours truly) didn't. I thought maybe it could be progressive, subversive, or at least funny to flip the script: to depict a man as emotionally intelligent, sensitive, and capable of true love and a woman as impulsive, commitment-phobic, and uncomfortable with vulnerability. Since stereotypes of women and men are so deeply ingrained in our psyches, my character was often thought of as "crazy" for having a masculine side and Chris's was often thought of as "a pussy" for having a feminine side.

The show seemed to be taking off well. It tested well with focus groups; it made emotionally numb comedy writers laugh; it even made some emotionally dead comedians laugh.

Imagine my surprise when, once we got picked up, I learned that I couldn't say most of what I had planned to say on TV. A lot of the stories I wanted to tell were "too dirty." On network TV we can't say *Jesus, God, ejaculate*—basically nothing people text about after ten P.M. You can't show a Coke if Pepsi is a sponsor; you can't have a sports jersey on a wall without jumping through numerous legal hoops. If you mention the NFL, I think you immediately just get stabbed in the neck. You also can't say something is "inside you." That rule alone killed like half the stories I wanted to do. After going to the Middle East and being able to say whatever I wanted onstage, I was very confused about being censored back in America the free.

When I was shooting this TV show, the bags under my eyes were very, well, baggy. And not like the sultry "that girl likes to party" nineties model type of smoky eye. No, it was more like the kind of eye bags that cause people to ask you if you're okay while looking very concerned. Pretty much every conversation started with "You seem tired" or "Rough night?" No matter how many cold compresses I put on my eyes or how many products my makeup artist put on them, I looked like a hungover panda.

I got through the insecurity by rationalizing that maybe it could be good for girls to see an example of someone in the media who isn't perfect. Someone who's human, who has a real face with real flaws and real eye bags. Maybe *this* was how I could be a role model. Maybe this was how I could try and crack the Beauty Myth that Naomi Wolf was talking about. I wished I had grown up with more realistic depictions of people on television, so maybe this was a gift and how I could actually contribute to a realistic physical standard. Creatively it made sense, too, given the symbolism of a character who has so much emotional baggage would also have, well, under-eye baggage.

One night I had people over to watch the show's live feed. I braced for having to see myself on-screen, which is always a complicated feeling. I'm grateful for what I get to do for a living, but I also think it's unhealthy to look at yourself as much as we all do these days. I have a completely unscientifically researched theory that humans aren't designed to look at ourselves as much as we do. From what I gather, there are no naturally occurring mirrors in nature. And no, ponds and ice don't count, you hater.

The show started. Another reason it is not enjoyable to watch shows that I'm in is that so much of making television is about running out of time and settling for something that's never as good as you want it to be, so I end up obsessing over all the improvements there was no time to make. I just drive myself crazy thinking of all the better jokes that I wish I'd had time to put in, or other choices I wish I'd made as a performer. As I braced to self-flagellate, I appeared on-screen, and the negative thoughts didn't come because my brain was too frozen in shock from at what I saw: me . . . but with no eye bags. I'd never seen myself without eye bags before. Most fetuses develop in amniotic sacs, I swear I developed in an under-eye bag.

I had dealt with eye bags all my life, so I assumed this was the result of some weird transmogrification of what happens when humans are made into pixels and reflected back to you with some electronic magic I'll never understand. But how could the camera add ten pounds yet subtract eye bags? Was I going crazy? Had the bags ever even been there in the first place? Had I become an insane dysmorphic actress who amplified her every flaw? Was everyone around me enabling my batshit crazy behavior? Or worse, was everyone around me tricking me, trying to make me think that I had flaws that I didn't have to slowly hack away at my self-esteem until I turned into a less charming iteration of Joan Crawford?

The good news and the bad news is that I later found out that the reason I looked so tired in person yet so rested on TV was because someone had been hired to "clean up" my face in post-production. The bags were so distracting that they were digitally removed. My reaction to this news was, and still is, complicated. I was relieved because I was pretty sick of getting attacked so much online for looking "tired" and "busted," but I was also sad. I thought about the girls in the Middle East and what they said about women in America and their appearance. I wondered if Photoshop and digital retouching could be America's version of women in the Middle East who choose to wear the hijab. Women in America may not cover our faces with scarves, but sometimes we choose or feel pressure to cover it with perfecting veils, be it an airbrush app or the most flattering Instagram filter.

Another thing connected to my experience in the Middle East was that once the show aired, people started recognizing me. I'm not trying to get sympathy because I'm probably the least famous "famous" person, but it took a minute for me to adjust to it all, so going out in public became weird and awkward. People would come up to me and give me jarring backhanded compliments like "You look *so much prettier* in person!" or "Don't listen to them, you're great!" I started wondering who this "them" was, and why they were so mad at me. I got obsessed with the idea that this amorphous "they" behaved one way to my face and another way behind my back. This awakened and fortified an old belief system I had that everyone is duplicitous and that you can't ever be truly safe with anyone. Like plaid schoolgirl skirts on adults, this was something that made sense in the nineties, and only in the nineties.

What does this have to do with the Middle East? Well, I got so paranoid and skittish that I found myself doing the very thing I had judged and resented years before in Dubai: When I left the house, I wrapped my head with a scarf. I obviously did it for a very different reason than Middle Eastern women do and it wasn't an official hijab per se, but there I was, voluntarily covering my head and face. I did it to avoid being recognized, being accidentally insulted, and getting confusing career feedback from strangers, e.g. "You're like the female Rodney Dangerfield!" I needed a way to avoid being in a situation where people came up to me and asked "Are you really the age you say you are?" and "Don't listen to the haters! They're just jealous!" in a grocery store parking lot.

People looked at me like I was slightly crazy for wearing a headscarf in 90-degree L.A. weather, but it actually worked because I stopped getting my feelings hurt in the frozen foods section. The headscarf gave me anonymity and safety, which was the only way I could protect my already fragile self-esteem. I finally understood what those girls may have been trying to tell me all those years ago. The experience had come full circle, and the symbol of oppression I felt so insulted by having to wear in the mosque I was now ordering in bulk on Amazon.

Taking refuge in a headscarf showed me that no matter how progressive and understanding we think we are, and how noble our intentions, sometimes we can be ignorant hypocrites. I will never understand what it's like to live in an oppressive culture like the Middle East where women are deprived of basic human rights, but at least I was able to finally understand that it could be more complicated than that, and that I certainly didn't know more about their experiences and emotions than they did. Or maybe there's absolutely no connection at all between these two experiences, and I'm just desperately trying to make sense of something that can never make sense to me. Obviously my going to the grocery store in a scarf had absolutely nowhere near the same stakes as a woman in the Middle East wearing a burka, but I had to be in that particular situation to finally understand what those girls were trying to tell me, which is that wearing what I thought was a freedom-denying hijab is actually what made them feel free.

I don't know if this situation was a lesson or a warning. Maybe those girls were showing me our natural tendency to normalize or acclimate to our oppression, even spin it as positive so we can get through the day. Maybe the lesson was to expose me to brainwashed people to illuminate how brainwashed I am. I don't know. One thing I do know is that my generalization that all Middle Eastern women were broken and defenseless led me to commit the exact transgressions I so disdained: These women told me their truth, and I invalidated it. While thinking they should be taken more seriously, I didn't take them seriously. While thinking their voices should be heard, I wasn't listening to them. While wanting them to be seen, I was ignoring them. The truth is that I was wrong about a lot of things. Goddamn it, I hate admitting that. I don't know if the girls were right either, but I do know that I was wrong to assume I knew more than they did.

I know this is not news to you guys—you probably think I'm wrong all the time—but it was breaking news to me. I don't know if it was being American, being a comedian, or watching too much or too little news, but my trip to the Middle East taught me that I had a very strong resistance to being wrong or changing my mind. I update everything else in my life obsessively—my phone, my computer software, my car—but I wasn't updating my ideas. I realized that if my thoughts were clothes, they'd be the oversized flannel shirt I wore as a dress in 1996.

I went to the Middle East with a very Anglocentric, naive idea of what these women's lives were like. When the girls tried to explain to me that their culture is more complicated than one sweeping statement, it was a threat to my worldview to have to delete all the old files in my head. It's like that old phone you have in a drawer that you know you'll never use again because your fingers are twice the size of the buttons now and they don't even make chargers for it anymore, but you can't bring yourself to throw it away because, well, it's yours. You're emotionally attached to it. The same thing happened with my beliefs. I became attached to my opinions, which live in a drawer in my dark labyrinth of a brain. My generalizations were an anesthetic that protected me from a much more complicated reality, and I was not willing to wean myself off that painkiller.

Going to the Middle East didn't liberate any women or instantaneously revise their culture. It certainly didn't change the world, but it did change my world. It made me notice how my paradigm is composed of a bunch of generalizations that I used to make me feel safe and superior. Our survivalist reptile brains love to put people and things in neat compartments. For me, these compartments ended up being "all men lie," "all police officers are good," or "all food goes well with ranch." If you're anything like me you've learned the hard way that only the last one is true.

From what I gather, generalizations and stereotypes were very important in tribal times, before alarm systems and locks on doors. Thinking "all noises in the bushes signals danger" was a very useful stereotype. What used to give us actual security now gives us a false sense of security. Don't get me wrong, my generalizations served me very well early on in life; for example, when I deduced that "all kids are going to make fun of your last name," I was pretty much right and planned a defensive strategy accordingly.

I mean, I don't blame them, but it was helpful for me to be prepared. Conversely, positive stereotypes helped me gravitate to healthy situations. For example, deducing that "all horses are awesome" and "you can always rely on MTV" ended up making me very happy because I was able to escape my real world by watching, well, *The Real World*.

Now that I'm an adult, my generalizations no longer serve me. I'm no longer in an unsafe situation, so I no longer need to protect myself in the same way. When we continually compartmentalize people, cultures, and genders, we tend to find what we're looking for even if it means projecting a mirage onto whatever you're seeing to manifest your assumption. I found myself actually ignoring and doubting any contrary evidence and looking for proof to substantiate my theories. And as we all know, we always find what we're looking for, whether it's actually there or not. See what I mean? That generalization isn't even valid because I can never find my keys no matter how hard I look.

From what I understand, this instinct has been around as long as our survival has been threatened, so I guess forever. I'm not a neuroscientist so I thought I'd quote someone who is so you don't think I'm bloviating about things I have no business pretending to know. Taxonomist and neuroscientist Santiago Ramón y Cajal wrote about six psychological flaws that keep talented people from achieving greatness. I would have loved to pretend that I just sit around reading old leather-bound books by famous neuroscientists from the 1800s, but I know you'd never believe me, so the truth is that I follow *BrainPickings* on Twitter and Maria Popova wrote an article about this. Santiago was complaining about how we look for evidence to support our theories back in 1897!

There are highly cultivated, wonderfully endowed minds whose wills suffer from a particular form of lethargy, which is all the more serious because it is not apparent to them and is usually not thought of as being particularly important. . . . As soon as they happen to notice a slight, half-hidden analogy between two phenomena, or succeed in fitting some new data or other into the framework of a general theory—whether true or false—they dance for joy. . . . The essential thing for them is the beauty of the concept. It matters very little whether the concept itself is based on thin air, so long as it is beautiful and ingenious, well-thought-out and symmetrical.

Yes, that's what I was looking for. Symmetry. Something to make sense of all the chaos. Generalizations may be a way we lie to ourselves because the truth is gross and messy and exhausting. Negative generalizations for me weren't even the most insidious. The positive ones sometimes caused the most disappointment. "All women are trustworthy" was a generalization I started making early in life as a reaction to getting the memo that all men were bad. My nascent psyche probably couldn't handle both men and women being bad, because that would mean feeling trapped in a perilous situation, so I deduced that since all men were bad, all women must be great. I really needed to believe that to get through the day. As a result, I put women on a pedestal, gave credit where credit wasn't due, and got hurt a lot. It was so hard for me as a woman, a supporter of women, and as fragile person looking for loving friendships that I literally would rather have gotten hurt before detaching from my delusion that every woman should be trusted with abandon.

When I decided I wanted to detach from old belief systems, it was way harder than I thought. Gray areas make me almost as uncomfortable as watching *Fifty Shades of Grey*. I did some research to see if refusing to update old worldviews was a human nature thing or a me being witless thing, and it turns out the whole thing is somewhat universal. Thankfully Stephanie Pappas wrote an article called "Evolution, Climate and Vaccines: Why Americans Deny Science":

> . . . *a 2010 study found that when people were shown in-correct information alongside a correction, the update failed to reverse their initial belief in the misinformation. Even worse, partisans who were motivated to believe the original incorrect information became even more firm in their belief in that information after reading a correction, the researchers found.*

So, for example, if you know the shortest route to the airport and someone tells you *they* have the shortest route, chances are that will make you believe even more firmly that yours is the shortest. So apparently we *Homo sapiens* have some innate need to defend our opinions, regardless of how incorrect they are. I'm half embarrassed, half amused by all the times I've done this in arguments with guys where I'm blatantly wrong, but physically can't admit it. Even when my brain says, "You're wrong, Whitney, you have got to stop talking," my mouth says, *"No, you're wrong!"*

I think I probably got this way because in our culture we're so shamed for being flawed or for making mistakes. This seems like another one of those nasty primordial needs to ostracize the weak for the good of the tribe, back when being wrong could have meant being eaten by a saber-toothed tiger. But as long as we equate lack of knowledge with weakness, we're all gonna remain very stupid. I saw a lot of pretending to know things growing up, which I blame on toxic masculinity and the generations before us having what seemed to be an allergy to vulnerability. My dad never asked for directions. My mom cooked without following recipes. And when people didn't know statistics, they just made them up: "Well, most people don't even care about politics." I mean, that's not a real statistic. When I bought my first piece of furniture from Ikea, it didn't even occur to me to look at the instructions because nobody had ever told me it was okay to not know something. Trying to assemble an Ikea side table myself led to a pinched nerve, some pretty epic emotional outbursts, and a lot of splinters. Basically everything except an assembled side table.

Maybe I heard the platitude "knowledge is power" so often that I internalized it, and thought that without knowledge, real or fake, I don't have any power. I was so embarrassed to admit that I didn't know something that I preferred to just defend whatever misinformation I made up than capitulate to the truth. In hindsight, it's so odd to me that I was insecure about not knowing things because when someone asks me "What does that word mean?" or "How do I do this?" I never think, "What an idiot!" In fact, the opposite is true. I'm always charmed and impressed by a person's ability to admit they need help. The truth is that if I had just been comfortable saying "I don't know" earlier in life, I'd actually know a hell of a lot more. Maybe even as much as I pretended to know. Case in point: Until I was twenty-six, I thought a 401(k) was a marathon. That's the kind of stupidity that happens when you're too afraid to admit you don't know something.

For the longest time I thought if I couldn't carry on a conversation about literally everything with authority, that I was an actual piece of garbage. The irony is we pretend to know things in order to be liked, yet nobody likes a know-it-all. They're very annoying. So why do we try so hard to be one?

In my case, in addition to the primordial brain dynamics I'm not qualified to outline, I think it's ego. Ego is a hard thing to explain, and there are plenty of therapists and books that are way better at doing it than I am. That said, I have a lot of experience with them, between having one and dating some big ones.

I personally see ego as a curmudgeonly middle-aged bouncer,

hair frozen in pomade icicles, leather blazer down to his knees, standing outside a nightclub. When people walk by, ego yells "You can't come in!" even though the nightclub has been closed since 2004 and it's three in the afternoon. But for me, my ego thinks it's protecting me. That said, since I'm not in any real danger when I'm having a conversation at a dinner party, it really serves absolutely no purpose but to sabotage me and weird people out.

My ego is like my hype man, encouraging me to make terrible choices. *Yeah! You got this, Whit! Totally say yes to that job you don't want just so people don't think you weren't offered it! Buy that over-priced ugly purse to impress shallow people! Pretend you know way more about the news than you actually know! Stay in that terrible relationship because you, my friend, do not fail at anything! Also, you can change other people with the powers of your mind even if they have no interest at all in changing!* My ego is a mascot that mindlessly cheers on scientifically impossible ideas and lame bathroom selfies.

My ego is like a veil that protects me from getting hurt, but also isolates me, preventing me from having true connections with people or an honest relationship with reality. Maybe it's my hijab, so to speak, that I use to hide and to carry on an ancient tradition in my family and culture. My ego is the armor that protected me as a child but now weighs me down as an adult. And sometimes it tells me to squat way too much weight, so it's also starting to mess up my knee. I've learned that as much as we've been through together and as good as its intentions may have been, it's time to break up with my ego.

These days it's my goal to be wrong as often as possible. It's my goal to say "I don't know" as many times as I can in a conversation. If you're not ready to flat out say "I'm wrong," which I totally get, I have some other phrases that are a bit easier on the ego. Try "I never thought about it that way" or "I may have a blind spot in that area." When we say stuff like this, something very magical happens: We start learning things.

If I'm in a relationship where I'm pretending to know things that I don't know, or am agreeing with opinions that I don't really agree with in order to be accepted or loved, I know I've become a puppet of my ego and have to step away. I need to course-correct and figure out why I'm being inauthentic. When you're afraid to be wrong or pretend you know and like things you don't, you end up in some pretty sticky situations. In the past this instinct led to disastrous ordeals like having to read a guy's poetry and going to hockey games preceded by an hour of Googling "how is hockey played?" in the parking lot.

Once I started saying "I don't know" and "I'm wrong," I may have felt dumber, but I also felt more free. My ego fights me every time, but how am I ever actually going to be right if I can't admit that I'm wrong? I just recently finally admitted that for the longest time I had been saying "let's play it by year" instead of "let's play it by *ear*." My whole life I heard the expression and could never tell if it was *ear* or *year*, so I guessed year (the one that makes the least amount of sense) and stuck with it. I know, if I had just dedicated thirty seconds of critical thinking to how ridiculous it would be to check in once a year while making plans with someone, I'm sure I would have deduced that it was *ear*, but I was too busy in my twenties making bad choices to use that kind of logic. When I first heard the expression, if I had simply asked, "Did you just say *year* or *ear*?" I would have saved myself a decade of sounding like a cryptic moron every time I made plans with someone. That said, to everyone in my life who heard me repeatedly misuse this phrase for years and never corrected me, you are my enemy for eternity.

In a culture where people are valued by how many articles they read that morning, what school they went to, who knows the most statistics, I say we do something radical and resist the default to need to know everything and be the smartest person in the room. I think deglamorizing knowing everything is the way we can actually really get some insight. In a time when being smug and self-righteous is almost stylish, I'd love to figure out how to make saying "I don't know" sexy, and not in a gross submissive school-girl-porn-scene type of way. We live in an age where we get our news from Instagram memes and our crazy uncles on Facebook, so even the most well-intentioned people are misinformed every now and then. I imagine admitting we can sometimes be idiots is the only way to avoid becoming an idiocracy.

I feel we've evolved into a society that prides expediency over accuracy, quantity over quality, decibel level over content. Some of the growth I'm the most proud of in the last couple of years has been developing the ability to shut up and listen, to ask questions instead of making assumptions. I'm hoping this is how I can stop myself from mindlessly perpetuating stereotypes and relying on generalizations to feel safe or smart.

I don't know a lot of things. I don't know how my fingers on this keyboard are making words on a big white document that I was supposed to turn in to my editor a week ago. I don't know how they bind all these book pages together and make them all stay stuck. Is it super glue or tiny yarn? Dunno. And if you're listening to an audiotape of this, I don't know why I sound so nasal. I don't even know how cell phones work, and one is in my hand most of the time I'm awake and half the time I'm asleep. Apparently the signal goes to space and back, but I know that only because of the punch line of a Louis C.K. stand-up bit.

The point is, I can't begin to pretend I know how a woman feels on the other side of the planet. I barely know how I feel half the time, so I'm better served trying to figure that out so I can lead by example, because as Vera says, I can't give away what I don't have.

I'd love to somehow make a dent in contributing to all of us stopping the cycle of pretending to know things we don't know. Maybe the first step in doing that is ending this book because if I write too much more, I'll be pretending I have more to say than I actually do. I've given you pretty much everything I know, and maybe for now, that's just going to have to be okay.

Ultimately, I think writing this book and admitting that I wasn't fine is how I got to a place where I actually was, well, truly fine. That doesn't make sense? Fine.

In the end, only three things matter:
how much you loved, how gently you lived, and
how gracefully you let go of things not meant for you.
—JACK KORNFIELD